# Raising Happy Children For Dummies®

## Tips for Creating a 'We' Mentality

A *'we' mentality* is a sense of personal family identity in ~~~~~~~~~~~~~~~~~~~~~~~~~ism. A 'we' mentality builds trust, support, loyalty, love, and a ~~~~~~~~~~~~~~~~~~~~~~~ teem. Here are some tips for building a 'we' mentality:

- ✔ **Encourage family traditions.** A family tradition is an ~~~~~~~~~~~~~~~~~~~~~~, such as preparing a roast on Sundays, watching football on the TV, or going on an annual camping holiday.

- ✔ **Create memories.** Memories don't have to be of expensive holidays or of receiving lavish gifts. They can be simple moments of being together or something funny that someone said or did.

- ✔ **Take time to talk.** Talk about your experiences and your needs and take time to listen to each other.

- ✔ **Work together to develop your family's rules and routines.** State the rules in a positive way and don't have too many of them.

Head to Chapter 4 for more about strengthening your family's identity.

## Communicating Effectively

Notice and think about how you communicate with your children on a daily basis. 'Talking at' your child and 'talking with' your child are two very different things – rather like 'laughing at' or 'laughing with' someone. Here are some tips for improving your communication with your children:

- ✔ **Ask open-ended questions.** An *open-ended question* needs a descriptive answer. Open-ended questions typically begin with interrogative words – how, what, where, when, who, how much, and where. Open-ended questions help a child develop his or her thought processes.

- ✔ **Watch your tone of voice.** Pay attention over the next week to *how* you say things to your children. If you don't like how you're saying things, change your tone. Have you ever heard your child admonishing another with your exact words and tone? Scary, isn't it?

- ✔ **Make eye contact.** If your message is important, deliver it while keeping eye contact. Maintain eye contact when you listen to their reply, showing that you're really engaged with them.

- ✔ **Repeat back what your children say.** Doing so shows them that you really understand them and are taking the time to listen. Paraphrase and summarise the gist of what your kids have said rather than repeating them, parrot-fashion.

Chapter 5 is all about improving communication with your children.

*For Dummies: Bestselling Book Series for Beginners*

# Raising Happy Children For Dummies®

## Disciplining Your Children

Managing your children's behaviour takes hard work, persistence, dedication, a sense of perspective, and a healthy sense of humour! Part III is all about disciplining your children, but here are some quick tips for when you're about to really lose your rag:

- Be firm and fair in stating your expectations.
- *Tell* your children – don't *ask* them – what you expect. Of course, be polite, but don't keep saying 'please' in a desperate way.
- Use the words 'I want you to . . .' when you introduce an expectation. These words clearly state what you want your kids to do.
- Use your body language and facial expression to convey that you mean what you're saying.
- Try being surprised when things go wrong rather than angry – doing so works wonders.
- Distract your child if they're having a tantrum. Pretend you find something really fascinating and get your toddler to come and have a look.
- Ground an older child, or send them to their room.
- Let your child know that you love them, but that you strongly dislike their behaviour.
- Press your internal pause button. Step back and take a deep breath. Leave the room and go and shout in the garden. Pound a pillow or swear quietly under your breath. Come back to the situation feeling calmer.

*For Dummies: Bestselling Book Series for Beginners*

# Raising Happy Children

## FOR

# DUMMIES®

# Raising Happy Children

## FOR

# DUMMIES®

by Sue Atkins

John Wiley & Sons, Ltd

**Raising Happy Children For Dummies®**

Published by
**John Wiley & Sons, Ltd**
The Atrium
Southern Gate
Chichester
West Sussex
PO19 8SQ
England

E-mail (for orders and customer service enquires): cs-books@wiley.co.uk

Visit our Home Page on www.wiley.com

For general information on our other products and services, please contact our Customer Care Department within the U.S. at 800-762-2974, outside the U.S. at 317-572-3993, or fax 317-572-4002.

For technical support, please visit www.wiley.com/techsupport.

Wiley also publishes its books in a variety of electronic formats. Some content that appears in print may not be available in electronic books.

British Library Cataloguing in Publication Data: A catalogue record for this book is available from the British Library

ISBN: 978-0-470-05978-4

Printed and bound in Great Britain by Bell & Bain Ltd, Glasgow

10  9  8  7  6  5  4  3  2  1

WILEY

# About the Author

**Sue Atkins** is a working mother of two children and was a former teacher and Deputy Head. She studied for her B.Ed (Hons) teaching degree at St. Mary's College, London, and has a diploma in life coaching from the Coaching Academy. She is also a neuro-linguistic programming Master Practitioner and trainer.

She set up Positive Parents – Confident Kids Coaching Ltd in order to develop her passion for helping parents to build self-esteem in themselves and their children.

Sue has written and published a number of books on self-esteem, parenting toddlers, and bringing up teenagers (*Music for the Soul: The Gift of Self Esteem, Are We There Yet? The Magic of Looking Under Stones and Finding Fairies!, If Men Are from Mars and Women are from Venus, Then What Planet's My Teenager On?*).

She has also written a number of journals for parents and teenagers: *The Positive Parent Journal, Keeping All the Balls in the Air Journal* for working parents, and *The Confident Kids Toolkit.*

Sue is passionate about making life with children easier and more rewarding, and is enthusiastic about helping parents to bring up happy, confident, well-balanced adults; today's children – tomorrow's future.

By introducing parents to new ways of thinking about themselves and their family relationships through one to one coaching, seminars, and books, Sue helps parents and their children to move forward and create positive change. In addition to running one to one parent coaching sessions, she is a regular speaker at events and workshops throughout the UK.

Sue enjoys salsa dancing (particularly round the kitchen table), singing loudly in the car, and lives on a farm in Surrey with her family, three dogs, two cats, and a hamster called Strawberry.

# Dedication

This book is dedicated to Will and Molly, my two wonderful children, and was inspired by my Dad and Mum who both passed away recently. My parents gave me the gift of self-esteem and the magic of realising that life is what you make it.

# Author's Acknowledgements

I'd like to thank my long-suffering husband Kevin for cooking, cleaning, and ironing while I became absorbed in writing this book. Also for his ability to sniff out lost commas and for his total support while I went on amazing NLP courses, and talked incessantly late into the night about making a difference in the world.

Special thanks to Dominic Demolder for all his technical support and formatting – I really must get the hang of the technical side of life one day.

Thanks to my wonderful friends and family who inspire me, make me laugh, and put up with me hogging the SingStar karaoke machine at parties. Thanks to all the children I've had the pleasure of teaching throughout my career – you really are the special ones.

## Publisher's Acknowledgements

We're proud of this book; please send us your comments through our Dummies online registration form located at www.dummies.com/register/.

Some of the people who helped bring this book to market include the following:

**Acquisitions, Editorial, and Media Development**

**Project Editor:** Rachael Chilvers

**Development Editor:** Brian Kramer

**Copy Editor:** Kate O'Leary

**Proofreader:** Helen Heyes

**Content Editor:** Steve Edwards

**Executive Editor:** Jason Dunne

**Executive Project Editor:** Martin Tribe

**Cover Photos:** © Tomas Rodriguez/Veer/ Corbis

**Cartoons:** Rich Tennant, www.the5thwave.com

**Composition Services**

**Project Coordinator:** Jennifer Theriot

**Layout and Graphics:** Claudia Bell, Brooke Graczyk, Joyce Haughey, Stephanie D. Jumper, Barbara Moore

**Anniversay Logo Design:** Richard Pacifico

**Proofreader:** Charles Spencer

**Indexer:** Aptara

**Brand Reviewer:** Jennifer Bingham

**Publishing and Editorial for Consumer Dummies**

    **Diane Graves Steele,** Vice President and Publisher, Consumer Dummies

    **Joyce Pepple,** Acquisitions Director, Consumer Dummies

    **Kristin A. Cocks,** Product Development Director, Consumer Dummies

    **Michael Spring,** Vice President and Publisher, Travel

    **Kelly Regan,** Editorial Director, Travel

**Publishing for Technology Dummies**

    **Andy Cummings,** Vice President and Publisher, Dummies Technology/General User

**Composition Services**

    **Gerry Fahey,** Vice President of Production Services

    **Debbie Stailey,** Director of Composition Services

# Contents at a Glance

# Table of Contents

# Introduction

$B$ ringing up children is a challenging, frustrating, and exhausting job because kids don't come with a handbook. But if they did, I hope *Raising Happy Children For Dummies* would be the one that at least helps you feel more confident about your parenting and gives you information to support and encourage you, and make you laugh along the way.

Parenting is the most important job that you'll ever do but is also the one few ever get any preparation for. Ironically, most people invest in everything *except* learning the skills needed for raising happy, confident, and well-balanced children.

The speed, pressure, and stress of modern living means you never seem to have enough time. These are different times – certainly different from your own childhood memories and experiences. Today's culture is about having it all and having it *now*. Children face the dangers of Internet chat rooms, exposure to recreational drugs, binge drinking, and casual sex. They spend vast amounts of time in front of screens – PlayStation, MSN, and the computer. And despite an abundance of other things they could do, they always appear bored.

My aims for you as you read this book are to:

- Develop a really wonderful and fulfilling relationship with your child that lasts a lifetime.
- Discover new ways to enjoy parenting your child.
- Find ways to communicate easily and effectively with your child, no matter what her age.
- Bring out the best in your child – and also discover the best in you.
- Explore new skills and choices in your parenting approach and style.
- Grow, change, and laugh together with your child and partner as you all go through this journey of family life.
- Realise that respecting each other as individuals is the magic that glues you all together.

# About This Book

This book was written from the passion I feel for children deserving to grow up with true self-esteem so they can become happy, confident, well-balanced adults. Children are tomorrow's future, one that creates a ripple in a pond of good parents. Happy children can become adults able to become whatever they want in life – unique and special in their own way.

You may be reading this book because you're thinking of starting a family, you're interested in picking up some new ideas, or you're going through a time of change and transition. Whatever your reasons, I believe you want to do a great job. You may have done a great job up to now, but perhaps you want to re-energise your family relationships or to feel more in control of your family life. Whatever your situation, if you care about developing effective parenting skills, this book is for you.

Many, many theories, experts, and books exist out there giving wonderful advice for raising children, but I think they overlook one crucial thing – every family is different, unique, and special. My perspective as a parent coach is to support you in discovering that all the answers lie within you.

I believe that you are the real expert for your own family, but at times I offer you advice based on parenting skills regarded as good practice. I also offer you my own experience as a deputy head and class teacher for 22 years and a mum of two children, aged 11 and 13. I am still a work in progress (as my daughter occasionally likes to point out to me).

My philosophy is simple: Your child deserves the best. She deserves you to be the best parent you can be. I hope through reading this book you develop more choices and can make new and different decisions based always on your best intentions for your child.

My approach is *coaching-based*, so I often ask questions to help you find your own answers to your family's needs and personal style. Parent coaching is a non-judgemental, confidential, and non-critical way to explore your parenting. My intention is to help you bring *your* answers to the surface and to help you gain clarity, direction, and confidence in your parenting.

I have tried to keep this book simple and easy to read, so it feels like I'm a friend talking common sense not jargon (but you are actually discovering something valuable and useful along the way). I believe all parents do their best, but sometimes you just can't see the wood for the trees – because it is *your* life! This book is an attempt to help you take a step back, see the wood, and maybe even smell the flowers!

# Conventions Used in This Book

To help you navigate through this book, I set up a few conventions:

- ✔ *Italics* are used for emphasis and to highlight new words, or define terms.
- ✔ **Bold** text indicates the key concept in a list.
- ✔ `Monofont` is used for Web and e-mail addresses.

I use alternate male and female pronouns in the chapters to be fair to both genders.

# How This Book Is Organised

This book has 19 chapters and 6 main parts.

Inside each chapter you find sub-sections that apply to that topic to make this book easier to pick up, find, and read topics that are relevant to you. Feel free to just dip in and out as needed.

## Part 1: Understanding Your Children and Yourself

This part is the solid foundation of all parenting. It contains the bigger picture – or the destination – of your parenting and helps you focus on what's really important to you. You discover how to make changes and gain courage to try out new ideas and fresh approaches. It also looks at the influences on your parenting and your parenting styles.

The part also looks at understanding your challenges and successes as a parent and helps you understand yourself better. You can identify the things you're good at and love about being a parent, while also pinpointing what you find difficult and a challenge.

You also gain an insight into actually understanding your kids – the differences between girls and boys, what children want from you as a parent, and what they really need from you, too.

# Part II: Improving Your Basic Parenting Skills

This part seeks to improve the fundamentals of parenting by helping you better manage your family's day-to-day routines. It looks at how to build the 'we' mentality of your family, which builds up the solid foundations of security and stability for your children.

Effective and successful communication skills, including listening more attentively, praising specifically, and gaining co-operation from your child easily, are all essential skills for parenting that I cover in detail in this section.

I also cover ways to remain flexible in your parenting, adapting to and recognising the changes occurring in your child as she develops independence. I discuss how to accept the changes as both you and your child grow and develop together.

The part also looks at the world of parenting from an adult point of view and helps you find balance in your parenting. I offer ideas for examining and revitalising your adult relationships, analysing your free time, and making sure you look after your own needs.

# Part III: Discipline

Different styles and approaches to discipline exist. The chapters in this part look at your type of discipline, the way you react to your children, and what is acceptable or not acceptable behaviour for you as a parent. It explores boundary setting, loving discipline, and how to create rules to fit your family that you all understand and can keep to.

The part looks at different strategies for parenting different age children – from toddler to teenager. You also find out how to focus on positive ways to handle conflict and to gain co-operation from any age of child.

# Part IV: Helping Your Child Cope with Common Problems

This part explores problems that children often have to contend with, such as the school-related issues of friendship, bullying, and exam pressure. Other issues I address include handling disappointment, bedwetting, bad dreams, and the changes occurring around puberty. It also explores bigger issues such as divorce, sibling rivalry, and bereavement.

## Part V: Being Different

Having a unique or special needs child affects the whole family. This part looks at the process of diagnosis and support, as well as common features of ADHD, dyslexia, dyspraxia, Asperger's syndrome, and gifted children. I also discuss the joys and challenges involved in having twins, triplets, and other multiple births.

## Part VI: The Part of Tens

In the Part of Tens you find some quick and easy positive parenting principles to live by: Ten ideas to build a happy home, ten things to do every day, ten things to do when it all goes pear-shaped, and ten great resources to support you in the day-to-day parenting maze!

# Icons Used in This book

Take a second look at these little reminders – so you don't forget! This icon highlights overall strategies to constantly bear in mind as you work to develop new parenting skills.

Pay attention to these practical suggestions to help you raise happy children.

This icon highlights anecdotes from my own life, and from my experiences working with parents and children in teaching and coaching.

Look for these positive ideas to help you remain optimistic in your parenting.

Watch out for these bits of information. The bomb draws your attention to behaviour to avoid when dealing with your kids.

Enjoy these inspiring (and sometimes silly) quotes by other people – some who are famous and some who are not!

# *Where to Go from Here*

As with most *For Dummies* books, you don't need to read this entire book from cover to cover. Perhaps some sections don't really apply to you at the moment or you just need ideas to deal with a specific situation. I've tried to include age-specific information where I think it's useful or relevant and kept to more general principles in other parts.

Read the chapters from first to last – or in any order you want.

If you have a question that's not covered in this book, feel free to contact me. Perhaps you want to find out more about parent coaching as a positive way to help you bring up your children. The best way to contact me is through my Web site at www.positive-parents.com. At my Web site, you can sign up for a free monthly parenting newsletter full of practical tips and interesting suggestions.

# Part I
# Understanding Your Children and Yourself

## In this part . . .

*R*ome wasn't built in a day – houses without solid
foundations and properly drawn up plans fall down,
and it's the same with raising kids. They need a foundation to grow from and you need a plan so that you know
where to start from and how it's all supposed to look in
the end! I'm going to help you become the architect of
your family's future. The first way to do this is to understand your children and understand yourself as a parent.

# Chapter 1

# Becoming a Confident Parent

*L*et me tell you the secret about being a confident parent: There really is no secret.

In fact being a confident parent is really a simple concept, but perhaps one you just hadn't thought of. Confident parenting involves:

✔ Taking control of your parenting.

✔ Planning what you want to achieve and focusing on it.

✔ Deciding to make some changes.

✔ Taking action.

You see, simple!

This chapter considers each critical action involved in becoming a confident parent.

## Become a better parent through parent coaching

I'm passionate about parenting and helping other people develop their confidence and skills as parents. Since starting my company Positive Parents – Confident Kids Coaching I've been very honoured to have worked with many parents, making amazing changes and improvements in their family life.

Parents often find that parent coaching is a life-changing experience because – at last! – they find a practical and *positive* way to move their parenting from where it's stuck to where they want it to be.

*Parent coaching* isn't counselling or therapy but a way to get ordinary parents back into the driving seat of their family relationships and to assume control of their lives. Just as a fitness coach gets your body into shape, a parent coach fine-tunes your parenting by providing a structure to help you focus on practical solutions that help you move forward and create change. Parent coaching is also non-judgemental, non-critical, totally confidential, and can be great fun. Put simply, parent coaching is a series of conversations one person has with another but with a purpose.

Sometimes you just can't see the wood for the trees in family situations. Having an objective and sympathetic person outside of your family to help you find your own solutions to family problems can be very helpful. Being a parent is challenging, tiring, and frustrating – but also hugely rewarding. All parents sometimes need a little help finding clarity, direction, and confidence in their abilities as parents.

# *Taking Control*

Who is in control of your life? Your kids? Your own parents? Your friends? Some talking head on television? Or you?

Actually this is a serious question. Are you *really* in control of your own life? Do you take responsibility for the way everything affects you? If you don't, you may be in personal and parenting trouble already.

Taking responsibility for stuff like going to work, emptying the dishwasher, and walking the dog is easy. But what about taking responsibility for the things you apparently have no control over? Do you take responsibility for the way things affect you? Most people draw a line at that point because being a victim of circumstances is easier than taking responsibility.

A victim takes the easy route and says thing such as, 'Well, you know kids – they just have a mind of their own'. A victim blames his children for making him feel tired, overwhelmed, or angry. By blaming the kids, the victim can sit back comfortable in the knowledge that the situation's someone else's responsibility to fix.

But by acting the victim, you give away what I refer to as your 'response-ability'. Of course everyone has a little of the victim in himself. But by letting your child take the fall, you're blaming him rather than taking control.

Victims are likely to become losers because they easily give up and say, 'It's not my fault. I trusted the kids, and they let me down – it's *their* fault.' But if you make a shift in your perception and empower yourself by following the tips in this book, you can make things work for you and become the *winner* in every situation.

The really successful and happy parent takes back control and responsibility. He's back in the driving seat, feeling more relaxed, happy, and energetic.

# Planning Ahead

Did you know that everything is actually created twice? First in your imagination and then in reality.

When you want to build your own dream house, you don't just buy a spare piece of land, get a load of bricks delivered, and start building (unless you're the third little pig!). In reality you start with your own ideas, appoint an architect to draw up some sketches, ask your partner and friends for their ideas, and fine-tune your plans until everything is just right. Only then do you finally start on the building work.

In fact you probably invest far more time planning your next holiday or deciding on a new outfit for your friend's wedding than you do planning what sort of adult you want your child to grow up into. This situation makes no sense!

Like all things of value, create your parenting twice. To have a harmonious family, you need a really clear picture in your mind of what you want to achieve. You need to visualise the finished product before you can start to put the pieces together.

## Dreaming of your child's future

Take some time now to imagine what you really want to achieve in your parenting. This vision is the bigger picture stuff – the destination of your parenting, your ultimate goal. Let your imagination go – dream a little! Make some notes in a journal or diary. Keep your journal handy while you work through the ideas in this book, and make writing in your journal a regular habit.

Write down *all* the ideas – big or small, silly or brilliant – as if you've already achieved them. Some examples include that you want your child to:

- ✔ Grow up to be independent and happy, confident and well-balanced.
- ✔ Respect and be tolerant of others.
- ✔ Enjoy spending time with you.
- ✔ Respect you as a parent and get on well.
- ✔ Have a great sense of humour and see the funny side of things.
- ✔ Become a responsible adult.
- ✔ Be kind and compassionate to others.
- ✔ Have tenacity and to study hard.
- ✔ Have stability and security in life.

Try this technique to discover your ideas for your child. Dream your ideal situation first. Then focus on it clearly and visualise it. Hear what you're saying – hear what your child is saying. Pay attention to how you're feeling. Make the whole picture brighter and closer to you, then step into it. Now write down everything that you just experienced. And dream some more!

## Breaking dreams into smaller goals

Just like a dream house, your dreams for your child can't be achieved in one go. You must break things down into sizeable chunks with a realistic timescale. Think in baby steps.

For the best results, try focusing on three types of goals:

- ✔ Long-term goals
- ✔ Medium-term goals
- ✔ Everyday goals

### Long-term goals: The philosophy of your parenting

Relax and consider: What are the one or two things you want your child to embrace about life?

My dad had a number of special little phrases that encapsulated his philosophy on life. 'Life is what you make it' and 'Get the balance right' were two of his favourites. My own philosophies include 'Enjoy the journey', 'Make a difference in the world', 'Laugh a lot', and 'Don't judge others'.

Write down your long-term goals in your journal or diary and then fine-tune until you're happy with them. Chapter 2 helps you clearly identify the type of parent you are and want to be.

Consider writing your long-term goals on a piece of paper and carrying them with you in your wallet or handbag to help you remember them when you're out and about in the real world.

### Medium-term goals: The annual health check

Each year (choose an easy date to remember, such as on New Year's Eve) relax over a cup of coffee and think about how your parenting is going. Be honest with yourself. Identify what's going well, but don't dwell on the stuff that's gone wrong. Just forgive yourself and focus on what you'd like to see happen in your family relationships in the next year.

Write down your medium-term goals in your journal or diary. Keep the journal in an easy to access spot (by your bed or on your desk). Read through your medium-term goals every month or so to remind yourself of what you hope to achieve as a parent this year.

### Everyday goals: Quick reminders

Think of your everyday parenting goals as your baby steps. Spend just ten minutes privately planning the little things that can make your parenting better. For example, an everyday goal may be to remember to step back from the situation, put a smile instead of a frown on your face, or see the funny side of a challenging situation. Chapter 7 includes many other ideas for useful everyday goals.

## Focusing on what you want

Focus, focus, focus – great parents get what they focus on.

Success, happiness, and being a great parent are *not* accidents that just happen to some people and not to others. These results are achieved by deliberate ways of thinking, acting, and being.

The changes that really matter are usually changes in *perception* within you, rather than the outside or external changes. And you can actually change the way you perceive something in a split second. Chapter 4 offers some useful tools for adjusting your perception.

## Become a better decision maker

Parents often find making decisions difficult because they're worried about making a mistake. No one likes to make an error, but what if you changed your way of thinking and saw it as an opportunity to learn how to improve as a parent?

Relax and realise that today's good decisions are based on yesterday's mistakes and experiences. Be happy with your mistakes, learn from them, and don't dwell on them – just move on.

As Richard Branson says, 'I have learnt more from my failures than my successes.'

Last autumn I went to my daughter's school to watch her play netball in the under 12's. She's a great player, enthusiastic and skilful. Standing behind the court, feeling frozen but enjoying the banter amongst the mums, I noticed something interesting. Every time a throw-in from outside the line occurred, she threw it to an opponent – definitely not where the ball should've been thrown! Eight out of ten times she was doing so because she was focusing on where the ball *shouldn't* go, instead of where it should. By encouraging her to relax and getting her to focus on where she wanted the ball to go and imagining it going there easily, she improved her game by simply thinking more positively.

Small changes really do make a big difference.

# *Making Some Changes*

In his bestselling book *Who Moved My Cheese?*, Spencer Johnson points out the difference between humans and rats. If rats discover what they're doing isn't working, they do something else; if humans discover what they're doing isn't working, they blame someone else!

The definition of madness is to keep on doing the same thing over and over again – but expecting different results. To keep getting up 15 minutes late and expect not to rush for the school bus is madness! If you want different results, you have to do things differently.

Parents who are stuck in their family relationships often say to me, 'But I've always done it that way' or 'That's just the way I am'. The truth is, if you really want to be the catalyst for change in your family and to begin to have success and different results, you need to step out of your comfort zone and try something different.

Only when you do things in a different way can you start to see your parenting get easier and more rewarding.

## Remembering win-win

To create success in your family life, you need to move away from an 'I win/you lose' mentality to a new perspective of really making an effort for the whole family to understand and co-operate with each other like a football or hockey team.

*Win-win* is a sharing mentality. It is the ability to work together. Thinking win-win creates mutual respect, shared understanding, and good quality family relationships as you all try to see the world from each other's perspective. Chapter 4 discusses this 'we' not 'me' mentality in detail.

# Taking Action

For most parents, taking action is the hardest part. The planning, focusing, and deciding are all relatively easy, but eventually a time comes when you reach the end of the diving board and have to jump off. Putting off action until tomorrow, next week, or next year is easy, but every decision needs to be enacted immediately. If you only manage something very small, at least you've actually started.

If you want to bring up a happy, confident, well-balanced child, start by talking with, listening to, and spending time with him on a daily basis at a time that feels relaxed, natural, and right for both of you. Now *that's* a positive first step to developing the long-term relationship you really want to build.

# Bringing Back the Bounce in Your Parenting

You can easily get bogged down in the socks and pants of life – the packed lunches you need to make, the dinners you have to cook, the grass you need to cut, the drains you need to clear out. Sometimes you need to reinvigorate your parenting, and the best place to start is with your kids.

Try the following technique to rejuvenate your parenting:

1. **Identify what you enjoy most about being a parent.**

   Some useful questions to ask yourself include:

   - What expression do you like to see on your child's face?
   - What's the best thing about that expression?

- How does it feel when your child laughs, giggles, or gives you that special hug?

- What's stopping you having more fun with your child?

- What do you think would be the biggest benefit to you and to your child if you spent more one-to-one time with him each day?

- How would more one-to-one time strengthen your relationship with your child?

2. **Write down on the Having Fun Together Wheel seven things you can do with your child.**

   Play hide and seek, ride a bike, play a board game, go for a walk in the park and chat, bake a cake, watch a game of football, go swimming, go shopping for ear rings! Be creative.

   Figure 1-1 shows a blank Having Fun Together Wheel.

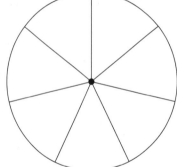

**Figure 1-1:**
The Having
Fun
Together
Wheel.

If you have trouble coming up with ideas for activities that you and your child can enjoy together, try asking your child what he wants to do. Consider filling in a wheel together.

3. **Try to do one activity from your wheel each week for seven weeks in a row – or each day for a week.**

   See the difference having more fun makes to your family life.

# Chapter 2

# Knowing What Kind of Parent You Are – and Want to Become

## In This Chapter

▶ Looking at what's important to you as a parent

▶ Identifying your values and influences

▶ Defining your parenting style

▶ Becoming an aware parent

*H*ow do you describe yourself as a parent? More specifically, how do you rate yourself as a parent? Do you believe that you're doing your best and have natural talent? Or do you think the whole endeavour is a bit overwhelming at times and you just keep getting it wrong?

The way you view yourself as a parent has a very strong effect on the way you influence your family and your kids. If you're confident and energetic, your family picks up on your positivity. But if you're constantly unsure or ill at ease, your family picks up on that too, and relationships can get tense.

✔ **Positive parents** believe in themselves. They enjoy life. They laugh. They are optimistic. They have lots of energy, passion, and creativity. They are great fun to be with. They focus on the solutions to family life not on the problems or challenges.

✔ **Negative parents** are unsure of themselves. They worry a lot. They appear anxious and tense. They frown and are stressed out. They lack energy and motivation. They are not much fun to be around as they drag everyone down with them. They see family life as a problem, something to be endured.

If you're not enjoying being the type of parent you currently are, perhaps you need to make a conscious change.

This chapter helps you look at what makes you tick, what's important to you, and what influences you – all in an effort to pinpoint what style of parent you currently are.

# Considering Your Parenting Values and Influences

The way you parent today is based on many things – notably your values and your influences. Identifying, understanding, and (perhaps) adjusting your parenting style means you need to examine your values and influences.

## Identifying your values

*Values* are the hot buttons that drive all your behaviours. Your values lead you to do something – and to decide afterwards whether your action was good or bad. Everything you hold dear to you stems from your own personal value system. Clarifying your values helps you to pass them down clearly to your children. Values can be related to your views about healthy eating, the environment, passing on your cultural traditions, your religious views or spirituality, your views about wealth, success, or social responsibility, or your views about education and your attitudes to the type of career your child may pursue.

So what values are important to you? Try the following to identify your core values (you can do this exercise alone or together with your partner to see if you hold the same values and are going in the same direction):

1. **Write down a list of all your values.**

2. **Look over your list and identify which of the values are most important to you *as a parent*.**

   Indicate your choices with a highlighter. You may include values such as being truthful, doing your best, being patient, being a good listener, being kind to others, being helpful, working hard, and so on.

3. **Narrow your list down to your top ten values.**

   Take your time, sit back and reflect on your list. Think about the values you most want to pass on to your children – the things you want them to remember when you're not around to remind them.

   Write down your top ten values in priority order – values such as honesty, kindness, integrity, being dependable and reliable, having determination, or the ability to finish a task.

4. **Narrow down your top ten list even further to just your top three.**

   Ask yourself whether you're living your life according to your values.

To figure out your values, you may have to do a bit of soul-searching, asking yourself questions about what really matters to you and what you deeply believe in. What are the issues that you're not willing to compromise on?

Values affect the direction of your family life – if you believe in security, comfort, and not taking risks, your children learn different values than from a family who teach their kids to be adventurous, take calculated risks, and are encouraged to be entrepreneurs.

You may discover that by writing your values down that you'd like to change, amend, or tweak some of them. Alternatively, you may feel really good about yourself and your family. Whatever you discover, enjoy exploring what your priorities in life are.

Being clear about your values makes parenting a lot easier because you know what you want to pass on to your children and you can live more consistently knowing where you're going. Living your values, whatever they are for you, also makes you feel loads happier.

What you do, say, and how you act really does matter. Next time you stand in front of a mirror, don't just ask 'Does my bum look big in this?' Actually *stop* and realise that who you are at this very moment is how your children see you. You're their role model. They're learning from you *all* the time. When someone cuts you up on the motorway, how you react, what you say, and how you behave are all ways of showing your children your values – such as respect for others, how to handle stress, and whether you're compassionate.

## *Considering your influences*

Adults parent in certain ways for a variety of reasons. Some common influences on your parenting include:

- ✔ **The way your parents brought you up.** Were your parents strict, permissive, authoritarian, or balanced?

- ✔ **Your personality.** Are you easygoing, patient, positive, and humorous – or negative, volatile, and anxious?

- ✔ **Your children.** Are they active, demanding, calm, nervous, determined, self-motivated, or lazy? Does your personality clash with your children's? Do you see yourself in your children? Do you find these similarities difficult?

- ✔ **Time, money, and circumstances.** Are you short of time and energy? Do you work? Is money short? Are you a single parent? Do you lack space at home? Do you need to make more time for yourself? All these factors can influence your parenting.

✔ **Your role models.** What role models were you given? Are you pleased to pass these models on to your children – or do you prefer to have your own style? Where do you get your parenting skills from – Richard and Judy, Oprah Winfrey, your mother-in-law, or your friends?

✔ **Your lifestyle, priorities, preferences, and tastes.** What is important to you in your life? How do you express your priorities to your children? How important are education, sport, TV, having a big house, religion, or compassion to you?

The following sections explore various influences in greater detail.

### *Your own parents*

The first time I recognised my mother's influence on my parenting style, I was shocked – I considered myself a totally different kind of mum! But when I'm tired, I've found myself telling my daughter (who just won't brush her teeth before bed) things such as, 'You'll end up with black teeth and no boyfriends!' The hard truth to swallow was that despite all my years working with kids and feeling I had a lot of experience, I was still under the influence of my early role models.

Consider some of the things your parents used to say to you. Write down a list of phrases and ideas. Maybe some of the following sound familiar to you:

✔ *Do as you're told – and don't argue with me.*

✔ *Do what you want, but don't get into trouble.*

✔ *Here's another present because I'm always away on business.*

✔ *I hate the fact you're growing up. I can't let you go easily.*

✔ *I'm a high achiever and I expect a great deal from you, too.*

✔ *I am firm, fair, and friendly.*

Read through the list above as well as your own list and consider which statements and phrases describe your parenting style. Which statements do you most relate to?

Taking on the parenting characteristics of your own parents isn't necessarily a bad thing. But when you're tired, overwhelmed, or under pressure, you may go into what I call *auto-parenting* – resorting to parenting in the way you've been brought up yourself (which may or may not be something you'd always choose) or you may go into your most 'natural' style of parenting, which for me is rather a bull in a china shop approach. Whatever your auto-parent is like, be aware that you're not in conscious control of the situation and that's not a good thing.

### Avoiding auto-parenting

What can you do when you start to feel overwhelmed or tired to make you remember to step back and avoid going into auto-parent? Well, you can start by beginning to notice when you feel tired, overwhelmed, or frustrated and notice when and where you start to experience these feelings.

Ask yourself:

- Do I feel overwhelmed at the same time every day, or only in certain situations?
- What causes me to feel like this and what can I do to change the circumstances or my attitude?
- How do my kids see me right now?

Your answer to the last question is revealing. Do your kids see an angry, out of control, scary parent; a defeated, exhausted, can't be bothered parent; or a distant, uncaring, and unemotional parent?

When you become aware of auto-parenting, you have the power within you to change the situation around. Become more aware of how you behave and if you don't like yourself, change. The following techniques help you to step out of auto-parent and help you to get back into control:

- See yourself pressing a Pause button inside your head to stop the situation from developing.
- Remind yourself that you may need to have a sit down, a cup of coffee, a read of the paper, or a dog walk to replenish or rejuvenate your energy. Work out what works for you.
- Think about the type of relationship you want to develop with your children and ask yourself: 'Is my attitude and approach here taking me closer or further away from my kids?' Consider your answer and change your attitude if you need to.

### Your teachers, friends, community, and society

Consider the other external influences that surrounded you as you grew up – as well as those influencing you today.

- Your teachers at school probably said things to you or about you that have stayed with you.

  I can still remember a teacher telling me, 'You really struggle with maths, don't you? What are we going to do with you?' That statement still affects the way I approach studying my bank balance today.

# Growing up is different today

The top seven discipline problems in schools in 1940 were talking in class, chewing gum, getting out of line, running in the corridors, making noise, wearing improper clothes, and not putting rubbish in the wastepaper bin. The top seven problems in 1990 were drug abuse, alcohol abuse, pregnancy, rape, suicide, robbery, and assault!

For many, children have become a real mystery, as though they're from another planet. Feeling they have failed, many parents ask themselves 'Where have we gone wrong?'

Don't be too hard on yourself: Children today *are* different. Massive shifts have taken place in Western culture in recent years. Never before in the history of civilisation has a generation grown up with such a massive cultural change. The world really is different to the world you knew and grew up in. Despite the fact that you live in and experience the same world as your children, you probably don't step back and analyse what it must be like for them. You may be too busy surviving yourself!

Today's fast-paced, non-stop, multimedia world has brought with it two problems:

✔ **As children grow up in this exciting world, they tend to develop the expectation that they must always be excited.** Today's kids don't expect to be bored. They don't understand that boredom is sometimes an inevitable fact of life. However, boredom is something all children need to develop the skills to cope with.

✔ **As children (and people in general) experience a new level of excitement, their thresholds tend to increase.** No matter how exciting something is at first, it tends to lose its excitement value, so people seek out something higher, faster, brighter, or louder to excite themselves. You can see why drugs are so appealing to young people – theirs is a world of constant buzz, where boredom isn't acceptable. Drugs provide the excitement and fulfilment so many children have grown up to expect and yet never seem to find.

Being bored doesn't mean something's gone wrong – it isn't a problem and doesn't need fixing. Today's world may be different but you can still help your children handle being bored in simple yet effective ways. For example, show your kids how to play Solitaire, hit a ball against a wall, practise catching, ride a bike, read a book, and not seek excitement constantly. These everyday activities may just save your child's life.

✔ Your friends praise, encourage, criticise, or complain to you all the time. Take a moment to consider how much you actively believe about yourself based on what they say. What influence do these people have on your parenting?

✔ Individuals in your church may have told you ways to behave or things to avoid doing.

✔ Your community and society in general have placed value on certain things while minimising others.

Start a list of these external influences. Which do you agree with – and which have you been accepting blindly? Think about how you can take control over yourself!

*The longer I live, the more keenly I feel that whatever was good enough for our fathers is not good enough for us.*

—Oscar Wilde

# Developing Awareness

So many parents are simply reactive and slapdash – responding without thinking about what they're doing. You probably take a great deal of time to buy a new house, car, or washing machine, and yet you may not take the time to really consider what you're doing when you raise your children.

A useful attitude to adopt while raising children is one of *aware parenting*, meaning being constantly aware of the bigger picture. By being aware, you react with *intention*, rather than by chance. Aware parenting doesn't mean you're boring and can't be spontaneous or natural. You simply hold a vision of where you and your children are trying to get to, together.

The destination of your parenting – the nurturing of unique, confident adults – is what really matters.

## Considering three types of awareness

Typically, parents need to be aware in three types of situations:

- ✔ **Situations where you have plenty of time to think through what you want to do before you act.** These situations include choosing a secondary school or deciding whether your son should take tennis lessons now that he's showing a keen interest in playing. You have plenty of time to reflect on the effect that your decision will have on your child. You make an informed decision, not an impulsive one.

- ✔ **Situations where you have to react on the spot, with little time.** Examples here include when your 3-year-old child refuses to eat what you're serving her for dinner or your 10-year-old wants to have a sleep over tonight and rings you at work. In these situations, you have to remember your principles and respond in a consistent way. But because you've made being an aware parent a habit, you can react quickly – and in keeping with your parenting style.

> ✔ **Situations where your reaction is completely reflexive.** These situations include when your toddler has thrown a wobbly by the sweets in the supermarket, your 11-year-old has just strangled her 13-year-old brother, or your teenage daughter has gone upstairs to her bedroom with her new boyfriend to listen to some music. If you develop the habit of being an aware parent, reflexive reactions that are in keeping with your values and parenting style can become second nature to you.

Aware parenting doesn't come naturally to many people. Thinking about what you're doing doesn't have to take away all the fun and spontaneity from life. Keep trying and don't be too hard on yourself.

## *Recognising your power*

If you are a thoughtful parent, you are nurturing your child's self-esteem *all the time*. As an aware parent, you can influence

> ✔ Your child's personality, interests, character, intelligence, attitudes, and values.
>
> ✔ Your child's likes and dislikes.
>
> ✔ How your child behaves at school, at home, and with friends.
>
> ✔ Whether your child is kind, considerate, judgemental, or selfish.

So harness your influence to help your child develop his or her best characteristics. What you do matters!

Whatever your parenting style, try to maintain your sense of humour. Humour diffuses tension, lifts your mood, and changes everyone's perspective. It shifts and changes your view of the world, often making the tense situation appear silly in the bigger picture of life. Laughing can relax you and make you feel more positive and balanced. So try to find the funny side to things and watch the tension and stress melt away.

A negative attitude is like a flat tyre – you don't get very far unless you change it!

You are a role model, whether you like it or not. Children have a strong desire to grow up to be just like their mums and dads. If you're an anxious parent, your nervous energy conveys anxiety to your child. If you're a confident, relaxed parent, your child learns confidence and calmness by watching you. If you are courteous, kind, friendly, and generous, your child has a much greater chance of turning out similarly. If you're rude, judgemental, aggressive, and aloof, your child (especially before adolescence) learns to be the same. So try to reign yourself in rather than screaming profanities at your spouse when you can't find the car keys!

Don't be afraid to assert your authority. You're a parent – your job is to set boundaries and stick to them. Rather than telling yourself you're powerless against the influence of the media or your children's friends, remember you do have a strong, guiding influence over your child. Today's numerous outside negative influences on your child make your role even *more* important. Have clear, fair, and consistent boundaries – limit your children's access to TV and video games and regulate what they're allowed to watch.

Everyone performs poorly when tired or stressed. Just be aware of this fact and forgive yourself. Raising a well-balanced, self-confident adult is hard work. Pat yourself on the back now and again for things you do right. You deserve that glass of wine!

# Chapter 3

# Understanding Your Kids' Needs

*C*hildren are all different. They are different at different ages. They are different from each other. They are different in different circumstances and they are different from what you expect. No wonder understanding your children is so difficult!

This chapter is about recognising that no two children are the same and that, as a parent, you should treat your kids as individuals, respect their differences, and help them grow and develop in their own unique and special way. You can talk to your children in different ways, depending on their needs. For example, a child who's sensitive may need to receive your messages in a gentle way, whereas a child who's easily distracted needs your undivided attention when you're telling him something.

Effective parenting is about you, as the parent, developing skills and abilities to understand your individual child so you can adapt your parenting to fit the needs of your child most effectively. Understanding your kids takes time and patience, but the reward is a strong and satisfying relationship with your child that lasts a lifetime.

This chapter looks at the six basic levels of all children's needs and goes on to consider the differences in needs between boys and girls. I offer ways to help you understand your children as individuals and to discover some new ways to express your love in ways that match each child's style of loving.

I help you discover ways to respond to your children's needs by giving security, stability, and meaningful praise. I also offer suggestions of how to listen to your children actively and more effectively and I look at different ways to support your children and show them respect.

# Exploring Your Child's Needs

Bringing up children today is a stressful business because you're bombarded with images of calm, obedient, and extremely clean children with happy, smiling parents all dressed in white, having fun. But that scenario only exists in Hollywood films! Most parents spend a considerable amount of time feeling anxious and guilty because they know that they're often 'getting it wrong' but forget that they're also 'getting it right' a lot of the time too. Most parents are a mixture of the two extremes of Mary Poppins and Cruella De Vil! We all have a mixture of strengths and weaknesses.

Nowadays the nurturing of children is a complicated business because many are brought up and influenced not only by their parents but by childminders, teachers, step-parents, nannies, TV presenters, and adverts.

Everyone has needs. From the moment you're born you require basic things such as food, drink, safety, comfort, warmth, and love. But before you know it, your kids are suddenly saying they 'need' those really expensive Nike trainers, a trendy haircut, or that designer T-shirt because everyone else has them.

As a parent you need to be clear about what's really important to you – your values – and you need to express them clearly to your children so you can find a balance between your values and your children's expectations. Keep the long-term objective of your parenting in front of you to maintain your perspective when your values are challenged, questioned, or argued over.

As children grow, their needs change and seem more complex but really the same emotional, physical, mental, and spiritual things still apply. Of course, how those needs are expressed by each of your children varies from child to child. Some children need more attention from you than others, some need more personal space or more help with their school work. These varying needs can seem demanding at times – but feeling you have to show a different side of yourself and your personality for each of your children is perfectly normal. Doing so is simply utilising your different skills in different situations and being flexible. Underneath, you're still the same person.

## Introducing the hierarchy of needs

In the 1940s, the American psychologist Abraham Maslow developed the *hierarchy of needs*, which suggests that every human being has needs that range from basic to more complex and abstract. As Figure 3-1 shows, specific needs must be met at each level in order for a person to feel safe, satisfied, loved, fulfilled, or inspired.

Maslow suggested that only when the lower order needs of physical and emotional well-being are satisfied can humans become concerned with the higher order needs of independence, responsibility, or self-fulfilment.

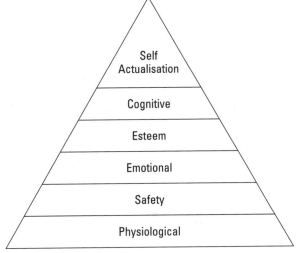

**Figure 3-1:**
Maslow's
hierarchy of
needs as a
pyramid of
increasingly
complex
human
needs.

When shown as a pyramid, the hierarchy of needs offers a clear explanation of the needs of children. In order for kids to be comfortable in their environment, with others, and within themselves, they must have specific needs met, in the following order:

- ✔ **Physiological needs.** Your child needs the basic requirements of food, drink, sleep, and shelter.

- ✔ **Safety needs.** Your child needs basic protection from the elements, safe limits, stability, and a feeling of safety from emotional and physical harm.

- ✔ **Emotional needs.** Your child must feel loved and that he can belong to a social group, both of which enable him to feel comfortable within his surroundings.

- ✔ **Esteem needs.** Your child must be able to achieve recognition within a group in order to develop self-esteem. Joining a group of other children is one thing, but to satisfy esteem needs and to feel truly welcome and comfortable, your child must feel accepted and recognised.

- ✔ **Cognitive needs.** Your child develops mental abilities and skills by acquiring knowledge, learning, knowing, and understanding himself and others.

> ✔ **Self-actualisation.** Finally, your child needs *self-fulfilment*, or realising who exactly he is. Children achieve self-actualisation by knowing about themselves and learning about who they are and what they are good at. From here they can go on to maximise their own potential.

Maslow's hierarchy follows the cycle of life and shows exactly what a child of any age needs, whether toddler or teenager. A baby's needs are almost entirely physiological but as he grows into a toddler, he needs safety, then love. Toddlers are eager for social interaction; teenagers are anxious about social needs; and young adults are concerned with esteem. Cognitive needs are the expression of the natural human need to learn, explore, discover, and create in order to get a better understanding of the world. Children are constantly exploring, discovering, and creating so they're always fulfilling this basic human need. While you, as a parent, can guide your kids towards self-actualisation, it depends on each individual person how far they want to explore or develop themselves in adulthood. Self-development and self-improvement are personal choices, so I don't cover that topic in detail here.

## Climbing the pyramid

Just like an actual pyramid, each higher level of need builds upon the level beneath it. Therefore, the foundations of each level must be strong in order for the child to be able to successfully move up to the next level. If one level is weak within a child, then the needs above that level will be very difficult to develop because all the needs are interrelated.

As a teacher I was very aware of the hierarchy of needs from my experience in the classroom. Children who arrived in school not well fed or well cared for, either physically or emotionally, weren't able to learn well (or satisfy their cognitive needs) because their lower needs had not been met. They couldn't concentrate on the lesson if they were hungry or they'd been shouted at or hit before they arrived at school.

Reaching the top of the pyramid can require a lifetime of effort. Some individuals never reach the highest level. Self-actualisation takes great patience, good communication, lots of love, and maybe a sprinkling of luck. Life doesn't offer any guarantees, and even good parents make mistakes and need to be prepared for disappointments. But the more you are aware of the important needs of your child and understand your responsibilities as a parent, the more likely your child can reach his full potential.

The following sections address the specifics of each level of need during a child's development.

# *Addressing Security and Stability Needs*

Children of all ages need to feel safe, secure, protected from physical harm, and free from fear. They need to know that their parents love them and will provide a safe haven with meals and a place to sleep free from violence. One way of creating a sense of safety is by ensuring your kids have a safe home environment.

Creating a safe haven – a real home – is very important to a child. Home is a place to relax, be messy, play, chat to family, create, discover, unwind, have privacy, be alone, and be themselves completely. Home is predictable in its familiarity. It is a place of love, security, and protection but also a place of respect.

Your home doesn't have to be a show home – just warm, comfortable, and safe for your kids, depending on their age. So when your children are toddlers, put up stair-gates and door protectors to stop them trapping their little fingers, have wires tucked out of sight, and remember that babies put everything in their mouths. As your children get older, talk to them about an escape route in case of fire. Always have smoke detectors, and a fire extinguisher in the kitchen.

Children also need daily structure and limits to feel truly safe and secure. Routines, repetition, and a stable environment build inner peace, security, and confidence.

Kids need some absolutes in their lives. Having clear rules and fair discipline procedures makes an enormous difference in creating a stable environment. The actual day-to-day rules you establish naturally may vary according to your child's age and level of maturity. Chapter 8 covers discipline in more detail, and Chapter 9 is all about using different strategies for different ages.

You can establish different rules for different children in your family – as long as you explain to your children why the rules vary. If your rules are based on real differences between the children, who genuinely warrant different treatment, most children can understand your reasoning and only get upset if they believe treatment is unjustified or unfair. For example, different rules for different children may be appropriate based on age. If this is the case, explain to the younger child that he can look forward to the same rule when he is the same age as his brother. Or one child may have trouble completing homework and need more supervision than his brother. The homework rules must be the same for all children ('Get the homework done on time and regularly'), but one child can do his work in his room or on the computer independently, while the other needs you to sit with him.

Children thrive on routine, security, and rules. If your child feels secure, he'll be happy to try out new challenges.

Ask yourself: If my child were describing our home to another child, what would he say about how secure, how safe, how peaceful, and relaxed he feels when he walks through the door? How do you feel about the answer – has it surprised you? If you've discovered something you aren't happy with, now is a great opportunity to do something about it and change a few things. What small change can you make this week to improve the situation? See how the situation goes for a week or two and ask the question again.

Parenting isn't an exact science – it's all about fine-tuning what you do from time to time and finding new ways to do things.

In order to be a good parent, you must have realistic expectations and delicately balance your own needs with your children's, which takes patience and understanding. Until your children can meet their own needs, you must do so for them. You have to help them develop the skills to take care of themselves physically.

# Addressing Emotional Needs: All You Need Is Love

All children want, need, and deserve is unconditional love. You have probably heard people talk about unconditional love, but you may not really know what it is. *Unconditional love* is

- ✔ Loving your children deeply and with no strings attached, regardless of what they do.
- ✔ Loving your children despite their behaviours or the mistakes they make.
- ✔ Loving free from any conditions or expectations to please you.
- ✔ Letting your kids know that they're worth any amount of trouble.

Showing your children unconditional love enables them to know that they belong and always have a place in your family no matter what. Children from affectionate families are better equipped to cope with the frustrations and disappointments of daily life. They develop self-esteem, self-worth, self-confidence, and ultimately self-belief from being unconditionally loved. And from this solid foundation, everything else in life becomes easier and more straightforward.

Unconditional love doesn't mean you become lenient with your children, lower your expectations, or just give them material possessions. Children need and thrive within their safe limits.

A very common parental pitfall is viewing discipline as an unpleasant, guilt-producing task reserved only for times of crisis. A far better way to view the job is to consider the effect of different discipline styles on your children.

Research shows that children whose parents are permissive, granting their kids a great deal of latitude, tend to lack self-control and self-reliance later on. And children whose parents are authoritarian, with a do-it-my-way approach, often become dependent and irresponsible. But children raised by parents who make a point of encouraging individuality while also enforcing rules and setting clear expectations of appropriate behaviour usually become the most well adjusted and independent of all. So by setting your children limits, you're actually being very loving.

 Your current self-image is the result of the repeated messages of unconditional love that you received as a child from authority figures in your life. The way you see yourself is the result of the messages you received from your parents, family, teachers, and other influential adults in your life. One of the key gifts you can give your child is the powerful gift of loving themselves. Show your child plenty of love and affection because doing so builds up his self-esteem and confidence for a lifetime.

Children who feel truly loved have such a strong sense of security that they are less needy. The healthiest adults are the ones who express their love to others easily because they grew up with unequivocal and unconditional love from their parents. Those who were forced to scrape by on something less than complete affection are the needy adults.

 You can never give too much genuine affection and warmth – or too much love – to your child. Don't think your child will become spoiled by all the attention. Holding back and being aloof sends out the wrong message. Children don't need the old school way of ' toughening up'. They are fragile, sensitive, small human beings who need hugs, fun, and laughter – just as much from their fathers as from their mothers.

## Showing love

One of the most basic ways to show children love is through your actions.

Most obviously, children need plenty of physical affection, not just when they are little, but throughout their childhood. Humans are tactile creatures and need physical contact with others. Touching releases endorphins (feel good hormones), reduces stress, and helps the immune system to work better. The rise in popularity of all sorts of massages, reflexology, and other tactile techniques is representative of the basic human need to be touched.

Children learn to love themselves primarily through experiencing love and appreciation from their parents. So you need to express this love clearly and frequently.

I like the idea suggested by Gary Chapman and Ross Campbell in their excellent book *The Five Love Languages of Children* (Moody Press) that every child has an emotional tank, a place of emotional strength that can fuel him through the challenging days of childhood and adolescence. Just as petrol tanks power cars, emotional tanks power children. As a parent, you must fill your children's emotional tanks for them to reach their true potential.

### Demonstrating your love in different ways

Imagine that you've been away from home for a few days and when you come through the door your children come dashing down the stairs to eagerly greet you. One child smothers you in hugs and kisses while the other jumps up and down asking if you've brought a present. Your partner takes your coat and bag upstairs, while your mum, who's been holding the fort, tells you she missed you and is so glad you're home.

Demonstrated in this scene are four very different ways of showing love. Understanding and reciprocating your children's and family's love languages can make a massive difference to how much everyone feels appreciated, loved, and understood.

There are actually five ways to show love and affection:

- ✔ **Words of affirmation.** Everyone likes to hear an encouraging word now and again but some children need an 'I love you' on a daily basis. This need doesn't mean that they have low self-esteem. Words of endearment and praise are vitally important to some children and are their key way of feeling loved. Kids who long to hear 'I love you' and 'I'm proud of you' will be amazingly encouraged by your simple words.

  Ask your child how he knows that you love him and if he says 'Because you tell me all the time and you're proud of me', then you know that their primary love language is words of affirmation.

- ✔ **Physical touch.** Perhaps your child thrives on cuddles and hugs and needs that goodnight hug and kiss from you. Whether you have a toddler or a teenager, physical touch is a vital part of showing love to your child.

  If your child loves to hold your hand, link arms with you, or give you lots of hugs, then his primary love language is physical touch. You can demonstrate your love for him by touching him affectionately.

✔ **Acts of service.** This love language shows a need to serve. My father-in-law is a great example of this way of showing love. He mends the kids' bicycles, sweeps up the leaves, repairs broken furniture, and changes light bulbs when he comes to visit. He never sits still and is never happier than when helping. Perhaps your child makes cups of tea for you, or lays the table.

If you ask your child how he knows you love him and he says 'Because you help me with my homework, sew my buttons on, and make my bed', then his love language is acts of service. He thrives on you doing little things for him (above the normal parental stuff such as cooking their dinner). Your child really appreciates you making a special costume for the school play, repairing his old teddy with one eye missing, or decorating his room unexpectedly when he's gone to stay with grandma.

✔ **Gift-giving.** This language isn't materialistic or selfish – the size of the gift is unimportant, its significance is the thought. Children who express their love this way paint pictures for you, or pick flowers for you as a special gift. You can return your child's love in the way he likes to be loved – perhaps by giving him a special key ring that you found at the market, a shell from the beach, or a fossil for his collection. Use your imagination.

✔ **Quality time.** Everyone enjoys spending time with loved ones, and who doesn't feel treasured when having an in-depth chat or a fun game with the family? For some children this is their primary way of receiving and expressing love, and yet for some parents this is the hardest to give because it requires, in some ways, more of yourself than the others. Hugging someone can be easier than spending an hour with them. Really being engaged and interested in spending time just chatting or doing something together with your child is a real gift, particularly if this is your child's prime way to feel loved. Make the effort to plan some quality time with your child and watch his face light up.

We're all a mixture of these languages and your child is no exception, but dig a little deeper and you discover that striving to learn your child's language is a very powerful gift to your whole family. The first time I started noticing the different ways my kids both showed love was very emotional for me because I realised it was a bit different to my own way.

Using the different love languages can help other family relationships, such as that between yourself and your partner. If you've ever felt 'unloved', it may be because your loved ones aren't showing love in a way you easily see. Recognising the various ways of expressing love is a tremendous help. I realised that I have a different love language to my husband – I love to spend quality time chatting to him and feeling heard, whereas he likes to make me cups of tea, run me a bath, and put the ironing away (I know, he's a saint!), but actually I've often felt 'unloved' when he doesn't sit down and simply listen to me.

Being aware of the different ways to express love may help deepen your relationships with your children.

## Appropriate affection at different developmental stages

Children need plenty of physical affection, not just when they're little, but throughout their childhood. However, what you did when your child was in nursery isn't necessarily appropriate when he reaches adolescence. This notion may seem obvious, but you'd be surprised at how many parents don't change their ways of showing affection as their child develops and then wonder why he's suddenly embarrassed or aloof.

When your child develops physically from one stage to the next, he's changing on the inside as well. Your child isn't just growing in shoe size, but changing the way he thinks, what he feels, what he thinks about himself, what he is capa-

ble of, and how he relates to other people, including you.

I remember my own son squirming as I gave him a big, noisy hug and kiss goodbye at the school gate in front of his friends. He was so embarrassed, possibly because I was also a teacher at his school. I'd forgotten that at 12 he'd rather I hugged him at home and played it 'cool' at school! I needed to develop sensitivity to his changing needs.

Teenagers still need displays of affection too – but remember to keep this part of your relationship more private. Find relaxed ways to show natural physical affection: Ruffle his hair or gently touch his shoulder.

## *Loving by listening*

Another way of showing children love is by genuinely listening to them. Children need you to stop what you're doing and to really pay attention to them with genuine interest. This type of listening shows respect and that you value what they say. Genuine listening also teaches them that you care enough to enter their world and empathise with their view of the wider world.

A huge difference exists between 'talking at' and 'talking with' your child. Rather like 'laughing at' or 'laughing with' someone, talking *at* a child resembles a lecture where you just go on and on, whereas talking *with* a child involves empathy, listening, and genuine interest. Guard against the conversation that always feels like a lecture, an inquisition, or a nag!

As a parent, you can easily fall into a *one-way dialogue*, where you are monitoring, instructing, or trying to pass on life's lessons without attempting to listen to your child's responses. One-way dialogues can be very demoralising – not to mention boring – for a child. Children, just like adults, want to be heard. They want their point of view valued, not corrected. Talking *with* your child shows that you're genuinely interested in what he has to say and that you want to spend time understanding him.

Here are some ideas on two-way or mutual communication, where both of you are truly listening and talking together equally:

- ✔ **Pay attention.** Concentrate on what your child is saying by putting the paper down or stopping gardening, making tea or whatever. Maybe the following sounds familiar:

    *'Dad, Sophie ignored me today all through lunch time.'*

    (Eyes watching television) 'Ooh, he nearly scored there . . . Go on. I'm listening.'

    *'So I felt really awful all afternoon. Are you really listening, Dad?'*

    (Eyes still watching TV) 'Of course I'm listening to every word.'

    *'No, you're not.'*

    'I can listen and watch the game at the same time. Go on . . .'

    *'Oh, just forget it!'*

- ✔ **Actively listen.** Turn off the television, put down the paper, leave the washing up, and look into your child's eyes so that he knows that he has your full attention. Stop talking. Actively listening requires a massive effort on your part (at first) to remember to stop what you're doing, turn to look at your child, and to truly listen without interruption, but it is a gift like no other to your child, regardless of his age.

    Actively listening involves your eyes as well as your ears. Let your child feel he's important and interesting. Turn your heart to face your child's heart for a simple (and hopefully not too corny) way to remember that you're speaking to one of the most important people in your life. Get down to his eye level if your child is small and remember how you feel if people fidget, play with their mobile phone, or look distracted when you talk to them – that's just how your child feels if you look disinterested in what he's saying to you. Actively listening is all about respect.

- ✔ **Actively ask your child's viewpoint.** Ask your child what he thinks about a problem. Try to get him to express what he would do to solve the problem. Here's an example from my own home:

    'I've got a problem with all the crisp packets that you leave stuffed into the sofa. I'd like your help in trying to solve this problem because I can't relax and watch TV if the room is a mess. What do you think we can do to sort this out?'

    *'Well, we could bring another bin into the sitting room and put it nearer to where I sit so I can reach it easier. It'll remind me to put the packet in the bin when I've finished.'*

✔ **Ask open-ended questions.** Questions that require more than a 'yes' or 'no' answer require children to share more with you – and give you an opportunity to have more to listen and respond to. Some open-ended questions include:

> 'What did you find the most fun today at school?'
>
> 'How did the hockey game go?'
>
> 'What did you enjoy most about the holiday?'

Where, what, and how questions are always good to get kids talking more openly.

✔ **Avoid interrupting.** Children think slower than adults. Give your child time to formulate his sentences and finish what he wants to say. When you cut off your child, you send the message that you don't really care about what he has to say. For example:

> *'I went to the school office today, Mum, to give in my—'*
>
> 'Form. Yes, that's a good boy. So did they give you back the form for me to sign?'

✔ **Be sincere and genuine.** Don't just ask banal questions for the sake of it. Be really interested in what your child is telling you. He's letting you into his world, and showing you that he wants you to be part of it.

## Loving by praising

Praising children is another way to express your love for them. Praise not only makes children feel good about themselves – therefore building self-esteem – but it helps them to experience important lessons about the value of working hard to achieve a goal or to behave in a certain way.

Pay attention to how you phrase your praise, for example:

✔ **Try to be specific.** For example, praise the non-smoking leaflet your son has designed for school genuinely by looking at the attention to detail, the words he chose, the colours he used, and the impact it had on you. Don't just say, 'I love it when you work hard at school'. Then there is no judgement or pressure put on your child, just a willingness to praise the positive.

✔ **Avoid linking the accomplishment to your affection.** 'I love you so much when you get a good mark for your History exam' or 'I'm so proud that you always do so well and get in the A-team at school'.

✔ **Praise your child's effort and energy, rather than focusing on a specific grade or review.** Children are painfully aware, by around the age of 9 years old, that their accomplishments are being graded and evaluated by others. Don't add to the pressure of securing a good grade or positive evaluation. Praise the improved spelling, not the 76 per cent mark.

For example, my husband and I rewarded our son with a trip to see Chelsea play Barcelona *before* we knew his exam results, in an effort to reward his time, energy, and commitment to studying for weeks beforehand. Similarly, our daughter felt our heartfelt praise and delight at her singing festival because she had to overcome her shyness at performing in public – not the fact that she received a certificate for doing so.

✔ **Limit the attention you pay to 'natural talent' and instead praise your child's effort and energy.** Link your praise to the quality of the work your child has put into the project.

Look at sporting stars such as Lance Armstrong, Tiger Woods, or Sir Steve Redgrave; they're successful because they work harder and practise more than their peers, regardless of how naturally talented they are. They're determined to put in time, energy, and commitment. Inspire this type of determination in your child and watch him soar with enthusiasm and self-esteem.

✔ **Offer praise *while* your child is doing something good.** When you see your child doing something right, reinforce the behaviour immediately with praise. Doing so is a powerful way to help children identify positive behaviours and ultimately like themselves more.

✔ **If you must compare, compare your child's performance or accomplishment to himself, not to others.** For example, after a good match, say something like 'You can really control the ball and throw it accurately to another player now. Well done, that's brilliant!' rather than, 'You always play better than Joe. I don't know why he's in the team'.

Beware of false praise. Don't praise your child for being good at geography when your child knows they haven't got a clue about any of the capital cities they were asked to learn and have always struggled with this subject. Don't pretend. Children can see through you easily – and don't deserve to be patronised.

Children want to feel accepted for who they are – not because they're clones of you or act 'perfect'. They want to feel special, unique, and loved for who they are, not what they do or say. Your praise helps them discover who they are and develop their senses of identity and self-worth.

# Loving by respecting

*Respect* means giving children freedom of thought and expression. It also means speaking gently and kindly to them and showing them patience and tolerance.

When parents are not respectful to their children, it can seriously limit the child's opportunities for self-discovery, keep them from forming an identity, badly damage their self-esteem and confidence, and prevent them from understanding and expressing their emotions properly.

Children need parents who champion and root for them. They need support when things are difficult or challenging. They need parents who will give them honest and sensitive feedback – both when they're doing well and when they're struggling and are disappointed.

The way you handle your child's trauma *after* an event – rather than the event itself – makes a big difference to how he handles the experience successfully in the long term. After a traumatic event such as divorce, being bullied, changing schools, listening to parental fights, or losing a loved one, your child needs to feel loved. Help him to feel better about himself (and feel like he belongs) by highlighting positive aspects of how he acted during the event. Or point to positive things he's done outside of the event.

Pride and respect are two different emotional expressions. *Respect* in the dictionary means 'admiration or esteem' while *pride* means 'pleasure or satisfaction with one's possessions or achievements'. Can you see the difference here? To be proud of your child means you are satisfied or pleased with your possession. To respect your child means you admire him and hold him in esteem for who he is.

I remember being in a local newsagent as a mother criticised her 5-year-old child to the lady behind the counter, who had merely asked 'How's it going this holiday?' The mother was rude, unkind, dismissive, and extremely hurtful about her daughter, who stood nearby listening as the mother told a stranger about what she thought of her child. The mother showed her daughter no respect.

Effective parenting involves a balance of nurturing, discipline, and respect for children. Evaluate your values and beliefs, your discipline strategies, your communication skills, and your work–life balance and put your child first on your list of priorities by showing him your utmost respect.

## Exploring your beliefs about respect

The following questions can help you focus on how you show respect to your child. Get a notepad and paper and write down your answers.

✔ **What thoughts come into your head when you hear the word *respect*?** What does respect mean to you? Is it about showing tolerance, acceptance, and common decency towards the people around you – your family, friends, and peers, people who are older or younger than you, people from different cultures or religions? Is it about being considerate of the consequences of your behaviour towards others? Is it about receiving respect from your child without showing it to him first?

✔ **Do you think your child should automatically respect you?** What are your reasons for your answer?

✔ **How do you feel about seeing respect as a gift that you give freely every day to your child?**

✔ **How do you show respect to your child with your words, body language, or tone of voice?** By listening to them, giving them time, valuing their drawings and paintings, and celebrating their many diverse talents?

✔ **Do you think children should just get respect for being a smaller and more vulnerable human being?**

✔ **How do you express your respect for the qualities you admire in your child?** Focus on your child's great characteristics, such as tenacity, resilience, kindness, humour, generosity, and all their positive attributes.

### *Noting – and avoiding – the seven deadly disses*

People can be disrespectful to others in various ways. I consider the following seven disrespectful behaviours to be the seven deadly disses:

✔ **Criticising** is a negative and often destructive way of talking to kids that really doesn't move the situation forward, such as saying 'That's the third time you've lost your jumper. You're hopeless at looking after yourself.' You can often find yourself stuck in this way of thinking and talking.

✔ **Blaming** means putting the blame on your kids and not taking responsibility for the situation yourself: 'I left you in charge while I went to the shop to get some milk and now there's food everywhere – it's all your fault.'

✔ **Complaining** is justified to teach your kids about your expectations but if you constantly use it to let off steam, your kids feel undervalued and unloved.

✔ **Nagging** is hassling over and over again for something you want to happen. 'Don't forget to do your homework before we go out on Sunday. Have you done your homework yet? You haven't done your homework yet, have you?'

✔ **Threatening** is using outcomes and consequences to get what you want, but if used inappropriately it can damage the sense of balance and respect within a household. 'If you do that again you won't get any pocket money this week.'

✔ **Punishing** if not handled sensitively can be too severe for the 'crime'. Always make sure your punishments are appropriate to your child's age and fit the severity of the misdemeanour and that your child learns from the experience so he doesn't make the same mistakes over and over again.

✔ **Rewarding disobedience** means ignoring the bad behaviour, which is just like condoning it, and saying something like 'Have this packet of sweets'.

If you notice yourself engaging in any of the seven deadly disses with your child, press your 'pause' button – just like the one on your DVD. Stop for a moment, take a deep breath, and try the following replacement techniques:

✔ **Replace criticism with respectful appropriate praise.** When you criticise, you judge your children with disapproval and put yourself on the defensive, which means your attitude is now negative so you tend to see only the 'bad' things your kids do. Instead, catch your kids doing something right and praise them immediately, which shows respect. Pay attention to the way you speak to your kids by imagining you're hearing the words outside your ears and if you notice you are criticising, stop and be clear about what you *do* want.

✔ **Replace blame with understanding.** When you blame your children, you're condemning them. Instead, try to listen and fully hear the story from their point of view. Doing so shows *empathy* (thinking 'If I was in your shoes, how would I feel?'). Children love to feel understood, so by attempting to tune in to your children's feelings and genuinely taking time to hear their side of the situation helps them feel valued.

✔ **Replace complaints with appreciation.** When you complain about your children, you are expressing resentment towards them – and this action typically just builds more resentment. Instead, try to appreciate your children by being thankful and grateful for their good behaviours and attitudes. Doing so builds goodwill all round.

✔ **Replace nagging and threatening with support.** When you constantly nag your children to do something, you're really scolding (and annoying) them. Kids switch off to nagging. Nagging usually means you're not getting through and you need to change your approach! Instead, support your children by being clear about what you want to happen and by when and praise them when they do it – doing so gives them help and guidance and creates a more positive family atmosphere.

✔ **Replace punishment with responsibility.** When you punish your children, you enforce a penalty for a crime. Instead, promote responsibility in your kids by encouraging them to be accountable for their actions. Teach them about consequences. If you've really had enough of the untidy bedroom or whatever it is that's driving you mad, you may say: 'If this room isn't tidy in 15 minutes, with all the clothes hung up and toys and magazines put away in their drawers, we're not going swimming today'. But you have to be prepared not to take your children swimming. You only need to use this tactic once for your kids to get the message that you mean what you say. In the long term this approach makes your life much easier.

✔ **Replace control with independence.** When you control your children you command, direct, and rule them. Instead, promote independence in your kids from an early age (according to their development) and help them grow up to be self-confident – and eventually independent from you.

Every time you feel a conflict or an argument about to take place, step back, press an imaginary pause button and ask yourself: 'Is what I'm doing or saying moving me closer or further away from my child in terms of building the long-term relationship that I want with them?' Doing so helps you detach from the mundane and to see the bigger picture, which is far more important.

# Realising the Differences between Girls' and Boys' Needs

All parents want a good future for their children – regardless of their gender. This is the 21st century, after all. Most parents are keen to raise their sons and daughters equally. Thankfully, boys going out to work and girls staying home to clean and raise the kids are no longer society-imposed roles. But to parent effectively today, you must be aware of your own ingrained stereotypes and how you pass them onto your children.

The general and trendy theory for about the last 30 years or so is that boys and girls have no differences apart from what parents do to them through conditioning. During my 22 years as a teacher, I've come across fanatical yet well-meaning parents in pre-school nurseries making boys play with dolls and girls play with Lego, which seemed rather a contrived way to let children play. Children left to their own devices with lots of choices soon find what they enjoy playing with, regardless of their gender.

Gender is certainly a complicated issue because, until recently, boys were believed to be more aggressive and violent than girls, but reports now suggest that girls demonstrate a higher level of indirect aggression at every age than boys. Boys seem to be more up front about their aggression: Threatening, yelling, insulting, name-calling, teasing, hitting, shoving, pushing, kicking, or destroying personal property. Girls, however, are more secretive in their approach: Ignoring, gossiping, telling secrets, spreading rumours, and using verbal ways to bully others, as well as being more likely to lie and steal.

Girls and boys are different in their needs. Not better or worse – just different. Many parents would agree that most little boys play and act differently from most little girls, and do so from an early age. Scientists generally agree that gender-specific behaviour is a complicated mix of both nature and nurture.

Here are some specific differences that apply to most girls and boys, but not to all because every child is unique:

- ✔ **The brain develops differently.** In girls, the right side of the brain (the language side) develops faster than boys, so girls are usually better at reading and talking, and have a much wider vocabulary than boys. Boys are more logical and are better at problem-solving and figuring out puzzles. To help your child develop in a balanced way, encourage your boys to talk to you and your girls to play with toys that need manipulation. When he starts school, you may find that your son has difficulty with writing and your daughter thinks she's bad at maths. Over time these differences iron out, but be aware of your children's different needs.

- ✔ **The brain is wired differently.** In girls, emotion is processed in the same area of the brain that processes language. Most girls find talking about their emotions easy. In boys, the brain regions involved in talking are separate from the regions involved in feeling, so one of the hardest questions for many boys to answer is: 'How do you feel?' So girls will feel the need to talk about people and emotions whereas boys feel the need to talk about things and activities.

  From the ages of 6 to 13, boys seem to 'switch on' to masculinity and want to fight and wrestle and make lots of noise! They have a need to connect with and spend more time with their dad as opposed to their mum, who featured mostly in the early years.

- ✔ **Girls and boys respond differently to stress.** Research by Dr Leonard Sax shows that a certain amount of stress enhances learning in boys but the same level of stress impairs learning in girls. Boys define themselves by achieving goals and accomplishing things by themselves, because they feel competent and in control. Girls define themselves by the quality of their relationships and have the need to share and nurture others. Be aware of how your child is reacting to the pressures of school and make sure your daughter talks through her concerns and your son feels suitably challenged.

Remember to be aware of the individual needs of your children – not only in relation to their gender differences.

Ask yourself some questions from time to time to see if you're stereotyping your children in the way you're bringing them up. Get a pad of paper and write down all your thoughts about your attitudes towards girls and boys and see what comes up for you. If you're happy with what you see, great, carry on; but if you're not, think about some new ways to get your values across to your kids. Ask yourself:

- ✔ **What are my values regarding, and my attitudes to, men and women or boys and girls in society?** Values are your principles and standards that you hold to be really important – things such as your integrity, being kind to others, trusting strangers. Values can also be about how you view boys and girls.

- ✔ **Do I think boys and girls are equal?** Should boys help clean around the house; can girls cut down trees? Writing down your views can help you gain clarity about what's important to you. You can then pass down your values to your children through the way you act as a role model yourself and the things you say and the things you encourage them to do.

- ✔ **What sort of man do I want my son to be? What sort of woman do I want my daughter to be?** Write down all the attributes, qualities, and skills you would like to develop in your children: Consider self-reliance, the ability to talk about feelings openly and honestly, having a healthy respect for both sexes, an ability to be courageous in life and take risks, the ability to be stable, reliable, creative, and to have basic life skills such as the ability to cook, iron, and manage a bank account. Ask yourself how you can get those values across to your children on a daily basis through what you say, how you act, or what you do physically.

Many books focus on the difficulties in bringing up boys and girls. Stephen Biddulph's book *Raising Boys* and Gisela Preuschoff's *Raising Girls* are books worth reading if you're interested in exploring this subject further.

Despite all these differences between the sexes, a great deal of overlap exists as well. If you focus on key skills such as building your children's self-esteem and confidence (see Chapter 6) and staying focused on helping your children relate and communicate effectively with others, you can easily overcome any differences.

# Understanding Your Child as an Individual

You probably expect adults to be individuals, to have likes and dislikes, to be good at some things and not at others. Likewise children have different tastes, styles, abilities, and personalities. For example:

- Some children are easy to care for and are not very demanding. Others are fussy, difficult, and challenging to care for.

- You may have two or more children who are very different from one another – even though you try to treat them the same.

Don't try to make your child into something he's not. Your efforts will resemble trying to change a geranium into a petunia: The process won't work and everyone will end up feeling a failure. Each day you are raising a totally individual human being with the little things you do and say. The secret is to celebrate and embrace your child's unique personality by responding to it positively. Dance around with him if he has a noisy and extrovert personality; be gentle and share doing the jigsaw together if he's sensitive and quiet; but above all, enjoy being with him doing small things. Spend time talking and listening to your child, praising things he gets right each day. Doing so helps your child to grow up mentally, physically, and emotionally strong, ready to take his place in the world.

# Part II

# Improving Your Basic Parenting Skills

The 5th Wave                    By Rich Tennant

"Mike! Wait! I gave you the wrong book!"

## In this part . . .

Parenting is a skill that takes practice and effort. Thinking about the basics is really worthwhile – considering what values are important to you as a parent; what sort of parent you are; how you support, encourage, and get the best out of your kids; and how you develop the family relationships that you want.

This part is all about improving your basic parenting skills, including effective and successful communication, and common sense ways to parent.

# Chapter 4

# Beginning with the End in Mind: Establishing Goals for Your Family

• • • • • • • • • • • • • • • • • • • • • • • • • • • • • • • • • • • • • • • • • • •

• • • • • • • • • • • • • • • • • • • • • • • • • • • • • • • • • • • • • • • • • • •

> *There are only two lasting bequests we can give our children. One is roots, the other wings.*
>
> —Hodding Carter

*W*ould you get in your car and set off from London to Edinburgh without a map? Probably not. So why do most families spend so little time planning their destination – what they are trying to achieve with their parenting?

Stephen Covey, the self-development guru, suggests that good families – even great families – are off track 90 per cent of the time. But he believes the key to successful parenting is having a sense of direction and a clear vision of the destination and even playfully suggests that 'The wonderful thing is that vision is greater than baggage.'

You can think of the importance of a destination in this way: An aeroplane can be 90 per cent off course throughout most of its journey and yet still arrive safely at its destination.

Every family is unique, with its own way of doing things and with its own baggage. But the great thing about sitting down together and talking about where you want to go is that you focus on the destination, which can make your lives together an exciting, purpose-driven experience.

# 1g Out What Your
# y is All About

We live in a stressful time. Families face difficult pressures on time, emotions, and money. Often, home becomes the place where everyone takes out his or her frustrations, tiredness, or irritability. But I believe that with a little awareness and making the effort to step back from the intensity of a particular situation, families can remain strong, happy, and supportive of each other.

What makes some families strong? Researchers have worked on finding answers to this question for years. I believe that the answer is not about experts' findings and opinions – but is about you and your family discovering for yourselves what makes you a unique, strong, and close family unit.

As I watched Kelly Holmes struggling to stay upright in *Dancing on Ice* – a television programme where celebrities who have never skated before perform complex routines each week – I found myself thinking about her competitive spirit, driving force, resilience, and attitude to life. Holmes is a brilliant runner and has surely practised passing on the baton in relay races hundreds of times. But she must also have dropped the baton many times. So what makes her special? Getting back up and having another go – and knowing where she wanted to get to.

So how do you pass on the baton of life to your children? Do you even know where you're trying to get to as a family?

I believe that the strength of a family comes from the inner beliefs and values of the parents. This means that each person is valued within the family; small individual acts of kindness towards each other are important; telling the truth is valued; and love is paramount. If you, as a parent, know what you're trying to achieve (for example, developing happy, confident, resilient, independent, and well-balanced adults), then life's challenges are less likely to blow you off course and, in the long run, you're likely to succeed.

Sit down around the kitchen table with a lovely meal and chat with your kids about the spirit or philosophy of your family. What bits about being part of your family are great? Which bits cause friction? Which bits are the key things that make your family special, unique, and wonderful? Write down your vision of what your family is and how you each act and interact. Identify specific ways that you can each reach your goals – as well as obstacles that may be blocking your current paths. Most importantly, start today to walk slowly towards your goals, *together as a family*.

The following sections cover some of the most important goals you and your family need to discuss in beginning to lay down your philosophy of what your family is.

## Examining how you relate to one another

Within your family you have the parental relationship, the sibling to sibling relationship, the parent to child relationship – not to mention the extended family relationships of grandparents, aunts and uncles, step-families, and adopted family relationships.

These relationships are a minefield of potential conflicts, misunderstandings, and upsets but also a wonderful opportunity to develop long-lasting bonds of respect, laughter, love, and memories.

When you express caring and appreciation for other family members, you strengthen these key relationships. Members of strong families find ways to support and encourage each other even when someone makes a mistake or gets something wrong. They make decisions, solve family problems, and do things together. Everyone participates.

## Relating by correcting and controlling

Most parents spend a lot of time talking and giving orders to their kids and get stuck in a groove of talking to them: 'Wash your hands', 'Stop teasing your sister', 'Do your homework', 'Stop that', or 'Go to bed'.

Think about your interactions with each of your children during the last week. What things did you talk (or yell) about with each child? Write down a list. Review the list and note whether each incident was friendly (helpful, happy) or unfriendly (angry, bossy, unkind).

Now think about the different ways you could have handled the situation or spoken to them. Picture the scenarios in a perfect world – what do you see, hear, and how do you feel? You need to constantly and gently analyse what you're doing well and not so well and change your behaviour. Don't beat yourself up and feel guilty – constantly and slowly improve your skills to become the best parent you can be.

The things you say and do with your children determine the kind of relationship you have with them. After you reflect on your relationship with your children, you may decide you need to make some changes.

For example, many parent–child relationships centre too much on control and correction. When parents control their children, they're trying to get the children to do things the children don't want to do. Or they are trying to keep children from doing things the children want to do. Forcing a struggling child into a car seat, keeping children from eating chocolate before dinner, and getting children to do their homework, eat their vegetables, or stop fighting with each other are all examples of controlling and correcting interactions.

A parent–child relationship based on correction can even become insulting, with comments such as, 'How can you be so stupid?' and 'You can't do anything right!' These types of insult are damaging because they don't give children useful information and only make them feel bad.

If you find yourself being very negative and insulting your kids, take a step back, sit down, and think about how you can change the words you use, your tone of voice, and your intention so that you can make the situation better next time.

Of course, parents *do* often have more power than children because they are bigger and stronger. But forcing people to do something they don't want to do is very difficult work. Parents focused on control and correction can end up spending all their time yelling at their children, trying to bribe, or force, them to do something. The trouble with control is it takes over the relationship. Control can easily be the only thing that parents and children talk about – not a very good basis for a balanced and healthy relationship.

So, are control and correction always bad? No, of course not. Parents must occasionally control and correct their children. But when control and correction are *all* that a child gets from parents, the child can become discouraged or even rebellious.

Really think about the sort of relationship you want to create *in the long term*. Don't let controlling and correcting your children be the only thing you focus on in your relationship.

## Relating to one another with respect

In order to make your relationships with your children more positive, think about what you want your relationships to be like.

- ✔ In what ways would you like to have more fun with each of your children?
- ✔ In what ways would you like to behave with your children?

✔ In what ways can you show your kids that you lik
want to spend more time with them?

✔ In what ways can you show your kids that their opi..
important to you?

After you have a picture of your relationships, think about ways you can ͻ
about developing your current relationships.

✔ How can you build more opportunities to show love and affection in
your relationships?

✔ How can you remove some of the control and correction from your
relationships?

✔ What things can you do to give some autonomy and independence to
your children?

✔ If your child was describing your discipline to a friend, what would they
say?

✔ How could you improve or change your ways of correcting your
children?

Think of someone you respect and admire in how they behave with their children and discipline them. Try copying their behaviour.

Adults are expected to be individuals, to have likes and dislikes, to be good at
some things and not at others. But you may find yourself surprised to think
that children are unique individuals with their own tastes, styles, and abilities
as well. All children have different rates of development and different personalities. Reminding yourself of this fact can help you be patient. You can
show your children you really care about them by accepting each child
as an individual.

# Involving the Entire Family

Examining your family requires both individual work and group work. Try the
following activities to get everyone thinking about what sort of family you're
all part of.

1. **Have a think by yourself.**

   Take some time and jot down your thoughts about the atmosphere in
   your home. Ask yourself:

   • Is it relaxed, frenetic, chaotic, noisy, tense, or happy?

   • Is it the sort of place where you can feel at ease, laugh, bring
   friends to visit, or feel safe?

- If your children were describing the family to a friend, what sort of things would they say?
- If a fairy godmother asked your kids how their family life could be improved, what would they ask for?

Your partner can go through the same questions, considering your home for him or herself.

2. **Look over your answers.**

If you're not completely happy with your responses, spend some time thinking about changes you can implement – this week – to make the situation better:

- Small changes might include both parents participating in getting the children up in the morning, both sharing the breakfast activity – one makes the packed lunch while the other puts the toast in – sharing all the numerous jobs involved in raising a family.
- Include the children in spreading out the tasks – laying the table, putting out the rubbish, bringing down the laundry basket, and so on.

Small changes make enormous differences and can transform your family life.

3. **Open up the discussion to the entire family.**

Choose a time when all the family can sit down together. Pass out some paper and ask everyone to write down his or her thoughts on the current atmosphere in your home.

Get a take away meal and get everyone involved in finding the solutions to responses.

Make sure that everyone has a chance to talk and be heard. Get a pepper pot that the person talking can hold and no one is allowed to interrupt.

Be prepared to hear some things you don't like, or don't agree with, but be prepared to take action in making changes.

Here are some examples of the types of questions you could ask yourself:

- What is the purpose of this family?
- What kind of family do we want to be?
- What kinds of things do we want to do?
- What kinds of feelings do we want to have with one another?
- How do we want to talk to each other and treat each other on a daily basis?

- What things are important to us as a family?

- What unique and special talents do we all bring t(

- What are our responsibilities to each other and to whole?

- What are our family values and principles?

Do this exercise regularly to really keep the lines of communication open. The families I've worked with tell me that they all enjoy doing this exercise – especially when it's over a very large pizza!

## Building a 'we' mentality

A *'we' mentality* is a sense of personal family identity. It is bigger than the 'me' mentality of individualism or the egocentric place of small children who think the world revolves around them. The 'we' – rather than 'me' – mentality is crucial in a family. A 'we' mentality builds trust, support, loyalty, love, and a true foundation for security and self-esteem. Consider the following ways to build the 'we' mentality:

- ✔ **Encourage family traditions.** A family tradition is any activity the entire family does together, such as preparing a roast on Sundays, watching football on the TV, or going on an annual camping holiday.

  Traditions have meanings that are special to *your* family. They create warmth, closeness, and memories that last a lifetime. Traditions also build loyalty, commitment, and a family history.

  What things do you like doing as a family? Perhaps you enjoy riding bikes, making models, listening to music, going to football matches, watching films, walking your dogs? Ask your kids what sorts of things they like doing with you.

- ✔ **Create memories.** Building happy family memories doesn't depend on how much money you spend or whether your children have the latest iPod, Gameboy, or trainers. Memories depend on the time, attention, and love you share with your kids. Memories don't have to be grand, they can be simple moments of being together or something funny that someone said or did.

- ✔ **Take time to talk.** Share your dreams, feelings, hopes, fears, joys, and sorrows. Talk about your experiences and your needs and take time to listen to each other. A natural time to chat and express yourselves is when you have some proper time. For me, it's when I'm taking my son to football training and we're in the car for half an hour. It could be when you pop up to say goodnight and you sit on the end of the bed chatting, reminiscing, or dreaming together.

✔ **Work together to develop your family's rules and routines.** Write down all the things that you want to see improved and start working out practical solutions to solving them – who does what, when, and how? Perhaps your son can take out the rubbish every evening after homework, your daughter can feed the dogs, Dad can empty the dishwasher in the morning, and Mum can walk the dogs every day after the school run.

State the rules in a positive way and don't have too many of them because it becomes overwhelming and no one sticks to them. Track how they're going (review them once a week until they work) – be flexible with them if they aren't working, and alter them if they seem overwhelming.

✔ **Develop habits that support each other through thick and thin.** Developing a stable environment in your family is necessary to deal with all the things life can throw at you – divorce, bereavement, redundancy, sickness, or accidents. A strong family unit can withstand all the blows and disappointments because it bends not breaks through change.

# Thinking win-win

*Co-operation* is the act of working together to achieve a common aim. Co-operation isn't putting your needs and wants and desires above anyone else in the family. Co-operation is the oil of family relationships. It helps families search for solutions and understanding even when things get difficult. Co-operation is a key skill in helping families move towards more harmony. If a family is experiencing turbulence between its members, how can it survive the storms raging outside in the big wide world?

The introduction of a questioning ethos, such as 'Are we all willing to search for a solution to this problem?', can help families get on better.

Your family needs to find solutions that are good for everyone instead of the competitive 'I win, you lose' resolutions. These typical 'I win, you lose' resolutions create tension and division. Instead, adopt a *win-win* approach as the fundamental and basic attitude underpinning your family ethos. The win-win attitude is about seeking to understand and feeling understood.

The key question in a win-win ethos is 'Are we willing to take a while to find a solution that makes us both feel happier?' Adopting a win-win ethos means taking a bit longer to listen and thinking of ways to be creative, but after a while it becomes second nature as a way of thinking.

I'm not claiming co-operation is easy. In fact, if you haven't tried it before, co-operating does take a shift in your thinking – particularly when your son is holding your daughter over the banisters by her hair because she borrowed his hair gel – but it does work in the long term.

No one likes to lose. Win-win thinking helps the whole family focus on creating something new and better together. Win-win thinking actually helps the family bond together more effectively.

Part of being a parent is making decisions where everyone appears to win – even if the situation doesn't seem that way to your children. An extremely important skill you need to develop in your children is the ability to brainstorm ideas and find solutions. Many parents forget that children are not born with this type of wisdom. Be patient with yourself and your kids as you teach them different problem-solving strategies. Bear in mind the following points:

- ✔ Get into 'accepting mode' because you're going to have to be tuned into your kids' ideas, which may or may not be great ideas to start with.

- ✔ Steer clear of judgements, evaluations, and lectures; and don't try to persuade or convince your children about your ideas straight away.

- ✔ Be patient. The win-win approach takes a bit longer than simply telling your children what to do.

- ✔ Talk about your feelings, let your children talk about their feelings, and work together on finding a way forward that pleases everyone without accusations or blame.

## Standing back from the wood and the trees

Standing back and remaining calm and in control can help inspire you to come up with different ways to sort out difficult situations. Stepping back takes practise. But after you see shifts in your family relationships, the power of stepping back can totally transform your life.

An exercise I regularly do with parents in workshops is 'Seeing it from the other person's point of view'.

I ask parents to stand on different parts of coloured circles and to look at the situation from the perspective of their child or partner, or even of an objective outsider. I ask them to tell me what they see, hear, and feel as that person; doing so can help shift stuck emotions or ideas. Here's what to do:

1. Write on four pieces of paper: 'My point of view', 'My partner's point of view', 'My child's point of view' (have a piece of paper for each child), 'A detached observer's point of view'.

2. Step on to each piece of paper and see the situation from that person's point of view. See what that person sees, hear what they hear, and feel what they feel.

3. Ask yourself: What have I learnt? How can I change a small thing to improve the situation? What small thing can I do now or this week to make a change?

# Staying Hopeful

Being positive and hopeful about your goals is often referred to as *the law of attraction* – you bring into your life all the things that you focus on. So if you get up and stub your toe, trip over the hairdryer, and burn the toast, you're not in a great frame of mind! The good news is that you can change your frame of mind easily and effortlessly by laughing at the situation and then noticing the good and positive things going on around you. Your daughter's made her bed, the towels are all hung up, the radio's playing that song that you like, someone's put the kettle on, and it's the day that you go to your favourite exercise class.

Suddenly you're back in control of your emotions and life looks better. Practise noticing positive things and guess what? You see even more great things! I've read this saying many times, and I really think it expresses a truth: *You get what you focus on*. For example:

✔ Negative parents focus on the problem and have difficulty seeing beyond it. Negative parents criticise a lot; they judge, complain, and argue. They're full of despair, negativity, and have a victim mentality. They give up easily, do anything for an easy life, and then moan about the outcome. Negative parents blame others for their lot in life.

✔ Positive parents focus on things that are going well in their lives. They stay hopeful, and more positive things seem to happen to them. When faced with a challenge or a change, positive parents know that it's only a temporary setback and they focus on the future.

Staying hopeful and positive gets easier with practice. Here are some techniques to help you get into a positive frame of mind and to stay in it.

- ✔ **Start a positive parenting journal.** I give parents who come on my workshops such a journal to write in. I recommend they write at night and focus on what went well during that day. Doing so provides a great way to fall asleep with happy memories of the day, so you can wake up in a positive frame of mind.

  Your journal can be full of little things or big things – what you write is totally personal. Try to celebrate the positive and let go of the negative. Always focus on the solution, not the problem.

- ✔ **Practise positive body language.** Your body language – the way in which you hold your body and display expressions on your face – is a powerful tool that communicates your attitude to your kids. Try smiling (even if you don't feel like it); not only does smiling release natural endorphins that make you feel good immediately, you look more pleasant and approachable to others. Do something physical such as jumping up and down, dancing around the kitchen table, or moving your body in some way – it sounds crazy but it changes the chemicals in your brain and gets feel-good emotions moving around your body that naturally lift your mood and attitude.

- ✔ **Use positive language.** When you hear yourself slipping into negative words, stop. Imagine you're an outsider listening to your voice – what do you think about the things it says? Use more up-beat words to describe situations and feelings. Instead of feeling 'okay', are you feeling 'great', 'determined', 'curious', 'focused', 'fortunate'? Take charge of your emotions and make a difference to your life by simply changing your vocabulary.

I have a poster on my wall with a picture of a vibrant woman with a huge smile on her face. The words on the poster help me to remember life is all about your perception of it:

*It's a problem – Actually it's an opportunity.*

*I'm never satisfied – I want to learn and grow.*

*Life's a struggle – Life's an adventure.*

*It's terrible – It's a learning experience.*

# Looking back from your rocking chair

Imagine you're well into your 70s. Your children have grown up and had families of their own. Take some time and imagine this very clearly in your mind. Picture yourself surrounded by your wonderful family. Consider:

- How do you feel?

- What do your children say is the best thing about having you as a mum or dad?

- What do they love most about you?

- How do they describe you to their children?

- How do you *want* them to describe you to their children?

- How does a difference between how they describe you and how you want to be described make you feel?

- What steps can you take to ensure that your children describe you as you'd like?

You can ask your future self just one question. What is that question? Perhaps you ask:

- What have been the highlights in your family relationships?

- When your kids look back at their childhood, what do you want them to remember?

- What memories have you built in them that will last forever?

- What wonderful stories about their childhood will they share with their own children?

- What steps can you take from now on to make sure that happens?

Looking back before you've even arrived is a great way to help you focus on where you're going because it helps you to create the compelling future that you want. Have fun discovering new goals and setting new visions for your family.

# Chapter 5

# Communicating Effectively and Connecting with Your Children

Communication is, in many ways, a full-time activity. But as a parent you may not stand back and think about how you speak or listen – the two vital components of communication – to your children.

One of the biggest issues I come across as a parent coach is helping parents overcome the barriers and misunderstandings brought about by poor or ineffective communication.

## Looking at Ways You Communicate

Before you begin radically overhauling your communication style and skills, you need to evaluate how you listen and speak with your children on a daily basis. The following sections cover some of the most essential – but often overlooked – aspects of communication.

# *Considering your questions*

Questions are very powerful. They're the currency of good communication, unlocking confusion and facilitating understanding. The key to really effective communication is asking the right questions and then sitting back to really listen to the answers.

Real listening isn't merely waiting for your turn to speak. I cover listening skills in the later section 'Listening properly'.

Parents can have a huge impact on the development of their children's language skills and mental development by asking open-ended questions. An *open-ended question* needs a descriptive answer, whereas you can answer a closed question quickly with a short yes or no. Open-ended questions help a child develop his or her thought processes. The ability to communicate is significantly improved by having to think properly about an answer.

Open-ended questions typically begin with interrogative words – how, what, when, who, how much, and where.

Questions beginning with 'why' are also open-ended, but you may want to use them sparingly or avoid them altogether. Why questions tend to make children feel defensive, as if you're criticising them. Think of your feelings if someone said, 'So why did you spill the breakfast cereal all over the table?' or 'Why didn't you ring me at 10 o'clock like you promised?'

Improving your questioning skills is pretty straightforward. Begin by observing your questions and taking a moment to phrase each so that it is open-ended before you utter it.

I often recommend to the parents I work with that they put up sticky notes around the house with a list of the interrogative words that typically start open questions.

Beginning to pay attention to the types of questions you ask may feel strange at first. This feeling is okay because you're engaging in a new habit. Like everything in life, the more you do it, the more likely it becomes second nature.

'Talking at' your child and 'talking with' your child are two very different things – rather like 'laughing at' or 'laughing with' someone. As a parent, you need to guard against conversations that feel like lectures, inquisitions, or nags. Open-ended questions really change the feel of your conversation. Parents who incorporate more open-ended questions into their talks with their kids often find dramatic improvements quickly – not only in the quality of conversations but also in the length and enjoyment of their exchanges.

## The power of asking effective questions

The types of questions you ask your children can yield amazing results. Children with parents who ask effective questions often

✔ Communicate more effectively with others.

✔ Are less frustrated at home or at school.

✔ Are more empathetic to other people.

✔ Are able to make small talk with people of all ages and all kinds of backgrounds.

✔ Know how to move conversations from small talk to deeper subjects.

✔ Read and use non-verbal communication well.

✔ Discuss rather than just shout out their thoughts.

✔ Argue rationally and articulately as they get older.

✔ Speak in public without being paralysed with anxiety.

Open-ended questions leave the door open for better answers. In explaining or describing, children use language more fully and this helps them develop their language and thinking skills.

# *Taking stock of your tone*

I remember when my mum used to call me. If she said 'Susan', it usually had an edge to it and meant I was in trouble, but if she called 'Sue', everything was okay and it was just probably time for tea. Her meaning didn't just lie in the words she used – it was also in her tone.

This situation's a bit like when my husband asks, 'Everything alright?' and I say 'Fine!' but my tone and body language say something completely different. My face gives me away because I look more detached, my eyes look colder, I'm not smiling (which is a dead give away because I smile a lot) and my body is tense, straighter, and less cuddly.

Children are extremely sensitive to the tone of your voice. Pay attention over the next week to *how* you say things to them. If you don't like how you're saying things, change your tone.

Many parents don't realise that the tone their children use can actually be a parent's fault. Your children may be mimicking your tone of voice. Have you ever heard your child admonishing another with your exact words and tone? Scary, isn't it?

### *Avoiding matching your children's tone*

Children are masters at getting under parents' skins – and sometimes drawing us into their angry rants. Kids know exactly how to say things to make you hot under the collar: Infants give plaintive cries, toddlers throw tantrums, and teenagers whine. You may try hard to remain calm when your child acts up, but sometimes your temper gets the better of you. Your child whines to you, and you find it easier to answer back in a similarly whiny voice. Unfortunately, you end up matching the tone of your child, and your emotions and volume escalate until you have a full-scale battle on your hands.

The key to changing any type of unacceptable tone is simply not to match it. No match. No game.

Try answering a whine with something pleasant and no-nonsense: 'Let's not speak in that tone of voice to each other.' A simple statement like this can nip a potential whine-fest in the bud.

### Modifying your tone

Your tone of voice is very important when you talk with your children because it gives them a signal about your mood. Your tone carries information about your emotion; whether you're feeling sarcastic, angry, gentle, or encouraging.

You use a higher pitched voice when you talk to babies, which shows you to be friendly and approachable. Deeper voices carry more authority and you use a deeper voice when you want to get a job done. Children read these clues in your harsh or soft tones, your loudness, and your speed of speaking to read what mood you're in.

Be aware of these hidden ways of communicating and consider:

- ✔ What tone could you adopt to change the atmosphere in different situations?

- ✔ What phrase could you remember to use that would lift everyone's spirits?

- ✔ What can you do to remember to listen to your tone of voice when you're speaking to your kids?

- ✔ What would be the benefits of doing this exercise regularly?

Remember the following tips to help you control your tone:

- ✔ Recognise when your child is speaking to you in an inappropriate way and try not to answer back in the same tone.

- ✔ Take a couple of deep breaths when you hear a word, phrase, or tone that gets your heart racing. Press your internal 'pause' button to calm yourself down and think before answering.

✔ Use a sweet tone. Although you may feel like Mary Poppins or that you're overdoing things, using softer volume and an air of gentleness yields results with kids.

✔ Listen for models of good tone. Listen to TV, people at the shops, or parents in the park for voices with appropriate tone. Recognise how you should sound and practise adopting these people's vocal characteristics. With practice, your adopted tone begins to sound natural.

✔ Praise your child for speaking in a normal conversational voice. Positive re-enforcement builds self-esteem and goodwill and helps your child realise that he doesn't have to whine or yell for you to listen.

Adjusting your tone takes a bit of practice – like most things worthwhile in life – but the effort is worthwhile in the long run.

## Studying sympathy and empathy skills

Empathy and sympathy allow you to walk in someone else's shoes. They give you the ability to understand another person's perspective or situation and to offer emotional support. *Empathy* means being able to identify with the emotions that someone else is feeling. *Sympathy* is a feeling of concern on behalf of someone who is distressed or needy.

Your toddler sees your sad expression and gives you a hug; your teenager sees a homeless family on television and wonders what he can do to help. The sympathy felt by the toddler and teenager in these examples builds on empathy. These emotions allow one person to notice, understand, and respond to the distress in another.

Empathy and sympathy allow your children to see other people's perspectives. They form the basis for *altruistic behaviour*, the act of helping someone else without gaining a tangible benefit in return. Children who are able to develop qualities of empathy and sympathy tend to be more tolerant and compassionate, more understanding of others' needs, better at handling anger, and more likely to have good social skills and relationships.

Empathy and sympathy are at the core of compassion, caring, and concern for others. Both come into play in almost every area of life: school, work, friendships, parenting, and romantic relationships. In his work on emotional intelligence, psychologist Daniel Goleman found that children who excelled at reading people's feelings nonverbally were popular, emotionally stable, and performed well in school, even though their IQs were no higher than those of other students. Children who lack these qualities may be more aggressive and more likely to have trouble with their social relationships.

Sympathy and empathy may come more naturally to some children than others, but you can play a tremendously important role in teaching your children to understand their feelings and to try walking in someone else's shoes by setting a good example and by talking about and exploring feelings with your children. By regularly and naturally talking with your children about their emotions, you can help your kids build skills that will come in handy in every aspect of life, from school to work to relationships.

How sympathetic are you when your child is trying to talk to you? More important than all the words you use is your attitude. If your attitude is not one of understanding, compassion, or sympathy, then your child will experience anything you say as insincere, false, and uncaring.

Hearing parents tell their children to 'shut up' or say things that humiliate or embarrass them in front of other people distresses me. These parents berate them, interrupt them, and speak to others in front of them as if their kids don't exist. I suppose they're demonstrating that they have the upper hand and are more powerful. Unfortunately, these actions do nothing to enhance a child's self-esteem, create family unity, or enhance communication.

Sometimes sympathy does come naturally. Interacting sympathetically takes thought and effort to let your children know that you have a sense of what they must be going through.

Let your child have time to formulate his sentences and finish what he wants to say. Children think slower than adults. When you cut your child off, you're sending the message that you don't really care what they have to say.

Here are some tips for improving sympathy and empathy skills in your child:

- ✔ **Ask questions about feelings.** This helps your child think about his own emotions as well as the way other people feel. For example, if your child has a bad dream, ask him to tell you how it made him feel, or if he says something mean to a friend, ask him to think how he feels when he's treated this way.

- ✔ **Label emotions.** Doing so validates the emotion, and helps your child develop a vocabulary for expressing feelings. Saying things like 'I'm sad that Grandma's ill', and 'I get frustrated when you cry but won't tell me what's wrong' teaches children to identify and express emotions with words.

- ✔ **Read nonverbal cues.** Reading body language, facial expressions, and tone of voice is important, so point these out to your child. Watch the television with the sound off and try to guess what people are feeling just from their body language. When you're at the shops, or at the playground, try to guess how people are feeling even when you can't hear what they're saying.

✔ **Include feelings in play-time.** Use puppets to act out situations, sing songs about feelings, make drawings or hats for different emotions, and point out expressions in books and magazines.

✔ **Use your voice.** When you read a favourite book to your child, try to express different emotions (bored, angry, excited) with your voice alone, and see if your child can guess which one is right.

## Keeping communication clear and positive

When you communicate with children you must be extremely clear about what you want to happen. Use short instructions and really mean what you say. If your kids can sense your energy and attitude, they're much more likely to get your message quickly and effectively.

Keep the following tips for clear and positive communication in mind:

✔ **Make eye contact.** Parents often try to communicate with their kids from different rooms. Unfortunately, the noise level just goes up and up while the actual communication goes down. Your child is highly unlikely to know you mean business unless they can see your face and hear the urgency in your voice. If your message is important, deliver it in the same room as your child.

✔ **Say what you mean and mean what you say.** Choose your words carefully. If you have time – and the message is important – think through what you want to say before you say it to your child. If the message is particularly important or difficult, consider writing it down. Be clear, concise, and mean business.

✔ **Talk positively and calmly – even in difficult or challenging situations.** If your child yells, 'That's not fair', instead of jumping in with an explanation or shouting back at him, try asking, 'What do you think would be fair?' Wait for the answer and ask a follow-up question. If you find yourself thinking of your response while your child is talking, then you're not really listening to him.

✔ **Create quality talk time.** Quality talk time is when you have plenty of time to really engage with your child, actively listening, and interacting naturally and fully with him. It's also a time to talk about difficult topics or to tell them about your views on drugs or sex if they're older kids.

## So how are *you* doing?

Consider the various communication skills in the 'Looking at Ways You Communicate' section, including asking open-ended questions, minding your tone, sympathy, actively listening, keeping things clear and positive.

✔ Which of these communication skills would you say you are best at?

✔ Which of these skills is your least effective?

✔ What do you think is the main reason for this?

✔ If you could develop and improve in one area, which one would you choose?

✔ How would an improvement in one area affect the quality of your communication and relationship with your child?

## *Listening properly*

You probably know a few people who are excellent communicators – people who make you feel good after you've spent time with them. They seem genuinely enthusiastic and interested in you. So what is these people's secret? Most likely, they are *actively listening* – a skill that great communicators may have naturally but one that you can develop over time.

Most people must develop good communication skills, and listening can be a difficult skill to master at first.

Take time to actually analyse how you listen to your children. You may think you're pretty good at it. But what are you doing *while* you're listening to your child? Tending to the laundry, cooking the dinner, and emptying the dishwasher are all important tasks, but when you combine them with listening, you're not able to listen as completely to your child. Your child feels more valuable when you give him your full attention.

How do you feel when you're talking to someone and he or she keeps on peeling the potatoes, reading the newspaper, or emptying the bin? You probably feel angry, frustrated, and even ignored. (I know I do!) So why do you do it to your children?

Sharing your worries or successes with someone who is really listening is much easier than trying to connect with someone who's otherwise occupied. As a parent, you can demonstrate to your kids that you're really listening by stopping what you're doing for a few minutes and giving your child your full attention. Often the sympathetic or happy silence in life makes all the difference.

The following sections cover various techniques for improving your listening skills.

### Listening with your eyes

I encourage parents I work with to look into their children's eyes to show them that they're really listening. The act of engaging another person visually helps make listening an active, effective habit – and it helps you remember this new skill.

When you engage in active listening, you intentionally focus your eyes on the person you're listening to, which improves your ability to understand exactly what your child is saying.

As an active, visually engaged listener, you should then be able to repeat, in your own words in your head, what your child has just said to you. Repeating back your children's words does not mean you agree with them, but rather that you understand what they're saying.

### Listening with your heart

Next time you're talking with your child, try physically turning your heart towards your child's heart. The movement helps you remember that you are concentrating on your child and what he is saying. (And focusing for a moment on your heart is a nice way to remind yourself that you love your kids, even if you are busy.)

Listening with your heart also means you're not judging and that you show you love them through just listening. Don't be in a hurry – stay focused and try to empathise with each word your child says.

Listening with your heart helps give your child the gift of self-esteem. Parents need to feel where their children are coming from. Empathy enables you to know about their world and share their interests in a balanced way that respects their independence and privacy.

If kids are ever going to listen to parents, parents need to listen to them. And if you start listening to your children when they're 4, they may still be listening – and talking – to you when they're 14!

### Repeating back what you hear

By actively listening to your children and then repeating back what they say, you show them that you really understand and are taking the time to listen. Repeating back what you hear by paraphrasing and summarising, clarifies what they've said to you and shows that you have respect for them, and respect definitely helps foster goodwill.

At first, repeating back another person's words may seem rather unnatural, but if you do it with the best of intentions, you don't sound patronising and the communication between you and your children really improves.

Be careful not to repeat your child's exact words, parrot fashion, because that sounds false. For example,

> I don't like Lily anymore. She gets on my nerves and follows me about at break time.
>
> *You don't like Lily anymore because she follows you around at break time.*
>
> That's just what I told you!
>
> Instead, try: *It sounds like Lily has upset you and you're a bit fed up with her.*

When your child comes home with a great long story complaining about all his homework or whatever is upsetting him, pick out the important bits and summarise it. Then ask how you can help.

Think of the repeating technique in this way: Words aren't just an everyday form of communication but a powerful vehicle for encouragement, teaching, love, intimacy, and forgiveness.

Listen first. Talk later. And always keep your word. It builds trust.

# Helping Your Children Handle Their Feelings

A direct connection links how kids feel and how they behave. When your children feel good, they behave well. How do you help them feel all right? By accepting their feelings.

Parents aren't always very good at accepting their kids' feelings. You hear parents saying things like, 'Put your jumper back on. You're not hot; it's cold in here', and 'You can't be feeling angry about that, you're just tired from last night.'

Denying how your child feels is a real block to effective communication because your child feels angry, confused, and frustrated by having his feelings denied, ridiculed, or dismissed.

A simple but effective way of helping your child handle his feelings is to simply acknowledge those feelings by saying something like 'Oh, I see . . . '

Simply allowing your child to have his feelings accepted and not having you rush in with your own take on the situation, helps your lines of communication because your child will feel supported.

Many parents have a natural tendency to negate their children's emotions, feelings, and experiences – no matter what age the children are! Listen to how you respond to your children. Perhaps you sometimes say things like:

- *No, you don't really mean that.*
- *You're just tired.*
- *You can't be tired. You've just got up.*
- *What do you mean you didn't have a good time?*
- *That's not right.*
- *If the teacher was cross, you must have done something wrong. You're always talking too much.*

Imagine if your friends, family, or work colleagues said things like this to you. How would you feel?

Most people, when they are upset, hurt, annoyed, or frustrated, just like having someone to listen, someone who doesn't offer advice, pity, or philosophy. Your children are exactly the same – they're just mini-people!

Perhaps you grew up having your own feelings denied and now you repeat the same pattern with your children. Stop. Discounting others' feelings is a habit, and like any habit, you can work to change your actions.

The following sections offer advice on how to respond to your children's emotions.

## *Acknowledging your children's emotions*

If I've had a bad day and I'm upset, the last thing I want to hear from my friend is advice, amateur psychology, her point of view, or a dismissive comment such as, 'Oohh, you're just overreacting. You'll feel differently tomorrow!' I want her to listen, really listen, to me. I want her to empathise with me.

When someone acknowledges my feelings and makes sympathetic noises, I can get all the bad feeling of the day out of my system. In fact I often formulate my views and opinions by talking through all my bad feelings with someone else.

Children are no different. If they just have a listening ear and a sympathetic parent who gives them the time they need, they often help themselves and solve their own problems.

Empathy is key to becoming a better parent. This vital skill doesn't come naturally, though, unless you practise it.

Use the following technique to practise and develop your empathy skills.

1. **Consider an emotionally charged statement that your child recently said to you.**

   Examples of emotionally charged kid-talk may be, 'The science teacher shouted at me and everybody laughed' or 'I'd like to punch Matt on the nose!'

2. **Write down (or in an actual conversation, think) of the word that describes the emotion that you think your child is feeling.**

   For example, in the science teacher situation, your child may be feeling embarrassment; with regards to Matt, he may be feeling anger.

3. **Write down (or formulate in your mind) a sentence to show that you *understand* what emotion your child is feeling.**

   To respond to the science teacher situation, you might say to your child, 'That must have been really embarrassing.'

   What you're doing here is helping give a name to a feeling. Your children may not know exactly what they're feeling, but they know they're feeling something.

Parents often don't think to respond to their children in the preceding way. Sometimes they worry that they'll make the feelings worse. Actually, the opposite situation is true. Children really appreciate having someone acknowledge their experiences. They find this recognition comforting and can relax.

One of the most illuminating and helpful parenting books I have ever read is *How to Talk So Kids Will Listen and Listen So Kids Will Talk*, by Adele Faber and Elaine Mazlish (Picadilly Press Ltd). The book shows these communication skills in action in a down-to-earth, no-nonsense way using funny cartoons to illustrate their points. This is a good book to explore the topic in more depth.

## Making a wish come true – in fantasy

Sometimes just having someone around that understands how much you want something makes bearing the situation easier. This notion is particularly true for children. In fact, you can turn this dynamic into a bit of a game, so long as you don't appear to be teasing them.

The following conversation shows how this strategy works:

Dad, I want crunchy nut cornflakes!

*Oh, we've run out of those. I wish I had them in this kitchen right now.*

I want them!

*I can hear just how much you want them. I wish I had a magic broomstick to whisk me off to the supermarket and fly me back in time for your breakfast.*

I wish you had a magic carpet that could do that too. Well, I think I'll have toast instead.

*Great. I'll get moving on that then.*

Sometimes just having a parent understand how much they want something makes your child able to bear the reality of not having it. So relax and explore the fun way to grant your child's wishes from being able to ripen that banana immediately to having the best computer in the world that can magically do homework in their own style of writing, to having the best binoculars in the universe that can see Pluto right from your kitchen table. Try it – it works!

## Respecting that their emotions may differ from yours

Empathising with your children takes a great deal of effort. Yet doing so gives your kids massive comfort in knowing their feelings are understood – not negated or solved for them.

No matter how tempting it is, try to hold back from giving advice to your children or dismissing their emotions – especially if they're different from yours.

Children need to have their feelings *accepted*, which means they need to be recognised, and *respected*, which means valued. You can show you accept and respect your kids' feelings by listening quietly and attentively, giving a feeling a name, and making your child's wish come true – even if only in imagination.

All of your child's feelings can be accepted and recognised but you need to make clear that certain actions must be limited – such as kicking, hitting, or pushing. Try using a response such as 'I can tell how angry you are with your sister, but tell her in words. Don't hit her.'

For the next week have conversations with your children where you just accept their feelings and acknowledge them. Don't sound patronising and repeat their words back too exactly, though. Your children are going to find the new you surprising. This novel approach may feel awkward at first – for everyone involved – but stick with the techniques and you'll see enormous benefits to your family relationships.

# Praising Your Children Effectively

Children need to be given a strong, healthy self-image because from this solid foundation everything else in life becomes easier and more straightforward for them. Every time you show respect for your children through listening effectively, giving them choices, or granting an opportunity to solve a problem for themselves, you are watering and nurturing their self-confidence, self-worth, and self-esteem.

Praise is about making positive statements about your child either in public or privately and is a wonderful way to raise your child's confidence and self-esteem.

All too often, parents mean well and praise in generalities like, 'That's fantastic', 'That's great', or 'That's beautiful'. Children really don't understand non-specific praise. To be effective, you need to state exactly what behaviour, action, or accomplishment you are praising.

*Descriptive praise* is a very powerful tool and a useful skill to develop. You break your praise into three specific parts:

 ✔ **Describe what you see.** State what you see in detail.

   Consider the following description of what you see when looking at a drawing your child created at school: 'I see a turquoise paddling pool with blue water and orange fish around the side and lots of people laughing. It makes me remember being on holiday in Spain when we had a great time at the BBQ with all our friends. It makes me feel excited.'

   This description gets down to the important details of what you're praising and helps your child understand *what* you are valuing.

Or consider this example that I used with my 11-year-old (and extremely untidy) daughter: 'I see a really clean floor without any of your clothes on it, an organised desk with all your pencils in the pencil case, a properly made bed with the duvet pulled up and the pillow at the top, and your clothes all hung up in the wardrobe.'

After hearing a wonderfully elaborate description, your child feels good about himself. He is then able to praise himself.

✔ **Describe what you feel.** State what you're feeling in simple yet specific language.

For example: 'I feel really excited and happy when I look at your art work' or 'It's really nice to be able to walk in here and feel relaxed. I'd like to spend time in here with you having a chat.'

Sharing your feelings in this manner opens up a positive line of communication and helps build rapport and understanding.

✔ **Sum up the whole experience in a simple phrase.** Finish off your praise with an energetic capper.

For example: 'We have such good memories from that holiday!' or 'Now that's what I call organisation!'

# Gaining Co-operation from Your Children

Take a few minutes to think about what you insist that your children do during a fairly typical day.

It doesn't matter if your list is long or short, or whether your expectations are realistic or too high – what matters is how much energy, time, and effort you expend on getting your kids to do what you want.

Most parents I work with use a mixture of the following tactics to get their children to co-operate:

✔ **Accusing and blaming:** 'Oh not again – you've filled the bowl right up to the top with milk so it's pouring all over the floor. What's the matter with you? How many times do I have to tell you to pour slowly?'

✔ **Insulting:** 'Let me take that into the sitting room. You know how clumsy you are.'

✔ **Lecturing and moralising:** 'I can see I've been wasting my time teaching you manners, because you just snatched that magazine out of my hand.'

✔ **Threats:** 'If you do that again we'll have to go home.'

- ✔ **Warnings:** 'Be careful – that's hot.'

- ✔ **Commands:** 'Right. Go upstairs and tidy your room. Now.'

- ✔ **Sarcasm:** 'Oh, brilliant you've left your Geography textbook at school. That's really going to help you pass the exam tomorrow.'

- ✔ **Being a martyr:** 'We give up all our time and spend all this money on you and you don't even appreciate it. I don't know why we bother.'

- ✔ **Comparisons:** 'Why can't you be more like your sister; she's always so neat and tidy when she goes out?'

- ✔ **Prediction:** 'You're so selfish. You'll end up with no friends at all.'

Just writing these words made me squirm because I've said most of these things to my kids (well, I am a work in progress!). There are alternatives to getting your kids to co-operate without damaging their self-esteem.

While parents can (and should) work on accepting and respecting children while interacting, children need to behave in certain ways that are appropriate.

If getting your kids to behave in an 'appropriate' or 'acceptable' manner feels like an uphill struggle on occasion, remember that this is one of the built-in frustrations of parenthood that no one bothered to tell you about. Part of the problem of developing co-operation lies in the *conflict of needs*. Conflict of needs is the conflict between what you have to teach them – such as brushing their teeth – and what they want to learn. You, as the parent, need to teach your children cleanliness, politeness, routines, and systems – but actually they couldn't care less!

Getting my daughter to brush her teeth and pick up her dirty clothes from her bedroom floor were part of my frustrations. With my son, the aggravation lay in bringing down the hundreds of glasses he accumulated in his bedroom over a week. A lot of my energy went into the frustrating business of trying to teach my kids what society expected of them – but the more I insisted, the more they resisted! I seemed to be more of an enemy than Darth Vader. My children's attitude became 'I'll do as I want' and mine became 'No, you'll do as I say!'

## Finding a way to get through to your children

Write down all the things you nag your children about (tidying up after they finish with something, cleaning themselves, eating healthily, and so on), and then do the following:

1. **Describe what you see or describe the problem that you have.**

   For example, in response to all the dirty glasses in my son's room, I may say, 'I see dirty glasses over the floor in your room. I don't like running out of clean glasses in the kitchen.'

2. **Give information.**

   Giving information is a lot easier for your child to take than an accusation.

   For example, I can say, 'Dirty glasses and crockery belong in the dishwasher.'

3. **Say it with one simple phrase.**

   I can make my point by adding, 'Will, the dishwasher!'

4. **Talk about how you feel.**

   By expressing your feelings honestly you can be genuine without being hurtful to your kids.

   I may say, 'Running out of clean glasses annoys me. I can't relax when I know your room is full of dirty glasses.'

5. **Write a funny note.**

   Sometimes nothing is as effective or as powerful as the written word. Writing a note, particularly if it is light-hearted in tone, can really make a huge difference.

   I can write something like, 'Dear Will, we would really like to have a dishwashing experience because we've heard from the other glasses that it's like being in Disney World. So how about giving us a real treat and taking us downstairs for the ultimate experience? Cheers, Your Glasses.'

   Put the note somewhere obvious and watch what happens. In my case, my son came downstairs with a big sheepish grin on his face and seven glasses to be washed. Mission accomplished – but in a friendly way.

The preceding five steps encourage co-operation and without creating bad feelings. This technique takes the sting out of your communication and brings in some humour.

Be genuine and patient. Don't expect a round of applause and a happy kid jumping up to please you the first time you walk into the sitting room, trip over the school shoes, and say 'Shoes belong in the basket by the coats.' You may have to practise this technique as a family for quite a while.

Keep a note of all the successes you have because they'll encourage you to keep going. I encourage the parents I work with to write in it their journal last thing at night so they fall asleep focusing on all the positive things that happened that day and wake up the next day feeling positive too.

# Helping Your Kids Gain Independence

Independence is the ability to do things for yourself. When your children are young, wanting to do things for them is natural, but it's also important to recognise that kids will never have any degree of independence if you don't teach them to take care of themselves physically, emotionally, and psychologically.

If you do too much for your children, you encourage feelings of helplessness, worthlessness, frustration, resentment, and even anger. As a parent, you're in a continual process of letting go of your children; accepting this is often difficult. You need to allow your children to make their own mistakes because doing so helps them understand the pressures and realities of the world.

At the same time, you can't expect your children to suddenly become independent. You need to begin this process gradually and from an early age. Children need to know that independence means facing failure and disappointment, and involves taking risks.

It takes patience and time to teach everyday skills to kids, but a useful tip is to teach skills backwards: Do everything for your child up to the final step, then let him or her complete the task at hand. So allow your child to give their shoelace that last tug, or get a plate for their sandwich, and gradually, over days, weeks, and months, you'll add more and more steps until your child is starting at the very beginning of the process and tying his own shoelaces or making his own lunch. This process ensures that your teaching sessions always end with success for both of you.

The life lessons you allow for your kids still need to be gentle experiences. Encouraging independence is a balance between being overprotective and too liberal. Lessons in independence can start as early as you choose – from letting your child try to do up his coat buttons to allowing your teenager to drive himself to a party.

## Showing respect for their development

Development in children is extremely variable because children develop at their own pace mentally, physically, and socially. While 'normal' milestones exist, there's quite a range around all these norms. You can't rush children through any of their development. Just think how it must feel to be 6 years old and hear your parents say 'Eat up all your peas. Let me do up your zip. You're tired out; go and have a sleep. I think you should go to the loo now . . . ' Imagine your reaction if your partner or a friend kept telling you and reminding you to do things all day long. Your response probably isn't printable!

If a child's struggle for independence is respected, he develops tenacity and self-respect for himself. Often, by just waiting and encouraging your child, he can develop this attitude of tenacity, perseverance, and resolve to life generally.

To help your children be able to tackle issues for themselves as they age and develop, you need to introduce them to problem solving. You can also help them develop the ability to weigh up the pros and cons of situations and to look at a problem from both sides.

 Flexible parenting is being able to go with the flow of certain situations, bearing in mind your children's ages and maturity. As your child grows and matures, his abilities, concerns, and needs change, so your parenting needs to change over time too. Good parenting is flexible because it fits in with your child's stage of development and maturity. It means recognising where the balance lies in allowing your child to replace your rules with his judgement when the time is right.

No exact answers exist for when true independence starts to evolve because children are unique and mature at their own speeds. They handle responsibility in their own way and in their own time. The best answer to working out how mature your child is and how much responsibility he can handle is to spend lots of time getting to know your own child. Then you'll know naturally how to handle this new shift in responsibility.

To find out if you're ready for the shifts in responsibility and independence that occur as a child develops, get some paper and write down your answers to the following questions:

- ✔ What needs to change for you to move easily into this different role of delegating some responsibilities to your kids?

- ✔ What stumbling blocks may get in your way? What do you need to do to get round them?

- ✔ In what ways do you need to change, develop, or grow to make way for your child's emerging autonomy? Would developing a new hobby, getting a new job, or learning a new skill help you through this transition?

## *Avoiding too many questions*

All parents at some point overwhelm their children with question after question: 'So how was your day? Did you hand in your homework on time, find your tie, and play football at break? What did you have for lunch? Did you remember to have vegetables? Was Joe okay with you today?'

Unfortunately, when children feel overwhelmed, they retreat into themselves. Asking too many questions is an invasion of their private life and individuality.

Children open up and chat when they feel ready or want to share their news or their day with you. My son used to tell me his day was 'fine' when he got in the car, only to show up in the bathroom just as I was about to get into my longed-for bath – and when he should be getting ready for bed – to share the details with me. His timing was less than ideal, but these were the best chats we ever had. They flowed naturally, and we just shared and opened up to each other. Our chats remind me of what parenting is all about: Being open and flexible and grabbing the magic moment.

Rather than launching into a series of questions after your child has been at school or out playing, try just saying something like:

- ✔ 'Hi! It's great to see you!'
- ✔ 'Welcome home!'

If your kids are tired or need to relax, just sit in the comfortable space of silence or relax in the car listening to the radio. You don't need to fill every moment with full-on conversation. They'll talk when they're ready, and if you are open and available they'll know when to come to you.

A simple friendly greeting can really work. Go on, try it. This book is all about small changes that make a big difference.

## Controlling jumping in to the rescue

Growing up and becoming independent is all about letting children make their own mistakes appropriate to their age and development. The ultimate goal is that they one day function on their own, away from you, as independent individuals.

Don't always run to the rescue. Let your children wobble and fall off the climbing frame in the garden (if it's not too dangerous!); make a cake that falls apart when you cut it; and figure out how to manipulate the flat pack shelving for their bedroom. Your children need to discover, learn, make mistakes, and find their own answers.

One way to help children develop their problem-solving skills is to avoid rushing in with all the answers. When children ask questions (which can be rather a lot at around 3 years old!), give them a chance to think things through for themselves and to formulate their own ideas and concepts of the world.

For example, when your 4-year-old says, 'Why does Nanny always come to visit us on a Wednesday?' ask the question back as a rhetorical question to see what your child comes up with: 'So why *does* Nanny always come over on a Wednesday – what do you think?'

Letting things go unanswered is quite a hard skill to develop at first because you naturally want to rush in to answer the question. But by standing back, you're helping your child think for himself – you offer him an opportunity to grow, learn, and feel a sense of personal achievement.

## *Protecting their dreams without overprotecting their experiences*

Parents often try to protect their children from disappointments and failures, which is a natural and even honourable thing to do. But protecting can have the effect of preventing children from striving or dreaming – or even trying to go for things beyond their comfort zones. Overprotection may stifle their aims and aspirations later in life.

You may now be thinking, 'Well, that's all very well, but what's so bad about helping them or solving their problems? I don't want them to have to go through what I went through.'

The problem with this rationale is that if your children become continually dependent on you for everything, they lose confidence in their own judgement. Over time, feelings of inadequacy and anger tend to pop up. (This dynamic is not exclusive to parents and children. Adults, too, can develop over-dependent relationships and lose the ability to function for themselves.)

In the long term, protecting your children doesn't do them any favours in life. You just end up creating negative feelings and damaging their self-confidence.

You're trying to achieve a balance between genuinely helping your kids when things are a bit overwhelming and difficult and allowing them to experiment, make mistakes, and learn from them in a safe environment. You need to assist them to become responsible, independent adults able to cope on their own – so neither dash their dreams nor sugar-coat their lives.

For example, when your child comes home and says, 'I want to earn some money doing a paper round', don't crush his aspirations with, 'Well, that's a joke because you'll never get out of bed in time. Look at last weekend – you didn't get up till 11.30!' Instead, try saying, 'So you want to try a paper round? Tell me about it.'

Similarly, if your child suddenly says, 'I want to be a doctor when I grow up.' Don't dash his dreams with: 'Well, with the grades from your last exams, dream on.' Try saying 'So you're considering a career as a doctor . . .'

Although these responses may sound like common sense, they really do require skill to formulate and determination to implement into your conversation. Try communicating better with your children and watch the changes transform your relationships.

# Chapter 6

# Approaching Parenting With Common Sense

. . . . . . . . . . . . . . . . . . . . . . . . . . . . . . . . . . . . . . .

### In This Chapter

▶ Shifting your viewpoint

▶ Changing as your child changes

▶ Enhancing a child's sense of self

▶ Moving towards independence

. . . . . . . . . . . . . . . . . . . . . . . . . . . . . . . . . . . . . . .

**C**ommon sense is sound practical judgement derived from experience rather than studying, and this chapter is about practical, skill-based parenting. I include different techniques and strategies for positive ways to build your child's esteem. I also talk about adapting to changes as your kids grow, and choosing your battles when your child is striving for independence.

## Seeing Life through Others' Eyes

Of course, all people see the world from their own viewpoints. Although this tendency is natural, it sometimes can be very powerful and helpful to try and see situations from another person's point of view. The following two exercises can help you consider other points of view.

### Standing in someone else's shoes

Often when I'm working with parents, I ask them to do the following exercise to get them to imagine they're seeing a problem – or a difficulty or their family life – through the eyes of their child. Doing so utilises a *neuro-linguistic programming* (NLP) technique. NLP was devised by Dr Richard Bandler and John Grindler in the 1970s and is a common sense way to understand and improve your thinking, your ways of communicating, and to positively transform your feelings.

Although the following exercise is simple, it often results in a massive 'Eureka' moment, encouraging parents to shift perspectives and gain real insights into the problem from a different view of the world.

1. **Get a piece of paper and write your child's name on it.**

   If you have multiple children, make a separate sheet of paper for each child.

2. **Place the paper on the floor and then stand on the paper.**

   Try to see the world from your child's point of view. What do you hear, see, and feel about your family or a particular situation as you stand in your child's place? Stand in the special space for each of your children for as long as it takes to get a real picture of what the situation looks, sounds, and feels like for your child. Take your time – the feelings may come up quickly but they may also take some time to emerge. Don't judge what comes up, simply let yourself experience the world from a different viewpoint.

3. **Get another piece and write your partner's name on it. Stand on the piece of paper.**

   Try to see the world from your partner's point of view. What do you see, hear, and feel about your family or a particular situation?

4. **Get another piece of paper and write on it 'Independent outside observer'. Stand on it.**

   Try to see the world from this unknown person's point of view. What do you see, hear, and feel about your family or a particular situation?

5. **Ask yourself what you discovered from standing in multiple places and considering the same situation through multiple viewpoints.**

   Write in your journal the ideas that surface to help you clarify and remember what you learn from the experience.

Consider what insights you've gained from the exercise and decide if anything in your family needs to change. Choose a small step, not a great leap that may leave you feeling overwhelmed, and make a small difference in your approach. Notice the difference it makes to your family relationships this week.

## Considering how your child describes you as a parent

The following are some coaching questions I ask the parents who I work with. The focus of the questions is to get parents thinking about how their children would describe their parents and their family lives.

Thinking about how your children would answer the following questions helps you shift your perspective from yourself and your own point of view. Doing so also helps you begin to develop a better understanding of each member within a family.

Ask yourself the following questions, scribble in your journal, and see what comes up for you.

- ✔ If you were describing yourself to a stranger, how would you describe yourself as a parent (or step-parent or partner-parent)?
- ✔ What does living with you feel like?
- ✔ What do you sound like?
- ✔ How do you act?
- ✔ How do your kids rate family life?
- ✔ What is it like coming home to you?
- ✔ What's the atmosphere like in your home most of the time? (For example, is it noisy, relaxed, frenetic, tense, chaotic, loving, or a host of other descriptions?)
- ✔ What do your children see, hear, and feel as they step through the door at the end of a day?
- ✔ How would your kids rate family life on a scale of 1 to 10 (10 being the best)?
- ✔ Imagine the 'perfect' family life scenario. What are you seeing, hearing, and feeling inside?
- ✔ What small changes can you make to begin creating this perfect scenario?

In life you can only change, control, or influence your own state of mind or attitude to things. But by you making those small changes, the whole dynamic of your family relationships can and does change, shift, and transform.

For example, one of my clients had low self-esteem and felt she wasn't doing a very good job as a parent. After a few sessions with me she began to visualise herself as a more confident parent with improved skills, and a positive, clear, and directional intention in all her interactions with her children. She learnt how to get herself into a positive, confident state before interacting with her three teenage sons and she enjoyed practising her new skills of actively listening and taking more of a positive interest in her sons' activities, music, and hobbies. This change of attitude got her back into the driving seat of her family relationship and enjoying the journey.

# Adapting to Changes as Children Grow

The only time I can think of when 'one size fits all' is when I bought some cheap socks from the £1 shop at Christmas. They really do stretch to fit everyone!

However, parenting isn't like a pair of socks. While the basics of good parenting apply to all children, the way these ideas fit into your family always varies due to your child's age, personality, and interests and your unique and individual family.

Entire books are written about child development, but Chapter 3 covers the highlights of your child's development from a stage-by-stage perspective.

As your children develop from one stage to another, they're changing on the *inside* as well as on the *outside*. They're not just growing in shoe size – but in how they think and feel and in what they're capable of.

Read about each developmental stage *before* your child gets there, so you can remain prepared and flexible to the changes. Being prepared like this is a key skill in being a great parent.

Each stage of development seems to me to have a central question for parents attached to it, for example:

- ✔ **Infancy:** 'How can I help my child feel more secure?'

- ✔ **Toddlerhood:** 'How can I help my child feel more in control?'

- ✔ **Early childhood:** 'What can I do to help my child feel more grown-up?'

- ✔ **Middle childhood:** 'How can I help my child feel more competent and capable?'

- ✔ **Early teen:** 'How can I help my teenager feel more independent?'

- ✔ **Late teen:** 'How can I help my adolescent understand herself better?'

The following sections consider the phases – and the questions attached to them – in greater detail.

## Infancy and toddler time

'How can I help my child feel more secure?' is the central question of infancy. Refer to Chapter 3 for more information on security.

'How can I help my child feel more in control?' is the central question of parenting toddlers.

Your toddler's constant use of the word 'No' stems from her strong desire to be independent. Other common displays of unreasonable negative behaviour include your child refusing to be strapped in the buggy, turning down food she loved last week, and insisting you do an impossible task – like getting a favourite toy she's left at home when you're now in Manchester.

All these nos and negatives are natural, but they can drive you to distraction. Following are some ways to deal with this phase in a positive way.

- ✔ **Toddler-proof your home.** Incorporate stair gates, put glass vases out of reach, and install door stoppers to prevent fingers getting crushed. These preventive measures not only increase your child's safety, they cut down the need for unnecessary battles.

- ✔ **Have regular meal times and bed times.** Routines provide security for your child and help make sure she's not too tired or hungry.

- ✔ **Keep your use of 'no' to a minimum.** Try to stay positive; eventually your child will begin to copy this style of thinking and speaking.

- ✔ **Be patient.** Remind yourself that this stage doesn't last forever!

- ✔ **Don't be over controlling.** Don't take over and do everything for your child. Let your toddler try things out for herself.

- ✔ **When you must say 'no', do so in the right manner.** Saying 'no' is appropriate – particularly when your child's safety is in question. Don't get angry or alarmed. Keep your tone calm but firm.

- ✔ **Use clever tactics of distraction to make life more interesting.** Get silly and suddenly announce, 'Oh, I think I hear the tickle spider coming to see you!' and walk your fingers up your child's arm. Get your child to close her eyes, put something in her hand, and see if she can guess what it is. Make supermarket shopping into a game where your children have to look for the spaghetti hoops or weigh the fruit. Draw on your child's back with your finger, and see if she can tell what you're drawing. Be inventive and let your imagination go.

- ✔ **Offer limited choices.** Doing so helps your child feel more in control of her life. If you're getting a struggle, it's probably because your child feels she doesn't have enough power. Give a child choices so she has a feeling of power and control. For example, getting her to eat breakfast or not isn't negotiable, but offer her a limited menu of real options you can live with: 'You can sit down at the table and have cereal with us or you can make some toast and eat it on the way to school.'

✔ **Use praise to encourage good behaviour.** Toddlers thrive when you praise them.

✔ **Don't waste time arguing.** Arguing drains your energy and is pointless. Instead, press your 'pause' button, take a deep breath, and move on to something else.

✔ **Lighten up.** Remember your sense of humour and ask yourself 'Does this really matter?'

## Early childhood and the middle years

During these phases of a child's development, a parent's main questions are, 'How can I help my child feel more competent and capable?' and 'How can I help my child feel more grown-up?'

As children grow up, they begin having (and expressing!) their own opinions. Doing so is a natural part of their development. So you must decide on what issues are actually important to you and then be flexible on less important things. This distinction is often the hardest part for parents because it requires a change of attitude.

These years are full of changes, and provide a good time for you to start building the foundations of communication and give-and-take. You need to be prepared to understand your child's viewpoint (see 'Seeing Life through Others' Eyes' earlier in this chapter) and then your child will be more likely to understand yours.

Growing up is a slow process – you often take three steps forward and two steps back! Maturity takes its own course. You often feel that your child has progressed forward and then slipped back and regressed in behaviour. That's all perfectly normal. Just be aware of it because it helps you understand your kids' development pattern better.

A useful trick to determine whether you're communicating appropriately with your child is to imagine that she's a guest staying with you or that she's someone else's. Ask yourself, 'Would I say that if it wasn't to my daughter?' If the answer is 'no', then don't say it.

Accept your children for who they are. Show respect for their emerging opinions even if you don't agree with them. Don't try to change them into something you want them to be. Early childhood and the middle years are a time for emerging independence and if you want your children to think for themselves and show initiative, they will inevitably make a few mistakes along the way. The secret is for both children and parents to learn from them. Experience truly is the best teacher.

# Early and late teens

As your child develops into an early and later teen, your parental questions become, 'How can I help my teenager feel more independent?' and 'How can I help my teenager understand herself better?' Some key questions I ask parents of teenagers are:

- How do you describe your style of parenting at the moment? (For example, are you stifling, controlling, flexible, relaxed, or some other description?)

- Are you clear on your priorities and values that you're trying to teach your teenager? If you're not sure what's important to you, jot your values down on a pad and arrange them in order of importance for you. Consider whether you're passing them on clearly by your own actions and words.

- How do you listen to your teenager? Do you listen when you're doing something else at the same time, or do you stop what you're doing and give your teen your full attention?

- What sort of body language and tone of voice do you use with your teenager? Do you match your child's tone of voice or try to lift the tone into a more positive, pleasant, matter of fact but taking no prisoners sort of voice?

- Do you anticipate confrontation? You need to stay centred and anchored even when your teen reacts in a negative or disgruntled way. The only behaviour and attitude you can control is your own mental state.

- How do you feel about your teenager's emerging independence from you? Are you frightened to let her go?

- Do you both know where you stand as a parent? Are the house rules clear, fair, flexible, and relevant to your child's current age and level of responsibility?

- Despite the 'It's my life' bravado that your teenager often displays, how do you show your unconditional love and support of your teenager?

- How do you develop your teenager's self-esteem at this very fragile stage of development?

By asking yourself questions, you look at your relationship with your teenager from a more detached viewpoint, which helps you to gain clarity and recognise areas for change.

Knowing where you stand with your teenager is difficult because this is a great time of change for both of you. As a small child, your teenager looked to you for all the answers; now she just wants a lift to the next party and finds you totally embarrassing!

---

## Remembering yourself

During the challenging times of parenting, remember to take time out occasionally to rest, relax, and have fun yourself. Likewise, maintaining healthy relationships with your partner, family, and friends is critical to your ability to be a good parent.

Relationships outside the ones you have with your children provide support and back-up to help you cope. Keeping your own life going gives you a sense of proportion.

Your children are with you for such a short time really – you need to remember they will leave the nest one day and you still have to carry on with a sense of purpose and fulfilment in your life.

---

Instead of seeing the teenage years as a time of confrontation, try seeing them as a time of growth and change, and an opportunity to develop a more adult relationship with your emerging adult. This period's a butterfly time – get it right and you've cracked it. A whole section in Chapter 9 is dedicated to teenagers.

Parenting isn't about winning or losing – the role's about helping your child develop self-confidence in a healthy, balanced way. Parenting's about *you* remaining flexible.

Your role as a parent changes as your child grows. In fact, all parenting is about *change* and how you adapt to or face up to it. Do you put your head in the sand, like an ostrich, or do you embrace and celebrate change as a natural part of your child growing up?

# Building Up Your Child's Self-esteem

Self-esteem, confidence, and self-belief are essential qualities that children need in order to become self-assured adults.

*Self-esteem* comes from the Latin 'to estimate', and means how you rate yourself deep down. It is a belief and a confidence in your own ability and value. Self-esteem isn't the same as arrogance, which is a slightly aggressive, false sense of belief; rather, it's a gentle knowing that:

- ✔ You like yourself.
- ✔ You think you're a good human being.

    ✔ You deserve love.

    ✔ You deserve happiness.

    ✔ You feel deep down inside yourself that you're an okay person.

Some people think that self-esteem means confidence. Although confidence is part of self-esteem, it is rather more than that. Many apparently confident people have poor self-esteem. Actors, comedians, singers, and royals all appear to shine on stage – think of Robbie Williams, Marilyn Monroe, or the Princess of Wales – yet many of them are, or were, desperately insecure. Having public adulation is no guarantee of having self-esteem.

Einstein observed that for every negative message the brain receives, 11 or more positive messages are necessary to negate its effect. Clearly, keeping things positive pays. Don't forget that humans have 90,000 thoughts a day, and 60,000 of those are repetitive. Giving your children positive messages and helping them think positively can pay big dividends over the course of a lifetime.

# Considering self-belief and self-image

*Self-belief* is trust in your own abilities. It is the key that opens up a world of fearlessness, freedom, and opportunity for your children. Self-belief comes from you as a parent developing ways to praise, support, and encourage your children every day.

Self-belief is like a muscle; if you help your children use it regularly, it gets stronger and grows. With regular exercise, your kids can cope with whatever life throws at them. Using the same principle, if your child fails to regularly exercise this muscle, her self-belief becomes weak, limp, and flabby.

Children also need to be given a strong, healthy *self-image*. Self-image is the opinion that you have of your own worth, attractiveness, and intelligence. From that solid foundation, everything else in life becomes easier and more straightforward.

Children become very aware of your feelings and behaviour. They hear not only the words you say but the tone of your voice. They observe and create their view of their body from how you talk about your body and theirs. They model themselves on the things you do and say. So if you talk about your body as something to be hidden away, or dirty or embarrassing or not good enough, then your children pick this up and model it themselves.

Your current self-image is the result of the repeated messages and instructions you received from authority figures, beginning from earliest childhood. The way you see yourself today is the result of years of conditioning by your parents, family, teachers, and other influential adults and peers in your life. As a parent of a teenager who is questioning her body image, you need to give her a balanced, healthy, and positive view of herself.

## What is inner confidence?

The way children think about themselves determines everything they do, say, act, and believe. Everything a child sees in the outside world has a parallel inside. The outer world enables children to appear and behave in a manner that looks like they're self-assured, while the inner world gives children the feeling and belief that they're okay.

Likewise, inner and outer types of confidence support each other. Inner confidence is the belief you have that you're a good person and deserve love, and outer confidence is the extrovert confidence you display when you walk into a room full of strangers.

The four main elements of inner confidence are:

✔ Self-love

✔ Self-knowledge

✔ Clear goals

✔ Positive thinking

The following sections cover each of the four elements in detail.

### Self-love

Confident people love themselves. They care about themselves, and their behaviours and lifestyles are *self-nurturing*, which means that they look after themselves, taking time to replenish their energy, keep alive their interests, and nurture their health. The subconscious mind has been programmed by simple, repeated instructions and messages from others, so children need to learn how to enjoy being nurtured and discover how to do this for themselves.

Children need to learn to love, nurture, and care about themselves and to take responsibility for making themselves happy, fulfilled, and valued. They need to learn to respect themselves and accept that they are perfect and 'good enough' for being themselves just the way they are.

Your children develop the skill of self-love by you believing in them, nurturing their confidence, and building them up with your encouraging positive words.

### Self-knowledge

Inwardly confident people are also very aware. They don't analyse their navels, but they do reflect on their feelings, thoughts, and behaviours. If your children develop good self-knowledge, they'll be more able to meet their full potential.

Children with strong self-knowledge also grow up with a firm sense of their own identities. They're more likely to be comfortable as an individual and not just as a sheep following the crowd – a very important attribute during the peer pressure of the teenage years. Another benefit of strong self-knowledge is that your children are less likely to become defensive at the first hint of criticism.

Encourage your children to talk about how they see themselves objectively and positively. A lovely thing I did with my kids was to sit round the table as a family and write down why my son and daughter are special.

For my daughter, we wrote:

> Molly is special because she has a really bubbly personality.
>
> She is kind and loving, fun to spend time with, enthusiastic, helpful, chatty, noisy, and untidy.
>
> She is articulate, great at history, and thoughtful.
>
> She is great at cooking, painting, and drawing, and has great dress sense.
>
> She has the most beautiful singing voice and makes people laugh.
>
> She is a loyal and trustworthy friend and she loves animals.

The look on my kids' faces was truly amazing. This is a very powerful way to help your child feel truly valued. I did this at school too, and parents still come up to me and say that their child has the framed version up in their kitchen.

So the ability to help your children analyse themselves and what makes them tick helps them learn to understand their own traits, feelings, and behaviours and helps them to become really comfortable with their own identities. It is a very important step in developing a well-balanced, mature, and happy adult. You can get your kids to write one for you too!

### Clear goals

Confident people seem to be surrounded by a clear sense of purpose. These individuals have a definite idea of why they are taking a particular course of action, and they have a specific vision of the results they want to achieve.

If your children develop the habit of formulating and working towards clear goals, they'll be less dependent on others to make them do things.

Children who set goals have more excitement and positive energy because they're more motivated. They're more persistent, focusing on what they want. They grow up finding decision-making easy because they have a clear idea of what they want and how to get it.

Kids need a focus for their destination in life. Goal setting is simply setting your dreams in motion. Help your child write down her dreams – they then become goals with a date!

Teaching a child how to set simple, clear, achievable goals is a really positive step in developing a self-confident adult. Refer to Chapter 4 for more about setting goals.

### Positive thinking

Confident people are usually great company because they're in the habit of seeing the bright side of life and expect good, positive experiences.

Children who develop positive thinking skills grow up expecting life to be generally good. They think and see the best in people. They believe that most problems have a solution. They don't waste energy worrying about possible negative outcomes. They're open to change because they like the excitement of growth and development.

You're a role model. If you act and speak positively, your children will too.

## Creating quality time – or 'getting stuck in'

What's all this fuss about 'quality time'? What is it and how do you do it?

Quality time is an essential tool for building and enhancing your child's self-esteem. This time isn't about *what* you're doing but about *how* you do it. Quality time is a state of mind. It means fully engaging, really listening, sharing a passion or interest, being relaxed, and having fun with someone else.

## Assessing your involvement

Here's a little quiz to see if you really are actively involved in your child's life.

✔ Can you name all of your child's teachers?

✔ Can you name your child's best friends?

✔ Do you know your child's favourite activity at school?

✔ Do you know what book your child is currently reading? (Or even if they are reading?)

✔ Can you name your child's heroes – in sport, films, music, or on TV?

✔ Do you know *why* your child likes her music?

✔ Do you always know where your child is, and with whom?

✔ Do you know whether your child is happy, sad, popular, lonely, anxious, or untroubled?

If you don't know the answers to these questions, you may need to get more involved in your child's life.

Children with involved parents do better at school, feel better about themselves, have greater self-esteem, and are less likely to take drugs. Whether your child is a toddler or a teenager, she needs your involvement – and that means spending time with her.

Quality time doesn't mean (to me anyway) teaching my daughter equations. I don't want to be her tutor. I'm her parent. Yes, I help her with homework, but then we like to bake cakes, paint rainbows, and buy earrings.

If you'd rather be somewhere else, mentally, then go. You're not spending quality time with your child. Don't be on 'planet autopilot'. Your child knows when you're genuinely interested. You're better off spending an hour fully engaged than two hours pretending to be.

Of course, parenting isn't something you do when you feel like it. Parenting takes hard work and often means you have to rearrange job commitments if you're a working parent. When your child has flown the nest, you probably won't say, 'I wish I had spent more time in the office'. You'll regret you didn't spend more time with your child when you had the chance.

One reason why spending quality time is important is that you never know when your child is going to open up to you. For example, my son never opened up in the car on the way home from school because he was tired and hungry. So now when I directly ask him 'How was your day?' I do so at unspecific times – when we're just chilling or being casual in our activity together. The more time you're together, the greater the likelihood of finding out about that row at school today, that unkind remark, or that funny incident in the science lab.

Try to become interested in what interests your child – not just what you're interested in or think your child *should* be interested in. Swap your thinking around. Be led by your child. Paying attention to your child's interests helps her self-esteem and maturity – plus you may find out lots of new things.

## Showing respect

*Respect* is understanding that all people and things have value. By treating people with respect, the world is a nicer place to live in, whether at home, school, or out in the community. Showing respect is easy – all you have to do is treat people the way you would like them to treat you.

Respect is the key energy of a good family because it brings everyone together. Families built on respect can handle whatever challenges come along, including divorce, bereavement, redundancy, or any other of life's ups and downs. Families don't die from their setbacks – but they can wither and die from the energies of negativity, sarcasm, taunts, and guilt.

Respect is not the same as being your child's friend or equal. Remember, you're the parent here. Sometimes you need to assert your authority in ways that a mate can't. Children can easily become confused if their parents depend on them emotionally, particularly during a divorce or times of stress. Your child needs to act her age and have a carefree childhood as much as possible.

Respect isn't measured by whether people agree with you – but by how they behave towards you when you *disagree*. A parent who shows respect and unconditional love to the most difficult child in the family (at that particular time) creates a culture of trust that the whole family can learn from.

Respect simply means speaking politely to your children, valuing their opinions, paying real attention and not interrupting when they're speaking to you, and treating them kindly.

Children naturally look up to their parents and want to be like them. So if you are being a respectful role model, your child will respect you and develop the skills and behaviours required to respect others. Of course, children with behavioural problems may require professional support, but generally speaking, if you treat your children with respect, they will respond with respect towards you.

Even when children are contrary, rebellious, or argumentative, they're probably not behaving in these ways out of spite. Rather, they're going through particular stages of development and are trying to assert their individuality and their control over their own lives.

Many parents worry too much about whether their children respect them and don't think enough about whether they treat their children with respect. I feel distressed when I hear parents tell their children to 'shut up' or when they say things that humiliate or embarrass them in front of others. I suppose these parents are demonstrating that they have the upper hand and are more powerful. Unfortunately, these actions do nothing to enhance a child's self-esteem or create family respect or unity.

When your child speaks or acts in a disrespectful way, the first question you should ask yourself is, '*Why* do I think my child did this?' Not, 'How can I make my child respect me?'

Think about the ways you show respect to your children – jot down all the ways you speak, act, and behave around your children in different situations – on holiday, at the supermarket, when you're stressed, when you're relaxed, when you're with your friends, and when they're with their friends.

You can show respect in the way you communicate with your child:

- ✔ **Recognise the huge difference between 'talking at' and 'talking with' your child.** The difference is rather like 'laughing at' or 'laughing with' someone. Parents need to guard against the conversation that always feels like a lecture or a nag. These one-way dialogues can be very demoralising and boring for a child. Children, just like adults, want to be heard. They want their point of view valued, not corrected.

- ✔ **Choose your expressions carefully.** Expressions such as 'Don't answer me back!', 'If I want your opinion, I'll ask for it!' or 'You'll understand when you're older!' are rude and patronising. You may be in a hurry or stressed, so the best thing to say is that you're going to use your authority and you'll explain to them later about your decision. If you've built up a culture of respect in your family, your child will understand.

- ✔ **Agree to disagree.** You can help your children understand that reasonable people can disagree and are able to discuss their disagreements respectfully. However, at times you, as the adult, may have to make the final decision because you have greater wisdom and experience than your child.

Part of respecting a child is also allowing her to act her age and enjoy being at her stage of development. Let her enjoy living life in the present. Children grow up so fast that it's worth remembering childhood isn't a race to see who gets to adulthood first.

# Choosing Your Battles

No parent likes to fight or disagree with their child, but inevitably conflict does occur – particularly when your child is exploring her independence! Having a different opinion, of course, is a healthy sign of your child's development. But, as a parent, life has a way of catching you off guard and getting under your skin. You can end up losing your cool over the wrong things.

Don't be afraid to say 'no' – but be sure to reflect on which battles you want to fight. Save your big guns for big issues. Try stepping back from the heat of the moment and asking yourself, 'Is she doing or saying this to strive for independence and to assert herself?' If the answer is yes, you need to change *your* attitude and approach to the situation.

*If your kids are giving you a headache, follow the directions on the aspirin bottle, especially the part that says 'keep away from children'.*

—Susan Savannah

## Seeing the bigger picture

When you feel things heating up between you and your child, take a moment and ask yourself any (or all) of the following questions:

- Is this something worth arguing over?
- How do I know whether this is a battle worth fighting?
- Does this disagreement really matter – or is it just bothering me?
- Is this really a difference in taste, style, or opinion?
- Is this issue really that important – compared to building a positive, lasting relationship with my child?
- Is this really *my* battle to fight?
- Is the problem mine or my child's?

Take a step back, press your pause button, and think about what a detached observer would say to you now as good advice.

Let the siblings sort it out amongst themselves; sometimes they need to resolve conflict without you!

Learn when to step in or when to hold back. Going to war over minor issues will exhaust you – but it will also exhaust your child's respect for your judgement. She'll stop taking you seriously and that can erode your long-term relationship. Children whose parents constantly nag them and argue about every little thing soon stop listening to their parents and don't hear what's being said to them. If you make a big deal over everything, even things that don't really matter in the long run, how will your child know when things *do* matter?

'It's always better to strike when the iron is cold.' This gives you cooling off time, and when you feel more in control you can sit down and discuss the incident properly and calmly.

## Common-sense ways to handle conflict

Some conflict in families is inevitable, but how you handle conflict makes the difference between happy and unhappy children. Negative ways to handle conflict include:

- ✔ **Avoiding conflict**, which is frustrating and usually causes more stress and resentment later on.

- ✔ **Being defensive** and steadfastly denying any wrongdoing or any responsibility. This creates long-term problems when your kids don't feel listened to and the unresolved conflicts continue to grow.

- ✔ **Over-generalising** is when something happens and the situation gets blown out of proportion by sweeping generalisations that perpetuate conflict and keep you from solving things.

- ✔ **Being right** means deciding that there's a 'right' and a 'wrong' way to look at things. However, handling conflict this way makes your children feel judged. 'Winning' the argument often means that the relationship loses!

- ✔ **Forgetting to listen**, where you interrupt, roll your eyes, and predict what your children are going to say next instead of truly listening and attempting to understand your kids. This keeps you from seeing their point of view.

- ✔ **Playing the blame game**, where you criticise and blame your kids for the situation, which just exacerbates the conflict.

✔ **Making character attacks**, where you take a negative action that your child has done and blow it up into a personality flaw. This is disrespectful to your child and she thinks that you don't like her, rather than her behaviour.

✔ **Stonewalling** is when you refuse to talk or listen to your kids. This shows disrespect and, in certain situations, even contempt, while at the same time letting the underlying conflict grow. Stonewalling creates hard feelings and damages relationships.

Here are some positive ways to handle conflict in your family. Use CHOICES to set limits and to generate new solutions to old problems. Here's how the strategy works, with an example of your child not hanging up her coat and putting her schoolbag away:

✔ **Command.** Give clear instructions, specifying what you want the child to do in a non-humiliating way. 'Pick up your coat and schoolbag now.'

✔ **Humour.** Use humour or surprise your child by doing or saying something totally unexpected to diffuse a potentially explosive situation. Stand waiting patiently like a valet when your child enters the room.

✔ **Offer choices between two options.** 'You can pick up your coat now, or I'll pick it up and you'll owe me a job later.'

✔ **Ignore unacceptable behaviour.** Simply leave the coat and schoolbag on the kitchen table and forget about it.

✔ **Compromise.** Seek a solution that satisfies all parties. Pick up the coat but your child has to sort out her schoolbag.

✔ **Encourage problem solving.** Discuss the issue and come up with a solution together.

✔ **Structure the environment.** Rearrange people or objects to reduce conflict. Place hooks in the hallway for your child's coat and schoolbag.

Fighting can get out of hand, but backing off and avoiding conflict isn't healthy either. Get things out in the open in a controlled, safe way when you haven't completely lost your temper.

Ask yourself some questions to discover how you handle your anger and see what you discover. If you don't like what you find, talk it over with a partner, or seek some professional help.

✔ How do you manage your anger?

✔ What triggers you off?

✔ How can you help your child handle their frustration and anger positively?

You don't need to argue to be powerful. Being powerful is really about being in control, strong, centred, and grounded in maturity and wisdom. Imagine that you're an anchor at the bottom of the sea being strong, stable, and reliable, while your child is bobbing about on the surface being buffeted and thrown off course from time to time by her emotions and what life throws at her.

Chapter 10 has more age- and situation-specific ways of handling conflict.

## Keeping anger under control

Whatever life brings along, it is important to forgive easily, say sorry, show love and encouragement – and move on. Children shouldn't live in an atmosphere of resentment, where you hold grudges and your kids feel your hostility. It damages your bond of love.

Ask yourself:

- ✔ Which things about my child's behaviour really make me angry again and again and are they really worth it?
- ✔ How can I change or defuse the anger?
- ✔ How can I make things more bearable for both sides?
- ✔ How does my child know when I'm sorry?
- ✔ Is this particular argument moving me closer to or farther away from my child?

Think about how you can distract, divert, and relax yourself quickly when you feel your anger volcano rising. Perhaps you can relieve your tension by hitting a pillow, screaming in the garden, or swearing quietly under your breath in a cupboard (I have done this on a number of occasions!).

# Creating Independent Adults

From the moment you play peek-a-boo with your baby, you're preparing her for the process of moving away from you and discovering independence. As your child matures and gains in confidence, she grows into an independent being. You need to prepare her to leave the nest one day.

Of course, the inevitable feelings of separation that come from gaining independence can be difficult for both parent and child. Even in ordinary, healthy situations, children can experience some form of worry, apprehension, fear, anxiety, or distress. These feelings are completely natural for children when they're faced with unfamiliar or new situations. Your child may want to retreat from the situation or look to you for more reassurance. But as a parent, your job is to help her be the mistress of her own destiny and not at the mercy of her fears.

All children leave home one day – honestly! Along the way, they'll struggle to finish homework; choose their own friends and partners; run out of petrol; walk down long dark streets at night; and have one too many drinks. But *preparation*, not protection, should be your new mantra. How your children respond to these decisions and incidents is largely up to you – and how you prepare them now for the future.

Your job is to teach your children self-discipline, right from wrong, consideration for others, and how to make the best of their talents. Your job is not to try and keep your children safe inside playpens. You need to continually enlarge their worldviews, encouraging them to grow up, so they eventually don't need the safety of playpens anymore.

## Finding a balance

Introducing your children to independence requires a delicate balance and a slow, deliberate pace.

No map, handbook, or chart lays out the exact plan moving your child from strict rules to greater freedom and trust. Your child is unique and handles responsibility in her own way and at her own pace. You know your child better than anyone else. So trust your feelings about when to loosen the apron strings and by how much.

To help decide how much independence you can give your child, spend time with her. Simply spending time with your child enables you to understand her strengths and weaknesses, and assess her maturity and way of seeing the world. Don't confuse your child's physical maturity with her social and emotional maturity.

Help to train your child to take responsibility for her own life in steps. Gradually allow your child to replace your rules with her judgements as she gets older. Doing so is one of the most difficult challenges that parents face. Too much responsibility too soon can overwhelm and frighten your child, so be sensible and sensitive.

For example, you can use pocket money to start devolving responsibility. Controlling her pocket money enables your child to hone her money management and budgeting skills, and it gives her freedom to choose what she wants to spend it on. (My 11-year-old daughter quickly got wise to spending all her money on sweets when she realised that she had nothing left for a lovely little top she saw an hour later.) With older children, running a bank account helps them see that money can flow out as well as in.

The more responsibility you can give your child, the more she'll rise to this challenge of trust and the more she'll behave responsibly.

The key challenge for emerging young adults is finding their own identities. They're struggling to know who they are and where they fit into society. Teenagers are constantly asking themselves: Who am I? Who do I want to be like? Which group do I fit into? What am I good at? As a parent, you must guide your child through the phase of having to buy designer clothes to fit in, or of being labelled the 'clever one' or the 'sporty one', and into her own place in the world with a sense of identity and worth.

Encourage your children to discover, explore, and develop their talents and skills throughout their lifetimes.

## Going slowly

In addition to balance, your pace is important. Gradually allow your child to replace your rules with her own judgement. If at first you don't succeed, don't give up. Just go back a few steps and realise that perhaps your child isn't quite ready for a particular responsibility just yet. Here are some indicators to work out whether your child is moving towards independence. Does your child:

- ✔ Cope with unexpected change?
- ✔ Listen to other people's ideas?
- ✔ Recognise her feelings as they occur?
- ✔ Express her feelings appropriately?
- ✔ Control strong emotions and impulses easily?
- ✔ Take responsibility for her actions and behaviour?
- ✔ Act intelligently and maturely under stress?

Any 'No' answer indicates part of your child's life where she may not be emotionally mature, so you need to support her for a bit longer.

For example, I remember working with a dad who was having difficulty accepting that his 15-year-old son, Chris, was growing up. We looked at small ways to help him let Chris be part of the decision-making process in the house, focusing first on the bedtime routine. Chris's dad started to let go of the strict bedtime rule he'd instilled and slowly began allowing Chris to determine his own bedtime. The change enabled Chris to start to take responsibility for judging his need to have fun with his need for sleep and being able to function effectively at school the next day. The whole process involved trial and error. After a couple of weeks, Chris felt more empowered and trusted, and his dad felt good about letting the perimeter fence of his son's boundaries become more flexible. As their relationship deepened and improved, they gained a new respect for each other.

# Chapter 7

# Maintaining Great Relationships

**K**eeping all the plates spinning at the same time is a challenge for any parent. Your kids want your attention, your elderly mother needs you to take her shopping, your partner wants you to spend time together, your friends ask if they can drop off their kids for a couple of hours while they do some DIY – and there's a pile of ironing and just a pork pie left in the fridge!

So many people want a part of you and although you try to please everyone, you seem to please no one. And sometimes the people closest to you are the ones who unintentionally put you under the greatest pressure.

Some people are a positive influence on your life and some are not. Not many parents take the time to stand back and analyse their relationships. This chapter helps you take a major step toward identifying, and possibly getting back in touch with, the important people in your life – and hopefully reconnecting to yourself along the way.

## Keeping Your Relationships Healthy

As a parent, you're the driving force behind a great many relationships – with your children, partner, work colleagues, relatives, friends, and finally yourself. Still, there may seem to be enough time in the day for all the relationships you want to develop, change, or enjoy. If you're not careful, though, you can start running on empty and feeling stressed, anxious, and overwhelmed by trying to fit everyone in. And if you drop a few of these spinning plates, you may start to feel guilty about letting people down.

Making time for relationships in a structured way helps you gain control of them.

Actually, the problem isn't time. Everyone has the same amount. The problem's *choice*. The choices you make determine whether you're running your life, or your life is running you. And you do have choices.

Bearing in mind that not all tasks are equal can be helpful. The same goes for commitments, responsibilities, and relationships. The importance of various people in your life varies from time to time. Yet many people act as if this fact isn't the case.

You can do fifty things today and get little, if any, results for having done them, or you can do one or two small things that bring you a big return in terms of personal fulfilment. People who are in control of their relationships know the difference and are happier. They see time as life's currency and how they use it as a series of choices they make.

Choices shape your results and your life. You get the same twenty-four hours each day as the parent next door. If they seem to fit more things in than you do, look at ways to use your time wisely. You'll see a massive improvement in your sense of well-being.

## Looking after yourself

One of the key relationships you need to protect and nurture is your relationship with yourself. So many parents I work with are truly selfless and generous with their time, commitment, and energy towards their family that they forget to look after their own energy, interests, friends, or hobbies and feel guilty if they do nurturing things for themselves. They put themselves at the bottom of the priority list but forget that if they become ill, stressed, or overwhelmed that the family suffers too.

Looking after yourself is vital for your own well-being and that of your family. Take time out occasionally to rest, relax, recuperate, and have some fun with other adults. Parents who are stressed out and exhausted lack the necessary energy to inject enthusiasm, laughter, and fun into their family life and everyone suffers.

## Considering your relationships

Before you can choose which relationships you want to invest your time in, you need to become aware of your many relationships – and know what you truly appreciate from relationships in general. Try the following:

1. **Brainstorm a list of all your relationships.**

   Write your list on a sheet of paper. Be sure to include specific relationships in your immediate family, your extended family, workplace, neighbourhood, and larger circle of friends and acquaintances.

   Don't forget to include your relationship with yourself.

2. **Brainstorm another list of the values or principles that are most important in your relationships.**

   These might include friendship, laughter, compromise, balance, or spending time together.

3. **Evaluate your list of values and select your top three.**

   What makes each of your selected top values really important to you?

4. **Consider each of the relationships you listed earlier, in terms of the three values you identified.**

   Rate each of your relationships in order of the amount of time you're investing in them on a 1 to 10 scale (1 being the lowest and taking up the least amount of time, and 10 being the highest and taking a great deal of your time). This rating system shows you which relationships feel neglected, and which are over-invested in. You can see quickly and easily the relationships that feel out of balance and need working on.

   Table 7-1 shows an example of a filled-in relationship rating exercise.

5. **Evaluate your results.**

   Now you've shone a torch on some of your most important relationships and on what you value about them, which ones do you find the most stressful? Which ones take up most of your energy? Which ones make you laugh and feel good?

   How did you score with yourself? Did this result surprise you? For more ideas for continuing to build your relationship with yourself, see the section 'Making time for yourself'.

| Table 7-1 | Rating Relationships |
|---|---|
| *Relationship* | *Rating* |
| Myself | 2 |
| My children | 10 |
| My partner | 7 |
| My relatives | 3 |
| My friends | 4 |
| My work colleagues | 6 |

How about your relationship with your partner? For more on rejuvenating this relationship, see the section 'Maintaining your relationship with your partner'.

If you could change just one of the relationships you identified above, which one would have the greatest impact on your life? What difference would it make to your life if you changed it for the better and how would that feel? So what's stopping you? Start to focus on all the great benefits to making that change and make a start this week. This chapter can help.

You're a role model to your children in *everything* you do. If you're grumpy and frustrated because you never see your friends, you're not teaching your children about the importance of friendship and balanced relationships.

## *Making time for yourself*

Finding quality 'me' time is one way to reduce stress and boost energy. Parents often feel guilty about looking after their needs ahead of others, but doing so is a must. If you're not relaxed and healthy, the whole family suffers. And if you're the only adult in the home (see the later section 'Being a Single Parent'), getting a break can be even more difficult.

Everyone needs to take time out occasionally to rest, relax, and have fun. Looking after your own needs and enjoying healthy and normal relationships with your partner, family, and friends is essential. Doing so gives you a sense of perspective. Children do eventually leave home, you know!

Make time for yourself this week and put one thing in your diary just for you. If you need a manicure or haircut, or time to see friends in the pub, watch a film, read a book, or watch a football game on the telly, put it in your diary – without any feeling of guilt. And then make sure you do actually carry out the activity.

Another technique I recommend for busy parents who forget to nurture their relationships with themselves is the Make a Date with Myself wheel. Draw or copy the diagram shown in Figure 7-1.

1. **In each segment of the Make a Date with Myself wheel, write down one thing that you would really like to do for yourself.**

   Be as specific as you can. Relax and think about what a real treat is for you. You can choose something for every day or once-a-week special activities.

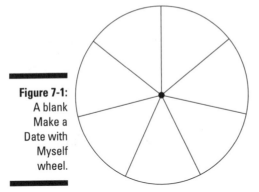

**Figure 7-1:**
A blank
Make a
Date with
Myself
wheel.

Take the time to discover a little more about who you are, what you like doing, and what feelings you'd like to feel more of, such as contentment, fulfilment, or excitement.

2. **Close your eyes and visualise what you'd like to do if money was no object, time was immaterial, and the kids were taken care of for an afternoon.**

Where are you? What can you see and hear and how do you feel? Turn up the brightness of the picture and enlarge it. Increase the volume of sounds around you. List some of these images and sounds in the Make a Data with Myself wheel.

3. **After you write your ideas in your wheel, write them down in your diary.**

Having a written record of your ideas enables you to really commit to looking after your own needs.

Make a real commitment to doing something for yourself each day, however small. Doing so will revitalise you and restore your zest for life.

## Maintaining your relationship with your partner

Relationships can change, become vulnerable, and lose direction when you have children. You and your partner are a team but sometimes your relationship can get lost among the nappies and sleepless nights. Partners often wonder, 'What happened to the person I first met? They used to be such fun.'

Sometimes your relationship with your partner can cause you stress and anxiety because having children completely changes your life and your priorities. Whether you are together, divorced, or separated, your relationship with your partner needs to be respected and nurtured to its best advantage in order to bring out the best for your whole family. (For more about dealing with ex-partners, see Chapter 13).

To revitalise your relationship with your partner, try the following:

1. **Take a minute to quietly focus on your partner's good qualities.**

   Ask yourself any of the following questions to get yourself thinking:

   - What are your partner's positive contributions to your family?
   - What makes your partner a good parent?
   - What makes your partner a great partner?
   - What are you most proud of achieving together?

2. **Write down seven actions that you can take to improve your relationship with your partner – one for every day of the week.**

   Examples may include going to the cinema, cooking a lovely meal, going out to do a shared activity without the kids, and sitting or chatting without the TV on when the kids are in bed.

3. **Rate the actions from 1 to 7, with 1 being the thing you most want to do, and 7 the least.**

4. **Do one action from your list every day.**

   Pay attention to how things look, sound, and feel in your relationship with your partner.

   - What impact are these actions having on your relationship?
   - How is family life improving because of these changes?
   - What else can you do to make life a little more fun?
   - What things can you do to introduce variety and spontaneity into your relationship as well?

## Developing relationships with your children

The relationships you develop and nurture with your children are probably the most rewarding and special of your life. Yet few parents actually sit down and step back from the day to day running of their families to think about the true value of their relationships with their children.

## Groups and individuals

I once coached a Mum who had three little girls all close together in age who she referred to as 'the girls.' When she started having trouble getting them to brush their teeth every morning, she couldn't work out why, until she and I spent some time exploring the way she talked to them. She spoke to her children as a group, not as individuals, so they didn't think she meant them specifically when she said 'Time to brush your teeth.' Just by using their individual names, she managed to transform the early morning school run experience into a much more harmonious and productive time for the whole family. It set the day up well for everyone.

Every parent I've ever worked with wants to make their relationships with their children even better – even if they're already great. Parents always tell me that parenting is the most important job they've ever done and they want to give it their best.

When you're in a relationship you don't often look at it objectively. So stepping back and looking at your relationships with each of your individual children helps you to notice whether you actually spend much individual quality time with them. The following exercise is a wonderful opportunity to plan your relationship with each of your children.

Focus on one child at a time if you have more than one. You need to give each child your undivided attention regularly. All children are unique in their interests and needs. They love to spend time with you alone doing something special.

1. **For each child, write down seven things that you can do to make your relationship with him even better and stronger.**

   Avoid writing down negative statements such as 'stop shouting'. Instead, focus on writing things that are positive such as 'praise Sam for doing something well' or 'give Sam more hugs and kisses' – whatever you feel can enhance your relationship with your child.

2. **Review your list of ideas and rate them 1 to 7 (1 being the best).**

   As you rank your ideas, ask yourself:

   - What makes number one such a great idea for me?

   - What difference will it make to me and my child?

   - What difference will it make to my relationship with that child?

3. **Write down your ranked list and put it where you'll see it on a daily basis.**

   You now have a bank of ideas to try out to further develop your relationship with each of your children – one for each day of the week or one a week for seven weeks.

## Nurturing relationships with friends and family

As the saying goes, 'You can choose your friends but not your family'. Close family members are often your greatest challenge because they tend to offer lots of helpful advice or criticise all your efforts. Trying to live up to others' expectations can put you under a lot of strain.

Consider your relationships with family and friends:

1. **Make a list of all the family and friends that you really enjoy spending time with.**

   Include people who uplift you, make you laugh, or support you in some way.

2. **Write down characteristics that make each of these people special to you.**

   Consider the following questions:

   • How often do you see or ring these people?

   • What can you do to expand these friendships or see these individuals more often?

   • Which person on your list would really make a difference in your life if you saw them or spoke to them more often?

   • What can you do to give more to this relationship?

3. **List some of the 'energy vampires' among your family and friends.**

   These are the people in your life who take more than they give back. After you identify them, consider:

   • What are the negative effects of spending time with them?

   • How often do you see them or speak to them?

   • How can you spend less time with them?

   • What would be the benefits to you if you saw them less often?

Imagine when you see or encounter these negative people that you are surrounded by your favourite colour and their negative comments can't reach you. Or try putting up an imaginary force field between the two of you so their words are blocked from bringing you down. How would creating such a barrier feel?

Life is what you make it. Don't wait for your kids to be this age or that age before you start to live your life. Start wearing your party pants now! Try any of the following tips and tricks to continue nurturing your relationships with friends and family.

- ✔ **Plan regular contact with those who matter to you.** Sometimes friends or family live far away, but with a little bit of planning, you can keep in contact via a regular phone call, e-mail, or text. The contact is worth the effort, particularly if these relationships make you feel good.

- ✔ **Surround yourself with positive people.** Invest in your relationships and enjoy living each moment of your life – have fun.

- ✔ **Think ahead.** Put a chat or meal with a friend in your diary. Keep planning ahead for something to look forward to.

- ✔ **Think of new ways to relax, have fun, and make new friendships.** Sure, parenting is demanding and tiring, but you need to have a balanced view of life and parenting. Having multiple support sources increases your energy and patience for your kids, helping you cope when life throws terrible events such as redundancy, divorce, or bereavement at you.

# Being a Single Parent

Being a parent is emotionally, physically, mentally, and spiritually demanding. Being a *single* parent is even more of a challenge because you're the only one setting limits, sharing wisdom, cooking dinner, looking for lost football boots and old geography textbooks, offering advice, and being a role model.

Children can easily take up your every waking minute. As a single parent, you must gather a support network around you of local parents, your family, friends, and community help such as mother and toddler groups or other single parents. If you don't look after yourself, you can exhaust all your reserves of energy and enthusiasm. Having a good support network enables you to make time for yourself, your friends, other adult relationships, exercise, relaxation, and fun.

# Taking care of yourself

The media often focus on the negative aspects of bringing up children single-handed, but parenting alone can be really satisfying because it can create an extra closeness and special bond with your child. But added stress is also possible because all the decisions and daily routines fall to you. If you're parenting alone, taking extra care of yourself is a wise move. To start taking care of your needs:

1. **Make a list of some of your favourite places, people, and activities.**

   Write down any idea that comes to mind. Your favourites can be as simple as a walk in the park on your own, a favourite meal, or a get-together with a good friend.

   - List types of exercise and outdoor activities that you like to do, such as walking, swimming, or playing football.

   - Don't forget the hobbies or crafts you enjoy, such as gardening, listening to music, or painting.

   - Think of the friends and relatives who support you and make you smile.

   - Include anything that *relaxes* you or makes you laugh, such as a hot bath and a good book, dinner with friends, or a funny or sentimental DVD.

2. **Go back over your list and put a tick next to each item you'd like to do more often.**

   Write at least two of these ideas in your diary for the coming week. Get into this habit and watch your life transform with more energy and fun.

3. **Plan some changes in your routine to incorporate the activities you've ticked.**

   For each activity, work out a practical way to put your plan into action and identify someone who can help you do it.

   For instance, perhaps you decide to go for a run in the local park once a week. You can organise a friend to look after the children – perhaps you can return the favour when your friend wants a break. Be practical and organised.

4. **Take action and get going.**

   All the planning in the world doesn't make a difference unless you actually carry out your ideas. You'll find making the effort is worthwhile because sometimes just taking ten minutes out for you can really lift your whole day.

Stay around positive people. The people you see every day can make a big difference to how you feel about yourself. When friends and relatives are positive, notice your good qualities, and have an optimistic attitude to life, their attitudes rub off on you and your family. You're more likely to feel great, have increased confidence, and to take greater pleasure in your life. Friends and relatives who criticise you without offering support or solutions can harm your confidence. Try to spend more time with people who give you support and have a positive outlook on life, because optimists live longer, smile more, and have better health.

Following are some additional ideas for single parents:

- ✔ **Get together with other parents at least once a week.** These parents may be friends and family – or you can try toddler groups or groups attached to your local school.

- ✔ **Find at least half an hour each day to unwind without your children.** Perhaps your private time is after their bedtime or first thing in the morning. Allow your mind, as well as your body, to take a break. And if you decide to take your break during the day, your children benefit from a period of quiet time too.

- ✔ **Contact a support group to see what they can offer.** Chat with other parents to see what they do to relax away from the kids. Look for support groups in your local paper, newsagents, or talk to other parents. Some parents often enjoy talking online and join forums on the Internet as a way to feel connected to other parents. Try www.baby-greenhouse.co.uk.

When you treat yourself well, others follow your lead. You and your children benefit when you care for yourself.

## *Introducing a new partner*

Parents are often concerned about introducing their new boyfriend or girlfriend to their children. Handle the situation with good intentions and it can all go smoothly. Here are some ideas:

- ✔ Acknowledge to yourself that your children are likely to view a date as a threat to their own personal time and experience with you, whether they voice their concerns to you or not.

- ✔ Be very clear with kids that adults need time with other adults, just as children need time with other children. If your child wonders why a total stranger is being invited to join the family, a good response is 'You are the most important person in my life, but like you I need to spend time with people my own age, so I'm going to start dating again. I know some kids don't like it when their parents date. What do you think?' Including your children in the discussion helps them to come to terms with the changes about to happen.

✔ Encourage your children to express their feelings, but don't allow them to dictate the terms of your love life. Children who are manipulative are usually fearful that events in their life are spinning out of control. Rather than viewing it simply as bad behaviour, recognise your child's attempt to regain control and order.

✔ Curb manipulative behaviour by demonstrating with your words and actions that a new love interest won't undermine your parent–child relationship. That may mean creating a sacred space of regularly scheduled parent–child time when your new boyfriend or girlfriend isn't part of the action. Try telling your children, 'I'm going to date, but it won't affect our time together. If I get serious, then you'll meet the person, but I'm not going to get serious until I know they'll fit into our family.' Never tell children, 'I'm not going to get serious with anyone you don't like.' That hands over all your power and may be a promise you can't keep.

✔ Make sure the introduction of your new significant other takes place only after you have a private conversation with your child about the relationship.

✔ When it comes to your new partner meeting your child, choose a setting where the focus is on an activity, not 'getting to know each other better'. This takes all the pressure off everyone to instantly like each other. Meet at a playground or go bowling – easier for your kids to be actively doing something other than having to make conversation with a complete stranger in a restaurant. Remember that casually introducing your partner at a huge birthday party may not give kids a true sense of how important the relationship really is.

✔ Have hope. If you lay the proper groundwork, and if your new boyfriend or girlfriend is really committed to you and accepting of your children, they can indeed develop a fond relationship. Don't rush it or expect it to happen naturally. Take your time and plan the transition.

# Part III
# Discipline

The 5th Wave    By Rich Tennant

"I always speak to the kids in a quiet and respectful way, but occasionally I wear this to add a little punctuation."

## *In this part . . .*

The most important thing children need is unconditional love. The next important thing they need is
structure. All children need rules, limits, and boundaries,
which give them security.

Having rules is important because over time your child
learns to manage his or her own behaviour through your
guidance, because they shift from being told what to do
by you, to developing their own self control. If you don't
teach children effective ways to control themselves, they
won't develop into well-balanced adults, able to behave
appropriately in society.

The tricky bit is knowing exactly what your boundaries
and rules are, and how to react if they're broken! This part
looks at different types of discipline and helps you figure
out what can work for your family.

# Chapter 8

# Getting Down to Earth and Practical: Disciplining Your Kids

*I*f you find disciplining your children difficult, this chapter may well save your sanity and get you and your children on the path toward an organised, respectful home life.

Managing your children's behaviour takes hard work, persistence, dedication, a sense of perspective, and a healthy sense of humour, but with time and effort – along with the tips and strategies in this chapter – you can succeed.

Expect the best from your children, get the basics right, and stay positive. Your kids will grow up into well-mannered and well-behaved adults to make you proud.

# *Understanding Your Child's Behaviour*

Children always have a purpose for behaving in the ways they do. They can behave 'badly' for any of the following reasons:

✔ **They're exploring.** Children sometimes do things to test situations and to get a response and reaction from their parents. With young children, what people may see as 'naughty' is really just a curious child trying to increase her understanding of the world. For example, a young child picking up a shiny wine glass to have a look at it isn't being naughty, she's just interested in the brightness and sparkle. She doesn't understand that she can drop it and cut herself.

✔ **They're looking for limits.** Kids need boundaries set by you. For example, throwing a cup on the floor for the eighth time or coming in late from a disco are both ways in which children see how far they can go.

Be very clear what behaviour is acceptable to you and don't back down. You can't have a stand off on every issue, so choose your battles wisely.

✔ **They're bored and seeking attention.** Children want your attention; in fact, it's the greatest gift you can give them. Because any attention is better than none, a bored child may start misbehaving just to get you to focus on her. Rewarding misbehaviour, however, is a *big* mistake because you reinforce the bad behaviour that you actually don't want. Of course, ignoring bad behaviour is really difficult because it automatically draws you in and winds you up.

As a teacher I had to guard against giving the 'naughty' children in my classes my attention. I reinforced only positive behaviour by giving lots of praise to children doing exactly as I wanted. Using this technique, you catch a child doing something well and then immediately offer praise, such as: 'That's really fantastic when you sit up at the table and hold your knife and fork so well' rather than 'How many times have I told you not to hold the knife like that?'

Being consciously positive is tiring at first and definitely needs a shift in thinking, but it really does work in getting results.

✔ **They're responding to the signals you send.** Parents are the ultimate role models. As a parent, you're constantly sending messages about the right way to behave with family, friends, children, teachers, shop assistants, and so on.

You send messages about how to behave in the way you talk to your children, the words you use, your body language, and how you react to their positive or negative behaviour. If a child hears you telling them off by shouting loudly – but then you say they mustn't shout – are you sending the message that only adults are allowed to shout?

Act out the behaviour you do want to see and watch what happens.

✔ **They're unhappy.** If children are tired, hungry, in a bad mood, or unwell, they're less likely to behave reasonably. Because children are not mature or experienced enough to recognise the signs of feeling tired or unwell, they may whinge or play up.

As an adult, you can recognise the signs of your child being sleepy or ill and make allowances for her. You can be clear about what you'll accept while also allowing more flexibility until the current blip passes.

Most children are lively, full of energy, and always on the go. Chapter 14 covers spotting the difference between normal energy and hyperactivity.

# Comparing Discipline Styles

Parents naturally differ in the way they react to their children. Some parents are very strict, while others are very laid back.

Whatever your personal style, your goal is to offer loving discipline to your child. *Loving discipline* develops your child's character, rather than punishes or undermines her self-esteem. This approach requires you to be a leader, role model, and mentor to your kids – not their friend. It means you care enough to say 'no' to your child when her well-being is threatened – but in ways that are gentle, kind, respectful, and compassionate. Loving discipline is never about dominating, controlling, yelling, threatening, criticising, or being violent. Rather, you set boundaries according to your child's age, maturity, and character. You notice when your child's doing something right and give her lots of praise and encouragement.

---

## Foods, additives, and behaviour

Although a number of different foods and additives have been linked to adverse effects in children, the research is controversial because few children fully responded over a long period of time to the elimination of food additives from their diet.

Exactly how foods affect behaviour and exactly what food triggers hyperactive behaviour isn't known. Some professionals believe that the success of diet changes may be due to the extra attention that a child receives while on the diet, and others feel that behaviour improvements may be due more to firmer parental control than anything else.

An initial, practical approach to consider is enforcing a more healthy diet with lots of fruit and vegetables. Eliminating fizzy drinks and sugary snacks can also help.

Of course, if you notice a significant change in behaviour due to a particular food or snack (like one of my friend's children who ate some blue sweets and became noticeably over excited), simply remove the specific food from your child's diet.

Take a look at *Children's Health For Dummies* by Katy Holland and Dr Sarah Jarvis (Wiley) for more about the effect of food on children's behaviour.

Stepping back and asking yourself about your style of discipline is important. The way you *act* affects the way your children *behave*.

Your discipline style may be based on how you were brought up – or it may be a reaction *against* how you were brought up. Considering your discipline style may raise memories from your past and can also explain what's going on in your relationship with your children at the moment.

The following sections describe some common styles of discipline.

## Controlling

If you're a controlling parent, you probably expect to be obeyed without question and you don't feel comfortable if you're not. You can be heavy handed in your approach and often find you make things worse, resulting in power struggles, particularly as your children grow up and become more independent.

Controlling parents need to guard against children doing as they demand but resenting them. This dynamic damages long-term relationships.

## Laid back

Parents who felt too controlled as children often react to these experiences by giving their children no boundaries at all, which can cause problems.

Sometimes this style of discipline just creeps up on parents. You may feel you've lost control of your child or you may find yourself thinking, 'What's the point; they'll do what they want anyway'. Or you may be too busy to notice that you've adopted this style.

The children raised with laissez faire discipline (meaning with unrestricted freedom) often feel ill at ease or insecure as they have nothing to push against and can feel abandoned and unloved. These children may start getting into trouble or doing things just to get attention.

If you don't put in some boundaries, someone else will – and you don't want it to be the police or the social services.

# Balanced, fair, and flexible

This style involves being clear about expectations and always handling the same behaviour in the same way.

This approach is my preferred style, and the one I try to use with my own kids. This style provides a clear structure with known expectations, but it also allows for flexibility because life is not an exact science. I prefer this style because it

- ✔ Allows my kids to have some say in what they can and can't do now they are getting older (they are 13 and 11).
- ✔ Helps my kids feel involved in taking responsibility for their own behaviour.
- ✔ Lets me set limits and allow for flexibility. I'm the adult, so I usually know when something is going too far. I like routines to be there, but I also like being flexible when I need to; our routines are adaptable depending on the circumstances.
- ✔ Allows room to grow and make mistakes. But everyone understands the general rules and limits to their behaviour.

Parents who feel confident in their parenting and believe in teaching children their values have realistic and flexible expectations of their children. They can be firm, fair, and flexible; but most of all they are consistent. Consistency provides security and a clear understanding of the rules for the whole family.

# Choosing your discipline style

The key thing to remember when making decisions about your discipline style is *respect*. Base your discipline choices on respect and recognising the needs of other people in the family.

No single correct way exists to discipline and raise your children. However, if you're more authoritarian and clear in what you expect from your children, you're more likely to be successful in getting the behaviour you want. Set rules and limits but explain why they are necessary, and take your children's point of view into account when you make the rules. Communicate regularly with your children and encourage them to be independent – doing so really shows your kids respect.

One important part of deciding on your parent–child relationship involves working out your priorities and thinking about the type of relationship you want with your child. Ask yourself the following questions:

✔ How do my children see me – as a friend, authority figure, disciplinarian, teacher, care-giver, partner, or equal?

✔ Am I happy with their perception of me?

✔ Am I different or similar to my parents?

✔ Do I want to make some small changes to improve or fine-tune my discipline style?

✔ What might these changes be?

What have you discovered about your discipline style and your kids' perceptions of you? If you're happy with what you discover, brilliant – keep on doing more of the same. If you're not happy with what you've learnt about yourself, think about a small change you could make this week to change things. Take control of your parenting style and notice the positive difference this can make.

# Getting the Behaviour You Want

Simply put, you can use two approaches for getting anyone – including your child – to behave as you want:

✔ Encouragement

✔ Punishment (or sanctions)

## Encouraging behaviours

The best and most effective long-term discipline strategy is the use of encouragement, or *positive parenting*. This means speaking positively with your children, encouraging and supporting them, and focusing on the destination of your parenting – bringing up happy, confident, well-balanced adults.

As a teacher, I found that by far the best way to get kids to co-operate was to catch them doing something right and then praise them. The same strategy holds true for parents – a fact that many forget. Instead, many parents get caught up in the negative cycle of controlling their child's poor behaviour.

If you expect the very best behaviour from your children, you'll get it. For example, I made a point when I was teaching never to read a child's report from her previous teacher because doing so could colour my judgement of the student and bring out the negative behaviours described in reports. I wanted all the kids in my class to start with a clean sheet.

Similarly, as a parent, you can focus on creating a positive rather than negative atmosphere for your relationships with your children. Focus on the good behaviour, praising and rewarding it quickly.

Try to give at least three rewards to every punishment to keep the focus on a positive approach to discipline. See the following sections for information on rewards and punishments.

Managing your child's behaviour has a lot to do with your attitude. If you see your child's poor behaviour as a problem and something that gives you stress and headaches, it will. But if you see your child's behaviour as a challenge, a growing expression of her independence, and a chance for you to become a better parent (and maybe a more patient person), you have a different mind set and a more positive outlook from the start.

You need to see your child's *behaviour* as challenging or difficult, rather than seeing your *child* as bad. This shift in thinking helps you work with your child not against her.

## Rewarding good behaviour

Rewards are the ways you give your children positive incentives for behaving well, trying hard, or being polite and kind. Rewards are really great motivators for your kids. This section covers several common types of reward that you can utilise to encourage desired behaviours.

Tailor rewards to the age and personality of your child. Rewards only work if your child values them and actually wants to receive them.

Whatever type of reward you choose to give your child, keep the following in mind:

- ✔ **Make clear why you're giving the reward.** This helps your child to understand what you expect from her and what she's done well.
- ✔ **Make a clear connection between the good behaviour and the reward.** Tell your child why she's being rewarded.

✔ **Be clear about the goal that your child can aim for next time.** This helps your child focus on the future and getting it right again.

✔ **Always keep your expectations high.** If you have high expectations your child will rise to the occasion and will often surprise you. Expect the best!

### Praise

*Praise* is a positive way to build confidence and is one of the most powerful rewards of all because a child *wants* to please you. Effective praise makes your child feel good by developing her self-esteem.

Children know if they've truly earned your acclaim or if you're manipulating them or overdoing it. For example, if you call your daughter a 'genius' she might wonder what you want, discount the praise as ridiculous, or think you're mocking her.

Praise is one of the easiest rewards to give. It costs nothing, requires very little preparation, and is hugely rewarding for you to give and for your child to receive.

Be liberal, generous, and sincere with your praise. But also be very specific in what you praise – mention the lovely colours in the rainbow your daughter painted, or the patience that she showed when playing with a child younger than herself. Flick back to Chapter 5 for more information on praise.

### Treats

*Treats* are special indulgences or luxuries that you allow your kids to have from time to time. Many types of treats exist. For younger children, sweets and extra TV are popular; for older children, money can be considered a treat. Of course, you know your own child best, so a treat for her may be staying up 15 minutes later, playing outside longer, having an extra story, or chatting for 20 minutes longer on MSN.

I think treats work best if you use them as a *privilege* or as an acknowledgement of something special rather than as a right.

### Time

Time – often called *quality time* – can be a powerfully motivating reward. Spending time playing, chatting, and being together can be a huge reward for your child. Unfortunately, many parents don't think to use time in this way.

The reward of time can be free and fun. It doesn't have to be educational or over the top. It can be as simple as spending time with your child making a model, flying a kite, watching a film with a pizza, or doing Suduko together.

---

# Distraction

A simple but really effective way to help keep the atmosphere positive in your home is through distraction. Distracting a young child can help her do as you want in a friendly, positive way.

Distractions don't need to be elaborate. For example, saying 'Come and look at this lovely butterfly' while taking your daughter away from pulling the petals off your favourite rose bush is a simple, positive distraction.

Of course, sometimes you actually need to deal head on with misbehaviour and disobedience. Use your own judgement to decide if distracting or punishment is appropriate.

---

### Stars and stickers

Stars and stickers are really just a visual way to show your approval. Your child can earn stars and stickers over time and display them in an appropriate spot. Displaying stickers enables children to see for themselves and show others how they're progressing and succeeding.

I love giving stickers to younger kids because they really seem to respond to them. You can find some great stickers – as well as display posters and tracking charts – on the market today.

Try giving your child a little reward, for example, after she achieves 10 or 20 stickers for a specific behaviour. Kids feel very proud of themselves when they reach these milestone rewards.

Beware of taking stickers away for bad behaviour. Doing so can demoralise some children.

## Setting up sanctions

A *punishment* is a reprimand, or a way of imposing something unpleasant on your child when she's done something wrong. Punishment is really about your child learning to face up to the consequences of her actions.

At school we used the word *sanction* rather than punishment, because it focused on the behaviour, not the child herself. Changing the term you use from punishment to sanction in your home may be a useful and positive step because doing so can shift your perspective on discipline.

A sanction is a way to penalise your child that is personal to her. Sanctions are more effective if you work out what your child particularly loves having or doing and take that away from her for a short time as a way to get her to co-operate with your rules. Sanctions come in many forms, including a child sitting on a step, going to her room, losing time on the computer, being grounded, or missing a party. Think about what sanctions may work in your home.

Although sanctions can effectively regulate a child's behaviour, you also need to include rewards and other positive incentives in your discipline plan. If you only ever punish your children, they'll find it hard to learn to take responsibility for their actions, regardless of their age. They'll feel de-motivated and fed up by your constant negative actions.

*When my kids become wild and unruly, I use a nice, safe playpen. When they're finished, I climb out!*

— Erma Bombeck

To make the best use of sanctions, remember the following:

- ✔ **A sanction only works if your child doesn't like it.** Different sanctions work best for different types of children. For example, going to bed early may be an effective sanction for one child but a reward for another.

- ✔ **Sanctions can be simple.** One of the best sanctions is a stern look of disapproval. Showing your displeasure can be a very powerful message to children.

- ✔ **A sanction that works well one day may not work the next.** Children are constantly changing; the things that they enjoy are changing as well. Be flexible with sanctions and revise them as necessary to match your child's current preferences.

- ✔ **If you threaten a sanction, you *must* carry it out.** If you don't follow through on a sanction, you send a message that what you say doesn't really matter. You lose your credibility and authority.

- ✔ **You must carry out sanctions quickly.** If you carry out your sanctions clearly and quickly, your child knows you mean what you say. Your child is much more likely to think twice before doing the same thing again.

- ✔ **Keep your own emotions out of the situation.** When you are angry or hurt, you don't deal with situations rationally. Try to keep your attitude towards sanctions as neutral as possible.

- ✔ **Don't make the sanction personal.** Apportioning blame doesn't help the situation.

Always match the punishment to the crime – and don't over do it.

# Saying 'no'

No is such a simple word but so many parents find it difficult to incorporate into their discipline strategies. Fortunately, when you use it effectively and appropriately, the ability to say 'no' can become a powerful behaviour-shaping tool.

Parents find it hard to say no to their kids for many reasons, such as:

- **Shortage of time.** Parents seem to be in such a hurry these days. Giving in and buying whatever it is your children want is easier than spending time explaining why you won't buy it or dealing with their sulks when they don't get it.

- **Fear of causing a scene.** Parents feel embarrassed if they feel other people are looking at them and judging them.

  While wandering around the supermarket with a happy and quiet child who is tucking into sweets or crisps may be easier than dragging a scream-ing child round, you can get your child involved without plying them with treats. Try making the whole experience a game and see how creative you can be. Engage your child by asking her to look for her favourite soup, find the butter, or help you weigh the grapes. This approach to shopping can be fun and provides good practical experience, too.

- **Seemingly abundant resources.** Many parents have (or think they have) more disposable cash splashing around these days. Even if your per-sonal finances are tight, when your child asks for a treat, you may think 'Well, it's only 80 pence so it won't break the bank.' Many parents don't think twice about spending more (or all) of their disposable income on their children, but is that a good message to send to them?

When you continually give in to your children's demands and requests, you send out one or more powerful messages, including:

- **'You can have anything you want.'** Giving in creates a child who has unrealistic expectations of you and the world. Your child will expect to get everything she wants – and you can be sure that her requests will get bigger and more expensive as she becomes more aware of all the goodies out there. It's sweets today, Nike trainers and Gucci purses tomorrow!

  While you may enjoy indulging your children's wishes, the world just isn't like that. Your children may be in for rude awakenings when they encounter the many situations in the real world where they actually can't have what they want. You may be preparing them for big disappointments.

✔ **'It really doesn't matter how you treat your things – you can always get more.'** Children who constantly get toys and treats lose their sense of awe and wonder for new things. Their expectations become inflated and they have no sense of gratitude or value for any of the gifts or treats they receive.

✔ **'I can't give you much time, but I can give you lots of things.'** If a child receives this message, don't be surprised if she doesn't place any value on these things or show any gratitude at getting stuff.

Things just cannot replace your time. If children don't get attention and input from you, among other things, they don't develop a sense of their own worth. They may feel they're not worth spending time with. So you may be showering your child with gifts, but their self-esteem may be diminishing as their stack of toys piles up.

✔ **'If you get upset, I'll get you a little treat.'** A child who always receives a treat when she starts to cry and shout or gets hurt is learning a dangerous lesson. Other children and the outside world aren't as generous as you. How will your child cope as an adult in a world where she most definitely won't always get her own way?

Developing the ability to say no is really about finding a balance between saying yes and no. Finding this balance takes practice, so try the following:

✔ If you are new to saying no and taking a harder line, start by saying no to requests for sweets, toys, and treats so you keep them for special occasions when your child will value them much more.

✔ Start saying yes to requests for your time – and find and make that time.

Parenting isn't about just enduring your child's childhood. Children grow up quickly – they'll be gone and not able to fit you in before you know it. Find ways to enjoy spending time with your children, doing things they like to do. Ask them how they'd like to spend their time with you. You don't have to visit Alton Towers every time! Discover what they can do, allow them time to show off their new skills and knowledge, and give them praise and encouragement.

✔ Cut down gradually on giving toys and treats. Think about what you really consider appropriate. Every family is different and has its own rules. As a parent, you decide what is best for your family. Work with your partner (if you have one) to establish these rules – and then agree to stick to them. If your child is old enough, explain the new rules to her.

Initially, saying no may be difficult. Your child may have trouble believing that you really mean no because in the past this wasn't the case. Your child will probably throw a wobbly the first time or two, but remember the bigger picture to your parenting – the values you want to teach her and hold on to.

Think about the consequences of giving in. Distract, explain, smile, or move on to something else, but stand firm.

Step back and reflect on not giving in each time you interact with your children. Ask yourself, 'Is what I'm doing teaching my child something I believe to be important?'

# *Setting Boundaries*

One of the big frustrations of being a parent is the daily struggle to get your kids to behave in ways that are acceptable to you and to society. A great deal of parenting energy goes into getting your children to take baths, say 'thank you', hang up their clothes, do their homework, or help around the house. You want courtesy, cleanliness, order, and routines and they couldn't care less. The more you insist, the more they resist!

Children like to know where they stand. Boundaries are a set of limits that are personal to your family – such as rules and structures – give children security and help them understand what acceptable behaviour is. By following and accepting your boundaries, your child develops a sense of autonomy and self-control, which is a crucial life skill.

Think about behaviour that is and isn't acceptable to you – such as getting your children to speak to others politely, using their knife and fork properly, or knocking on your bedroom door before entering. Insist that your boundaries are respected and acted upon.

As soon as you feel that your child is old enough, start talking about your rules and limits. Explain why you have certain rules and be clear about what you expect from her. Doing so helps your child understand where you're coming from and this builds respect and understanding, and makes you a good role model to follow.

You also need to follow the boundaries and rules you establish. Insisting that your child eats all her vegetables if you just tuck into your chips and leave your carrots is pointless. Similarly, you can't deny your child TV time while you sit and devour your favourite soap.

*Consistency* is the key to success with boundaries. Every time your child pushes the perimeter fence, push back and make your limits crystal clear. You can give a sanction, take away a privilege, or reward good behaviour (see the earlier section 'Setting up sanctions' for more on these terms and techniques) – but keep your messages on boundaries consistent. Your children will get your message eventually.

## Shepherding children

I remember hearing this story when I was training to be a teacher and thought it was a simple but thought-provoking analogy for parents.

A shepherd had three fields to raise a sheep in. The first field included a very tight pen. The sheep felt restricted, stifled, and held back within such a close boundary. The second field

had no boundaries at all, just wide open space. The sheep was absolutely terrified because it had no protection. The third field offered an adjustable boundary fence that the shepherd could extend as the sheep grew older and bigger.

So, which field are you creating for your child?

# *Valuing boundaries*

Setting boundaries is difficult for many reasons, including the fact that you may:

- ✔ Feel too tired or too busy
- ✔ Be confused about what's right
- ✔ Lack support from your partner
- ✔ Find setting boundaries overwhelming
- ✔ Feel guilty about disciplining your children
- ✔ Worry about lots of other things
- ✔ Feel angry
- ✔ Lack confidence
- ✔ Feel like disciplining your kids is all too much hassle
- ✔ Feel that you were too disciplined as a child and you don't want to repeat that experience for your child

How many of these excuses for not setting – and enforcing – clear boundaries can you identify with?

Whatever your reasons for not creating boundaries, the reasons for doing the hard work of establishing them are stronger:

- ✔ Children need to know how far they can go so they feel loved and safe.
- ✔ Knowing their boundaries makes children feel secure.
- ✔ Boundaries keep children safe from physical and emotional harm.
- ✔ Boundaries teach children to respect other people and other people's property.

✔ Boundaries teach children self-control.

✔ Boundaries help children develop into responsible adults.

Parents and partners need to back each other up and present a united front when defending boundaries. Enforcing boundaries as a parenting team can be difficult, especially if one partner is more controlling and the other has a relaxed, chilled-out style. But with positive attitudes, awareness of the bigger picture, and good old-fashioned communication about your different approaches, you and your partner can find a balance to help your kids get the best of both worlds.

## *Determining what's acceptable to you*

To effectively create and defend boundaries, you first need to take a few minutes to think about what issues or behaviours are really important to you.

Actually sit down and think about the behaviour you want from your children. Write short descriptions or lists of what you specifically expect from your kids. Consider lots of different scenarios, such as your expectations when your children are out with friends, sitting in a restaurant, having friends over, doing school work, and so on.

Try to visualise what your children are doing and saying in each of these scenarios. How are they feeling in these perfect scenarios? What has changed and why do they feel so much better?

Now visualise what *you* are saying, doing, and feeling in the perfect picture. Imagine the changes you've made to get to this picture and how you feel having easily made those small changes. Imagine the benefits from making them. Enjoy the huge feelings of success and joy you'll feel when this scenario happens.

Only by spending the time and considering what you expect from your children can you be clear about where you are going.

Every family is slightly different, and that situation's fine. But unless *you* know in your own mind what is and isn't acceptable to you, your kids don't stand a chance! Evaluate your ideas by asking yourself the following questions:

✔ **Are my expectations realistic for my child's age?** Parents sometimes establish rules that simply do not mesh with the realities of being a child. For example, taking a small child to a fancy restaurant and expecting her to sit still for ages is setting her up to fail and be naughty.

✔ **Are my expectations appropriate for my child's age?** Parents often forget to adapt rules as children grow up. For example, expecting your teenager to hold your hand when you cross the road is inappropriate.

Chat with your partner and share your ideas about how you can go forward in the same direction together.

## Determining what's not acceptable to you

Many parents I work with feel they should instinctively know how to control or manage their children's behaviour – that somehow disciplining should be 'natural' to them. As I explain to self-critical parents: Kids don't come with a handbook. Most parents have never had to manage another person's behaviour before. And even if they have managed someone's behaviour at work, it probably wasn't a child! Children are a law unto themselves. (For good reason do many actors say, 'Never work with animals or children.')

To help work out what behaviours you consider inappropriate, write down a list of the things that are absolutely not acceptable to you as a parent. Visualise specific scenarios (in the car, at a shop, at school, while hanging out in the living room, and so on) and identify specific actions that you deem unacceptable. Go through this exercise with your partner too, so you can stick together when guiding your children's behaviour.

Avoid writing an endless list of prohibited behaviours because doing so can be too controlling and restrictive. Strive to be clear on the things that you will definitely not accept – for me, that means spitting, biting, swearing, and physically hurting someone.

Combine this list with the actions and behaviours you came up with using the exercise in the earlier section 'Determining what's acceptable to you', and you have a set of values that can help guide you as you create boundaries.

Your list can be short or long. The purpose is to clarify your core values – the things that you're not prepared to waver on. Having a list helps you to focus your energy on dealing with the behaviours that are really important to you.

## Creating house rules

When I coach parents I often coach them to establish rules of behaviour within the home. House rules aren't meant to be a soul-destroying list (like the time I went camping in the South of France and visited a pool with 21 'Do Nots' followed by the message 'Welcome to our pool'!).

The Rules of Our House is a great opportunity for your children to get involved in making up your house rules and to feel they're part of the decision-making process. Creating these rules provides an incentive to co-operate.

For example, I've seen families working together as a whole group with older kids writing the following Rules of Our House:

> *We don't take anything without asking the person first (T shirts, make-up, trainers – even chocolate).*
>
> *When we go out, we say where we are going, with whom, and when we'll be back.*
>
> *Bedrooms have to be tidied, vacuumed, and dusted every Sunday.*
>
> *When friends come round, we are responsible for tidying up the mess.*

To begin creating house rules with and for your family:

1. **This week sit down with your family and have a chat about house rules.**

   Explain that you want to establish some house rules to help improve the atmosphere in your home. Note that house rules enable a home to run more smoothly. Highlight the importance of getting input and suggestions from everyone in the family.

2. **Ask each member of your family to think of at least one house rule and write it down.**

   Share ideas, collaborate, and have some fun thinking up practical solutions to your family's niggles. Listen to each other and respect all the ideas and then talk through the most practical and acceptable to you as the parent.

3. **Compile a list of the agreed upon rules and display them somewhere where everyone can see them clearly and easily.**

   Maybe one of your children can produce the rules on the computer so they look nice.

4. **Arrange another chat next week at the same time to see how following the rules is going.**

   Assess how the week went – what worked and what didn't? Now you can make further adjustments.

# Developing Consistency

The simple secret to disciplining your child is consistency. If you constantly use empty threats, change your mind, or let your child live with broken promises, you send a message that you can't be relied on.

Being consistent means being clear about your expectations and always handling the same behaviour in the same way. Consistency eliminates confusion because your children know how you're going to react and this gives them a sense of security and familiarity.

For example, if your child throws her toys at another child who's come round to play, you can say 'no' firmly and then remove her from the toys for a few minutes. Your child will get the message and make the connection over time – if you keep responding in the same way. Similarly, if your teenager keeps forgetting her keys and you lock her out for an hour, she's much more likely to remember to take keys the next time!

Unfortunately, being consistent takes energy. When you're tired, in a bad mood, or busy, you may feel like letting your kids get away with something just this once. But over time, making this choice erodes your authority. You may end up over-reacting to something minor (such as your child accidentally knocking over a drink, or leaving the door open) or ignoring something major, which confuses and upsets everyone.

Tiredness makes parents forget that most unacceptable behaviour is often just a plain old mistake. Children are not miniature adults acting childishly. Children are inexperienced and have to learn all that you and society expects of them.

---

## Precious patience

Yes, patience is a virtue – it's also a skill, a talent, and a gift. And as all parents know, sometimes patience can be hard to find.

The real challenge is to be patient when everything is going horribly wrong. Of course, being patient is hard when your toddler has lovingly written all over the wallpaper, or your 11-year-old has decided to bake cakes but left the mess for you to tidy up, or your daughter wants picking up from the station just as the football has started.

The secret to finding patience amidst the chaos is taking a deep breath and trying to see the bigger picture: The relationship between you as a parent and your child. Try lightening up and seeing the funny side, the pettiness and trivia of each incident, compared to the really important things in life. (Oh, and I often find the odd large glass of wine helpful!)

Your job is to guide, nudge, and steer your kids in the right direction – which requires lots of hard work if you really are to succeed. You need to have lots of energy, be very clear about what is (and isn't) acceptable to you, and stay centred when they cry, shout, sulk, or throw tantrums. You have to remember that your mother-in-law, neighbours, family, friends, your children's teachers, and society as a whole will thank you for raising well-behaved children.

# Tips for Successful Discipline

Sue Cowley, in her excellent book *Getting Your Little Darlings to Behave* (Continuum), suggests using the seven Cs – characteristics necessary to successfully discipline children.

The following tips are universally accepted as tried and tested ways to bring up well-mannered, well-disciplined, and happy kids.

## Being certain

Children need you to be absolutely certain and clear about what you want. Certainty gives them security, as well as clarity. Vague instructions stress everyone and send mixed messages to children.

This certainty is known in teaching as 'having clear expectations'. The higher your expectations for your children, the better they'll behave. But you must be clear about your expectations – and you need to let your kids in on the secret. Many parents forget to tell their kids what they expect from them and think that they'll just pick things up. Assume at your peril. Children need to be shown and told what is expected of them.

The following tips can help you be certain while disciplining your children:

- ✔ Be firm and fair in stating your expectations.

- ✔ *Tell* your children – don't *ask* them – what you expect. Of course, be polite, but don't keep saying 'please' in a desperate way.

- ✔ Use the words 'I want you to . . .' when you introduce an expectation. These words clearly state what you want your kids to do.

- ✔ Don't give in too easily. If you do, you send the message that what you say really doesn't matter that much.

- ✔ Use your body language and facial expression to convey that you mean what you're saying.

✔ When things go wrong, as of course they do from time to time, just be calm and state again what you *do* want.

✔ Try being surprised when things go wrong rather than angry – doing so works wonders.

## Being confident

If you're sure of what you want from your children, you appear confident. Your kids sense that you mean what you say and they're less likely to mess you about.

As parents start to feel more in control of their family life, they send out more positive signals. Their children pick up on this new confidence and react more positively, too. Sometimes I ask parents to 'fake it till they make it' – to simply act more confidently and assertively. This strategy works as a self-fulfilling prophecy: The more confidently you act, the more confident you become.

Everyone has to do things they don't like sometimes. But be bold – you really do know what's best for your children because you are the adult and what you say goes.

## Being consistent

Consistent parenting means being clear about your expectations and always handling the same behaviour in the same way. Consistency avoids confusion and increases children's sense of security and familiarity.

## Being calm

To stand back from a situation and not lose the plot takes a lot of patience – just ask my kids!

Staying calm – not shouting and simply being cool when you're confronted with a rude or difficult child or a completely trashed bedroom – can feel strange at first. But as a constant role model and an adult, your job is to maintain your self-control because you can frighten or confuse your child or encourage a repeat performance if she really enjoys winding you up!

The advantages of staying calm are twofold. First, you can deal with the situation far more effectively. Second, you're setting a good example to your kids by teaching them about self-control, which is an important life skill for any adult.

You can gain control by thinking of the situation as the child's problem because she isn't yet mature enough to act responsibly. Thinking of situations in this way shifts your perception to correction and learning, instead of resentment and anger.

## Being caring

Being caring means listening to your kids, talking with them, spending time together, giving hugs, and providing a safe and secure environment for them. Caring's also about remembering how it feels to be a child and putting yourself in your kids' shoes sometimes. It means lightening up, being playful, and having a laugh.

Being caring means being sensitive to the needs of your children and seeing the world through their eyes. It's remembering that childhood is a special and magical time and should be a time of laughter, joy, and discovery. Show you care by finding time for a cuddle and a laugh, or by listening to a story even when you're tired or bored.

Caring can be confused with allowing your children to do exactly what they want, but actually it's the opposite! If you appear too caring, you may appear a soft touch to your kids and they won't listen or respect you or behave in the way you want them to.

Treat your child with care and give consideration to her feelings. You may shout because you're tired but she may not understand and feel really hurt by your words or attitude. Just imagine how you'd feel if someone shouted at you at work. Try to speak to your child with respect.

## Being careful

Some parents are very cautious and over careful with their children. Their kids grow up over-cautious themselves and frightened to take any sort of risk.

Being careful is not allowing your kids to run riot. As a parent you also have a responsibility to teach your children the rules – including the rules of your house, the rules of school, and the rules of society as a whole. You need to prepare them for the big world, and caring means offering tough love sometimes.

Parents who are careful want the best for their children and that means guiding and teaching them in responsible ways.

## Being creative

Creative parenting and disciplining means you relax and think of new ways to relate to your kids. Perhaps you make your own reward stickers, get messy together, paint, draw, or cook. You can become a kid again.

I remember using puppets at school during Emotional Literacy lessons with older children as a way to get them to open up and talk about their feelings. This technique worked really well. Try a puppet or cuddly toy to get your children talking about their feelings and experiment using different funny or sad voices. Make up imaginary scenarios to help them explore different emotions or situations. Look for different ways to solve problems and get your children involved in coming up with ideas.

# Chapter 9

# Choosing Different Strategies for Different Ages

*H*ow does a 'typical' child behave? Well, in my mind a normal child is giggly, sometimes naughty, enthusiastic, loving, forgiving, incorrigible, bad-tempered, untidy, homework phobic, and has dreams and aspirations just like you. He may be shy, extrovert, good at sewing or bad at cooking, but he loves you and you love him.

This chapter examines age-specific challenges children face and appropriate parenting strategies – including discipline – that you can employ to aid in their growth and development.

# Taming Toddlers

Children of pre-school age are delightful to have around, but guiding and managing a pre-schooler often takes a lot of patience. Taming toddlers sometimes feels like disciplining jelly – all wobbly with no set rules!

Toddlers ask lots of questions and they love to imitate adults. They are learning to share and take turns; sometimes they want to play with others, and sometimes they just like to be on their own. They like to assert their independence, and getting any form of attention is much better than being ignored! Toddlers like to make decisions for themselves because it makes them feel important. They also get rather carried away and can be rather bossy! Toddlers all have lots of energy – often lots more energy than you. They play hard, fast, and furious and then tire suddenly and become bad tempered and irritable.

## Strategies for pre-schoolers

Successful parents of pre-school age kids use a variety of different strategies at different times – an approach that works in one situation won't always work in another.

Things you can do for your toddler include setting up a safe environment so your child doesn't hurt himself when he's rushing about exploring; and establishing a regular routine for sleeping, eating, and playing. Also establish a 'cooling off' place. This is a safe place where your child can go to calm down if he misbehaves, and gives you a few minutes to calm down too. This place is often described as a 'naughty step' but I prefer to keep things in the positive and call it the 'Chill Out Zone'! Toddlers only need about two to five minutes in this space, otherwise they forget why they're there.

One important strategy for use with your pre-school child is to watch your language. Use your words carefully to teach your children and focus on what to do rather than what not to do.

| *Instead of:* | *Try saying:* |
|---|---|
| Stop running. | Slow down and walk. |
| Don't touch anything. | Come and hold my hand. |
| Don't climb on the couch. | Keep your feet on the floor. |
| Stop screaming and shouting. | Use your quiet voice inside. |

## When all else fails

Sometimes children have a disruptive behaviour that happens over and over again. So when nothing seems to be working, try the when, what, where, and how method. Ask yourself:

✔ When does the troublesome behaviour occur?

✔ What happens just before and after?

✔ Where does it happen and with whom?

✔ How do I usually respond?

✔ How could I prevent the behaviour?

✔ What other approaches could I use?

The best method to find a more successful way to cope with behavioural problems is to take the time to think about options.

Parenting kids before they're at school is often challenging and works better when you remember to take care of yourself. Rest when you can, eat healthily, and relax. Above all else, try to maintain your sense of humour and to see the world from the eyes of your young, innocent explorer. When you discover your child sifting through sugar on the floor or finger painting with the guacamole dip, remember that someday this will be a great story to tell your grandchildren. So grab your digital camera and take a picture! You will look back and want to remember this. Honestly.

The first six years of parenting are like being a teacher. You teach your kids how to handle a beaker and a knife and fork, how to go to the toilet and open doors – everything they need to know to survive in life and make sense of the world. Most parents really enjoy this stage, despite how tired they feel!

## Avoiding tantrum territory

One in five 2-year-olds is estimated to have a tantrum each day – but remember that means four out of five don't!

The peak for tantrums is between ages 2 and 3, but tantrums can happen earlier and some kids go on throwing them up to the age of 6. (You can usually begin reasoning with a 5- or 6-year-old and talk things through.)

These emotional outbursts are usually called *temper tantrums*, but your child may be experiencing a number of other strong emotions in addition to anger. Tantrum triggers for young ones include:

✔ **Frustration at not being able to do something for themselves.** For example, being unable to tie shoelaces, pour a drink easily, or make others understand what they want can send toddlers into a tantrum.

✔ **Desire to be more independent.** For young children, simple things like strapping themselves into the buggy can prove too difficult, and they get upset.

✔ **Hunger and tiredness.** Toddlers are more likely to behave badly when they feel either hungry or tired. Their small stomachs and high energy levels mean that they frequently need nutritious snacks and meals. Establishing consistent times for eating, napping, and playing helps children pace themselves. Balance the day with active times, quiet times, times to be alone, and times to be with others.

✔ **Being refused something.** When young children are denied something they want – think sweets by the checkout – a tantrum often results.

✔ **Wanting attention.** Young children love to be the centre of attention. If you over-react to their screams, at least you're noticing them – and to a toddler any attention is better than none.

With some forward planning, you can cut down on the number of tantrums. Here are some practical tips:

✔ **Set a good example for your toddler.** If toddlers see adults flying off the handle all the time, they think throwing their own paddy is acceptable.

✔ **Give your toddler lots of praise to encourage good behaviour.** Refer to Chapter 8 for more information on using praise to reinforce behaviours.

✔ **Avoid the trouble spots.** Whenever possible don't take your toddler to the supermarket or other places where you know he'll be bored. (I once saw a young mum have her false nails done, which takes a good hour and a half. She couldn't understand why she had to keep telling her toddler to sit down and stop being naughty and crying.)

✔ **Look for signs.** Most toddlers give plenty of warning that they are getting wound up. You can use diversion (see Chapter 8) as a good tactic here if you pre-empt them.

✔ **Offer your toddler some control.** You can avoid some tantrums if you allow your child small choices. Let him choose the colour of his jumper or whether he wants an apple or banana for a snack.

✔ **Agree with your partner on how to deal with tantrums.** Arguing parents when a tantrum strikes can lead to even more confusion for your toddler and worsen the situation as he learns to play you against each other. Determine with your partner beforehand how you both want to respond to tantrums.

✔ **Keep a temper tantrum diary.** Write down when, how, and where tantrums occur. Try to notice patterns – the time of day, what happened immediately before the tantrum, or other triggers to your child's tantrums.

✔ **Keep calm.** Remaining calm and centred makes a difference because your toddler picks up on your energy. Hold your child close and talk calmly, slowly, and reassuringly while breathing slowly. When parents slow down their breathing, toddlers often copy and become more relaxed.

✔ **Ignore the behaviour.** Try walking away or pretending to take no notice. However, if your toddler is in full flight, this tactic may not be as effective.

✔ **Divert and distract.** Pretend you find something really fascinating and get your toddler to come and have a look.

✔ **Take some time out.** If you feel that you're just about to boil over yourself, make sure your child is safe and then go in the garden or into another room for a couple of minutes to give you both a feeling of space.

✔ **Make up quickly.** After a tantrum blows over, make amends easily and genuinely and have a hug.

# Changing physically and developmentally

Toddlers are wonderful, exciting, busy, and demanding. They've come such a long way in such a short time – but they still have a long way to go.

This section covers some of the significant changes your toddler experiences.

### Developing a sense of self

For the first 18 months your child was totally devoted to you and followed you everywhere. Suddenly he wants to stand on his own two feet and assert his independence. A toddler continually tests your limits as a parent and has temper tantrums when crossed. And despite a toddler's wilfulness, if you speak to him sternly, he may burst into tears.

The toddler years are a time of huge learning, growth, and change for your child. These years are often called the *terrible twos* because toddlers demand to do things their own way without help and only see things from their own point of view. With patience, you can help your toddler build up positive self-esteem and self-control, which will help him become independent and self-confident now and later in life.

As toddlers become more independent, their feeding and eating habits change. Your toddler may want to feed himself and yet at the same time want to be fed. Eating may also become less important to your child than other activities, such as playing.

### Developing social skills

Toddlers learn to gain and hold an adult's attention through social interaction – and they ask lots more questions. They'll happily chat away when a familiar adult engages them in conversation. You may notice that your toddler is becoming friendlier with visitors, too. He may even take his toys over to a chosen adult to try to gain attention.

## Development milestones for toddlers

The following are some general guidelines to the physical development of toddlers. Of course, each child is an individual developing at his own rate. If you have questions about your child's development, share your concerns with your health visitor or doctor.

By 24 months, a toddler can:

✔ run without falling

✔ walk up and down stairs

✔ turn pages of a book

By 27 months, a toddler can:

✔ walk on tiptoes

✔ jump with both feet

✔ stand on one foot

By 30 months, a toddler can:

✔ show a need to go to the toilet

✔ build simple block structures

By 36 months, a toddler can:

✔ hop on one foot

✔ begin to use scissors to cut paper

✔ put on coat and shoes, but can't tie bows

✔ climb stairs placing one foot on each step

Toddlers will play beside other young children, but they don't actually play with them yet. Remember, they only recently learnt the concept of owning toys – they aren't old enough to share them. Nor are they always happy to share attention with others. For example, if a new baby comes into your home, a toddler's initial reaction is unlikely to be positive.

If you're sensible and prepare your youngster for the arrival of a new sibling by giving consistent love and attention, your toddler soon adjusts. Try getting your toddler involved with 'helping' you get the wipes or the changing bag. Your toddler will feel more grown up than the baby and more important. He'll come to accept the baby more easily and gradually realise that the infant is a permanent fixture too.

## *Dealing with sleep-related issues*

Many parents face sleep-related problems during the toddler years.

Toddlers may demand elaborate, sometimes ridiculous, bedtime routines or refuse to go to bed altogether. Some toddlers wake up several times during the night and wander through the house.

Toddlers don't want to go to sleep for two main reasons. First, they're not tired, and second, they feel lonely. Here are some survival suggestions:

✔ Recognise that you can't force your child to sleep but you can encourage him to nod off by creating the right environment for him to feel relaxed and sleepy.

✔ Recognise that sleep needs differ. Some toddlers need nine hours of sleep a day, while others require 18. Most fall somewhere in between.

✔ Relax with your toddler rather than playing noisy or physical games right before bedtime.

✔ Set up a simple bedtime routine with your toddler and partner (and any other siblings) so everyone knows what happens before bed. Give him a bath, slow everything down, and read a story. This creates the routine that the day is coming to a close, and by relaxing and slowing down, he knows that he's getting ready for sleep.

# Discipline strategies for infants, toddlers, and pre-schoolers

Chapter 8 has an in-depth look at discipline, but here's an overview.

For infants:

✔ Use a simple 'No' in a firm voice.

✔ Remove your child from the situation.

✔ Divert their attention to something else by saying 'Wow, look at this!'

✔ Never shake or smack your child.

For toddlers:

✔ Use clear one-word commands, such as 'No' or 'Stop'.

✔ Remove your child from the situation.

✔ Distract their attention on to something else.

✔ Count to three to give you time to calm down or cool off and give your child an opportunity to think about the right thing to do.

✔ Use time outs in the Chill Out Zone (for example, sitting on the stairs or a chair).

✔ Hug, smile, and reassure your child soon after disciplining him.

Pre-school:

✔ Give simple explanations for your rules. 'You have to hold my hand crossing the road otherwise the cars can knock you over.'

✔ Use clear one- or two-word commands, such as 'No', 'Stop', 'Pick it up'.

✔ Remove or distract your child from the situation.

✔ Use time outs in the Chill Out Zone and count to three.

✔ Hug, smile, and reassure your child soon after disciplining him.

✔ Give choices and teach consequences.

✔ Rely on your ability to tell the difference between 'fussing' for a few minutes and potential hysteria.

✔ Resort to unusual as well as practical ways to make bedtime tolerable. Try putting the mattress on the floor if your child has learned to escape from his cot. Be sure the bedroom is clear of toys and other objects if you have a night wanderer.

Children can feel devastated if you lock their bedroom doors at bedtime. The resulting fear can live with them for many years. Try a safety gate instead, which works well without causing any major traumas or panic.

Children don't wake themselves on purpose. This sleepless stage won't last forever. Ask parents of teenage children with early morning paper rounds about how long it takes to wake up their kids!

Children often have nightmares from time to time, which I cover in Chapter 12.

# Navigating the Middle Years

During the middle years of development – 8–12 years – your children will generally have fewer illnesses. Their social skills are continuing to grow and they understand the ways of friendship and find making and keeping new friends easier. In fact, friends often become *very* important to children of this age; they usually love group activities and adventures.

In terms of physical development, girls will start to develop faster than boys during the middle years. Boys in this age group often enjoy rough and tumble play. Children aged 8 to 12 have good body control and enjoy activities designed to develop their strength, skill, and speed.

In terms of their developing mental skills, kids during the middle years are capable of more prolonged interest and their skills in reading and writing are good. Often, children in this group research information for themselves using the Internet, CD-ROMs, and reference books. They enjoy finding out information on subjects that interest them – anything from spiders to racing cars.

## Being patient if your child is lethargic

Rapid physical growth during the middle years may mean your child has a larger appetite but less energy. During this stage your child may seem 'lazy' or lethargic. For example, my son started staying in his room for ages listening to his radio and getting up incredibly late at weekends.

You need to be patient about these changes because the rapid growth of this period can be very tiring for your child.

Tell your child how you feel and what you expect from him. Be firm and assertive but don't accuse him of being lazy – that's focusing on his character. Instead, say, 'I don't like the fact that I have to keep on asking you over and over again to come and help me. I expect you to come when I ask you. It's part of being a family team.'

Show a little faith – if you ask your child to put his ironing away, wait for him to do it. Don't get irritated (a big challenge, I know!) and do it yourself. Expect good behaviour and sooner or later good behaviour will follow. For example, ask him when (not if) he can put his ironing away and assume that he will.

The rapid pace of your child's development can also cause him to be self-conscious and clumsy, which adds to his woes.

## Answering awkward questions

Kids during the middle years are interested in finding out more about sex and babies; they need parents to provide this information in a sensitive way. Children can, at times, be giddy and silly, especially when it comes to topics that they find embarrassing, such as sex. They often tell dirty jokes and use rude words. Although this behaviour shouldn't be encouraged, most children go through this stage. (Chapter 12 has lots more advice about answering awkward questions.)

Be patient with your kids if they seem embarrassed and try to be a good role model. Your children will quickly grow out of this stage. Honestly!

## Disciplining and negotiating

During the middle years, parents are faced with many challenges. The following are some tips for dealing with some behaviours that may emerge during this stage.

Your negotiation skills will be tested during the middle years. Children often become very argumentative and refuse to do things at home during these years.

Your best approach is often a firm one: While you need to discuss what you expect your children to do, you must also be firm that they contribute to the smooth running of the household by carrying out chores that are age-appropriate.

# Dealing with moodiness and emotions

These years can be a very emotional time for both child and parent as you both make that transition to a more mature relationship. Children at this age have often just started secondary school, which can bring many worries, fears, and tears. See Chapter 11 for more on starting secondary school.

Think back to when your child was a toddler and how his moods changed from one minute to the next. Well, a child's mood during the middle years can be very changeable too. One moment he may be outgoing, friendly, and affectionate and the next he's rude, demanding, stubborn, and bossy. Try to keep your cool and ignore the bad moods as much as possible.

Children in the middle years can be very dramatic and turn simple events into mini crises. My daughter started to say things like 'Nobody loves me' and 'You're the worst parents in the world' during this stage. These behaviours can upset you if you're not prepared for them.

Although this phase can be very frustrating for parents to deal with, biting your tongue and being calm is the best way to react. I know doing so is easier said than done (particularly in my house because my daughter's 11). Don't get upset or hurt by what your child says and does – he's looking to you for reassurance. At these challenging times, remind yourself that you're building a *long-term relationship*.

# Growing independence

Although kids in this age group are beginning to be more realistic about their skills, they sometimes overestimate their own abilities. They're more trustworthy, dependable, and independent. However, they may at times seek more independence than is good for them – or than you are willing to give.

Although you do need to make sure your child is safe and has clear expectations, at this stage you also need to listen to your child's point of view and come up with solutions that suit all concerned. (Boys, particularly, begin to rebel at this stage if they feel the rules are too strict and they're not allowed to express their opinions.) Try to involve your child in some of your discussions and try to work out solutions that are fair and reasonable so everyone feels involved in the agreements.

Negotiation skills are necessary for many of the situations you encounter as your child enters his teens. If you begin putting a system in place for dealing with these situations during the middle years, negotiating will be easier as your child progresses to the teenage years and beyond.

## Discipline strategies during the middle years

During the middle years (ages 8–12) you can be more flexible and possibly drop some rules in return for expecting firm obedience to the rules you consider really important. These rules may relate to your child's schoolwork, respectful and helpful behaviour at home, or rules about sleep-overs. Sit down and chat through your rules, negotiate, and explain them with your kids. You'll reap the benefits.

Here are just a few ideas to get you started – for more ideas on discipline, refer to Chapter 8.

✔ Ground your child.

✔ Send him to his room.

✔ Withdraw privileges.

✔ Give explanations for your rules.

✔ Give choices and teach consequences.

✔ Restore your relationship quickly afterwards – don't hold grudges.

If you think this time is tricky, just wait for the teenage years!

Kind words can be short and easy to speak but their echoes are truly endless.

During this phase many children begin to challenge adult knowledge. They're now good logical thinkers and can be very critical of adults. Where before you were your child's hero, you may now be the villain of the piece through no fault of your own!

This shift can be very difficult for parents because their relationship with their children changes. Parents may feel hurt and not as important to their children. Remember, though, that you're still central to your child's life. Maybe not in the practical, day-to-day care, but your child is experiencing many new emotions and needs you to bounce them off.

Don't take your child's comments too personally. Try to remain calm and reasonable. Easier said than done, I know, but you are still the adult and your child, despite his spurt of growth and development of thinking, is still a child.

# Surviving the Teenage Years

Young people today face many pressures, and many parents of teenagers struggle to know how to raise teens. As a parent, you're dealing with the mixed feelings of joy and pride but also the sadness of watching your child enter the adult world. Parents sometimes feel that their children don't need them any more. (Of course, this perception isn't the case – they just need you *differently* to toddlers.)

As your child becomes an adult, your relationship with him will change, but no reason exists to believe that it won't be as deep and enriching as it was when he was younger.

*It rarely occurs to teenagers that the day will come when they'll know as little as their parents.*

—Anonymous

## Following physical changes

Childhood doesn't seem to last for long these days, and research shows that children are entering puberty earlier.

The onset of puberty is usually accompanied with a sudden and rapid growth in height, weight, and size, increases in strength, and the sudden explosion of hormones.

Because of this sudden spurt of growth, teenagers sometimes feel uncomfortable and self-conscious about themselves and can often go through what my dad called 'an awkward phase'.

During this time, both sexes can become very concerned with their appearance, and many teenagers also start to suffer from acne, which can be very upsetting and distressing for them as they struggle to maintain their often fragile self-confidence.

Being physically mature doesn't mean that teens are emotionally mature.

## Considering other developmental changes

Mentally, teenagers are developing the ability to think introspectively and are able to look inside their own way of thinking. They're better able to plan realistically for the future.

By this age your child definitely knows right from wrong and will be more able to accept responsibility for his own behaviour. Socially, your teenager may have a wide circle of friends and a 'gang' made up of both boys and girls.

Many young people feel pressurised to grow up fast and to dress and behave like mini adults. But the adult world offers a minefield of temptation and excitement – drugs, alcohol, and sexual relationships to name only a few examples. Peer pressure can be very stressful. Teens really want to fit in and be part of the group – cool, stylish, and trendy. Staying connected to your teen – and not just becoming their taxi, hotel, and laundry service – is critical.

# Connecting with teens

Communication between child and parent can dry up during the teenage years, which is why so many parents identify with Harry Enfield's Kevin and Perry characters and call it the 'Grunt Stage'.

The stereotype of the teenage years is that it is a difficult time for all. While this stage *can* be rocky, you don't need to panic. The important thing is to keep the lines of communication open and to retain your sense of humour!

Following are some ways to break through and continue interacting with your teen in meaningful ways:

- **Channel enthusiasm.** Teens may grumble a lot, but they usually have a few things they actually enjoy doing. Try to direct your teenager's energy into activities – such as joining a karate or drama club – that give him a challenge in a safe environment.

- **Be watchful of media choices.** Be aware of the magazines and books your teen reads, programmes he watches, and Web sites he visits. Be prepared to talk about things you don't agree with and be prepared for him to challenge you in return. Learn to discuss, not judge.

- **Let your teen still be a kid.** Don't buy your daughter overtly sexy clothes, make-up, or expensive salon treatments and face creams because this creates undue pressure that she may not be able to handle.

- **Realise that mood swings are common.** One minute teens are excited and bouncy, the next tearful or angry. As a parent, you must be the stable one in your relationship.

  The safest person for a teenager to dump negative feelings on is his parents.

- **Acknowledge academic pressures.** Young people today face endless exams and coursework. It can be a real pressure for the less academic as well as the academic. Be patient, supportive, and encouraging. Everyone can succeed at something, and your teen may just be a late developer.

- **Recognise the need for your teen to have his own identity.** Teens need to know who they are and how they fit into society. As a parent, you need to accept that your child may want to be part of a group, may want to explore designer clothes, or may try to be 'the sporty' one or 'the clever one' for a while.

- **Hand over control and independence gracefully.** This can be the stumbling block for many families. Kids get tense because they want to do their own thing, and parents get angry because they worry and feel like they're losing control. Proceed bit by bit.

The journey from dependence to independence is an untidy, messy business, and the path rarely runs smoothly.

*When children reach the teenage years, we as parents often withdraw and pull away, thinking our children no longer need us. This is the exact opposite of what we need to do, despite what your teenager says and does. They need you now, more than ever.*

—Teenage coach, Sarah Newton

## Communicating effectively

Most parents find themselves lecturing, ordering, and jumping to conclusions – or even threatening their teenagers. If you always presume the worst and speak to your kids like this, you block an opportunity for communication.

Effective communication is the oil that lubricates a good family and builds a lasting relationship between teenagers and their parents. Here are some tips for good communication:

- ✔ **Remain silent most of the time.** Really listen to what your teen is saying. And think before you speak.

- ✔ **Use non-verbal communication.** Show you're really listening by saying 'I see', 'Uh-huh', and 'Mmm' occasionally. Look into your teen's eyes. Use a tone of voice and body language that show you respect your teen and are genuinely trying to understand where he's coming from.

- ✔ **Be sensitive to your child's body language.** Watch for signs indicating whether he's disappointed, worried, angry, excited, pleased, and so on.

- ✔ **Mirror back.** Reflect back the gist of what your teen has said to you in order to check you understood him clearly.

- ✔ **Avoid giving advice.** Don't offer suggestions. This is tough, I know, but believe me this tactic *really* works. Ask open-ended questions instead, such as 'So how do you feel about that?', 'What do you think would be the best thing to do then?' Sit back, listen, and allow your teenager to find his own answers. Only chip in if he asks you to or gets stuck.

Many teenagers don't like face-to-face chats. So it's easier if you are doing something else at the time, like emptying the dishwasher, driving them to a football practice, or peeling the potatoes.

# *Meeting emotional needs*

Teenagers, as well as adults, have emotional needs. If these needs aren't met appropriately, parents run into conflict.

Here are some examples of what you can do to respond to your teen's emotional needs while furthering your relationship:

- ✔ **Give your attention.** Take an interest in your teen's world, the things he likes, the music he listens to, the things he dislikes (and why), his worries, and his ways to have fun.

- ✔ **Appreciate your teen.** Notice when your teen gets things right or is helpful.

- ✔ **Accept your teen.** Show your teen that you love him even if he behaves rather erratically. Give your teen space and don't expect him to get everything right, every time.

- ✔ **Encourage your teen.** Show him you believe in him and lift him up when the going gets tough.

- ✔ **Show love and affection.** Keep it simple – giving him a friendly pat on the back or a hug, or ruffling his hair, can work wonders.

- ✔ **Show respect.** Ask for his opinions and ideas for solutions to problems.

- ✔ **Support your teen.** Attend football games, drama productions, and school events.

- ✔ **Comfort your teen.** Notice when he's feeling down, nervous, or apprehensive. Have a chat, watch a DVD together, or go out for a meal.

- ✔ **Note your approval.** Teens sometimes do good things! Point out behaviours you appreciate, such as owning up, helping others, tidying a room, or taking the dog out for a walk.

- ✔ **Show your teen security.** Doing so is critical. Your teen needs to know that you're there for him *no matter what.*

Golden moments often pop up when you least expect them. Often, teens like to talk when you've just settled down with a cup of coffee to watch your favourite TV programme, just climbed into bed exhausted, or just run a lovely hot bath. Be open to these opportunities for deep and meaningful chats at inopportune times. These moments connect you to your kids and help bridge the gap of empathy.

## How to switch off your teenager

Following are some classic ways to switch off your teenager. Try to eliminate the following interactions, statements, and phrases when relating to your teen.

Asking too many questions:

✔ Why did you do that?

✔ What did you say?

Being bossy:

✔ Just do your homework right now and don't argue.

Lecturing:

✔ Honestly, you should know better at your age.

Criticising or shaming:

✔ How could you be so stupid?

Pitying:

✔ I feel so sorry for you, you poor thing.

Rescuing them or doing things for them:

✔ All right, I'll do your homework for you so you don't get into trouble.

Jumping to conclusions:

✔ Late again! I suppose you've been up to no good!

Threatening and shouting:

✔ If you don't shape up, you're grounded for a week.

Always knowing best:

✔ I told you that would happen, didn't I?

Spending quality time with your teenager is a good habit to develop. This time doesn't mean just putting up with him. Quality time means you make an effort to enjoy his company and do something you both enjoy. For my family, quality time means going to support Chelsea FC as season ticket holders. We have a ritual of hot dogs, train journeys, heated debates about who played well, and discussions about controversial refereeing decisions. This is the oil of good communication that lubricates our family. What activities do you and your teen enjoy where you can give your full attention, listen carefully, chat, and ask questions?

## *Responding appropriately*

During the teen years you need to change your style of discipline because this stage is about understanding both sides of the situation.

You need to start understanding and empathising with your teen's point of view, otherwise discipline becomes a confrontation. Of course, this understanding must be a two-way process. Your teenager also needs to see things from *your* point of view.

So go with the flow and keep remembering the bigger picture to your parenting – bringing up the happy, confident, well-balanced teenager who will one day be an adult and parent.

The following sections describe behaviours that cause the most concern to parents, as well as some tips for handling them.

### Extreme moodiness

Anger and sullen responses are common teen responses. Additionally, your teen may resent being told what to do, which can often lead to him becoming even more moody.

Be patient and understanding. Due to teens' rapid physical and mental development, they can often feel overwhelmed by things and react negatively. Try not to take these outbursts personally and work with your partner to back each other up when dealing with discipline issues. Make sure you keep the lines of communication open. Even though your teenager may pretend he's completely in control and on top of situations, he does still need your guidance.

### Being idealistic

Teenagers need to feel important and part of the adult world. This stage is often characterised by your teen becoming idealistic. Many teenagers take on causes that they believe are important and start to fight for them.

You may feel your teen's idealism is a bit naive, but it is actually something to be proud of. Your teenager is beginning to take his role in world and community affairs seriously. He's now looking for ways to influence how the world works. Be careful not to make fun of your child's views because doing so can be very hurtful to him and have a negative effect on your relationship.

### Withdrawing

Teenage children sometimes withdraw from parents, labelling them 'old fashioned'. Teenagers often complain that parents are too restraining, and some even become rebellious. Sulking is a common reaction during this time too, which can be very frustrating for you as a parent.

Withdrawal can be very annoying for you, but try to avoid too many arguments. Choose your battles wisely. And don't feel offended when your teen thinks you're a fuddy duddy. You need to be yourself; it's your teenager who's learning about his identity, not you.

### Balancing freedom

Parents often worry about the amount of freedom to allow their teenagers and how to protect them from bad influences.

The line between being over-protective and allowing too much freedom can be a grey one and will depend on your particular circumstances, so use your common sense and judge each situation depending on your teenager's maturity.

Make sure your teenager feels his friends are welcome to your house and that you communicate with friends' parents. If you know the kids your teen hangs around with, you'll feel reassured. While you can't be with teens when they go out with friends, be aware of where they are going, with whom, what time they'll be home by, and how they are getting to and from their destination.

### The role of groups

At this stage your teenager needs less family interaction and companionship because he's probably very group-orientated. In fact, your teen may seem to spend more time with friends than at home with you.

This may be a sad time for you because your relationship is changing with your child. Prepare yourself by keeping your own life and interests going.

### Younger brothers and sisters

Sometimes teenagers who were always loving and affectionate with their younger brothers and sisters suddenly become resentful of them. This behaviour can be very upsetting for younger children, as well as the parents watching it.

## Discipline strategies for the teenage years

Parents often become confused about how to discipline children when they reach their teens. You need to strike the right balance between too little discipline (where your teenager might run untamed and wild) and too much (where they feel trapped and constrained and might rebel). Chapter 8 has some ideas about discipline, but here are the basics:

- ✓ Negotiate wherever possible.
- ✓ Ground your child.
- ✓ Withdraw privileges.
- ✓ Give explanations for your rules.
- ✓ Give choices and teach consequences.
- ✓ Restore your relationship quickly afterwards – don't hold grudges.

You must establish clear boundaries around this behaviour. Don't allow your older child to be hurtful and rough with younger siblings. And make sure your teenager has space of his own too, free from the younger ones.

# Negotiating

A vital skill in disciplining through the teenage years is the ability to negotiate. Following are the basic steps to successful negotiation:

1. **Stick to a main issue, focusing on the *behaviour* not the person.**

   Rather than harassing your teen about homework, try saying 'I'm worried because you haven't started revising for your biology exam yet.'

2. **Try to understand the issue from your teenager's point of view.**

   Put yourself in your teen's position or ask your teen what he's thinking: 'I know you've got loads of other stuff to revise, but is there a problem with biology?'

3. **Say openly how you feel about the issue – and what you'd like to see happen or change.**

   For example, you may say, 'I'm a bit worried that you'll leave your biology exam revision to the last minute and run out of time, so I'd like you to make a start on it by Wednesday.'

4. **Find out how your teenager feels about the situation and what he would like to happen or change.**

   Your teen may express himself emotionally, for example 'I hate biology and find it difficult!' Just listen to what he has to say.

5. **Start to discuss all the options.**

   Agree on a plan of action together. Keep an eye on the plan and monitor it to see if it's working.

   For example, you may say 'Can we get a good book from the school library or ask your teacher for a good revision book to help you?'

# Dealing with discipline

The way you discipline your child is individual to you and your child. Your approach is influenced by a number of factors, including your own and your child's personality. Refer to Chapter 8 for more details on discipline styles and strategies.

Some teen-specific discipline tips include:

- **Criticise the action not your teenager.** Constantly telling a child that he's wayward or bad only damages his self-esteem and reduces his self-confidence.

- **Consistency is the key to good discipline.** If some behaviour wasn't allowed yesterday, it shouldn't be allowed today. Check out Chapter 8 for more on being consistent.

- **Consequences must be realistic and occur straight away.** Follow through on your rules. If your teen consistently disregards your rule for coming home at a certain time, you need to enforce some form of boundary and loss of privilege to teach him about the consequences of his actions.

- **Look for alternatives to 'no'.** If the week is full of nos, try finding positive ways to direct your teen's behaviour. For example, a client's 16-year-old wanted to go to a nightclub with friends and stay over in the city unaccompanied. My client was horrified and wanted some strategies to help guide her daughter towards discovering that this wasn't really a good or safe idea. We worked on asking her what the dangers and snags of the evening were, and alternatives such as going with full adult supervision, going dancing more locally, and being picked up by parents.

  The powerful exercise that changed the situation was getting the daughter to stand on two pieces of paper with 'Detached observer' written on one and 'Mum's point of view' on the other and asking her to see the situation from these different points of view. The daughter really thought about the attitudes and perspectives of others and suggested they go locally and be picked up at a time agreed by all of them.

- **Keep your cool.** Watching a parent out of control, shouting, or crying can frighten your teenager, regardless of his age, and it doesn't provide the role model you want for your child either.

- **Catch your teen behaving well and praise accordingly.** Be aware of the type of attention you give your teen. Is it mostly negative? If so, look for positive behaviour and praise that instead.

- **Set fair and reasonable rules.** Agree with your partner on what is allowed and what isn't. You can only be consistent in your discipline when everyone is on the same page.

*The trouble with being a parent is that by the time you're experienced, you are unemployed.*

—Anonymous

## *Understanding what teenagers want from parents*

Despite the bravado and the mantra 'It's my life', your teenager still needs your support and understanding.

Underneath the clothes, make-up, hair, bangles, tattoo, or whatever it is you don't like, your teen is still the same person. Your teenager may talk a lot about freedom, but he's still making the transition to adulthood and wants your help and guidance on the way. Your child needs to know that you're still there for him when the going gets tough. Don't try to be a best mate; you have a unique and special relationship – you're his parent! Be there, be you, and hang on.

# Chapter 10

# When the Going Gets Tough: Handling Conflict

*I*f you're like most parents, the way you handle discipline problems is by reacting to your child's behaviour and not thinking about whether your reaction is good for your child or your overall situation at home.

Often, parents feel they must 'control' their children, when in reality the only person a parent can control is him or herself. As a parent, you can *force* your child to do something, but that's not the same as trying to work out *why* your child is acting in a certain way.

Every discipline encounter you have with your children can be an opportunity to help them grow into the kind of people you want them to be – or an opportunity for a screaming match.

A well-behaved child behaves well for a reason, just as a child who misbehaves has reasons, too. All behaviour has a purpose. This is the main reason why discipline problems can't be lumped together under one label and dealt with in the same way. (A child who talks non-stop is probably motivated differently to the child who talks back, for example.)

As a parent, you can't rectify a misbehaviour effectively until you understand the reasons for it. This chapter examines the real causes hiding behind the misbehaviour – attention, power, revenge, lack of concentration, and self-confidence – and suggests specific responses to each scenario. I also cover anger-management techniques and respond to questions about smacking, two relevant discipline topics for all parents to consider.

# Responding to an Attention-Seeking Child

Most children gain attention in school or at home in normal, positive ways. However, some children feel that misbehaving is their best way to get attention. These children are the ones who constantly speak out without permission in school or make strange noises at the dinner table that force everyone in the family to stop their conversation. Some children will even tell their parents about all the bad things they've done that day, just to wind them up.

I'm *not* in favour of giving any child a label because if you keep on telling your kids that's what they are, that's what they'll become (for example, the clever one, the artistic one, the clumsy one, the noisy one, the slow one). Labelling can destroy a child's fragile self-esteem. However, sometimes labelling the *behaviour* is a helpful way for parents to find strategies to deal with it. Never use labels when talking to or about your child.

## Common behaviours

An attention-seeking child frequently behaves in the following ways:

- Usually loud.
- Responds negatively to authority.
- Tries to force her way into peer groups.
- Frequently late to everything.
- Late in getting school work handed in.
- Frequently out of her seat at school.
- Picks on siblings and other children.
- Asks unnecessary questions.
- Often tries to be nonconformist in order to gain attention.
- Says the wrong thing at the wrong time.
- Often wears unusual or attention-seeking clothing.
- May swear or use crude language.

The effects of attention-seeking behaviour include:

- Frequent minor levels of misbehaviour that are designed to get a parent's time and attention.

✔ Parent often loses track of what they're trying to say or do because the behaviour is highly irritating but not really serious.

✔ At school, the concentration of the teacher and class is often interrupted.

✔ Everyone, including siblings, is antagonised by the behaviour.

✔ Other children may react by excluding the attention-seeking child.

## Underlying cause

An attention-seeking child is doing everything possible to let you, her teachers, and her peers know that she exists. This child feels invisible and is attempting to prove herself to others by getting everyone's attention.

Attention-seeking children are not very confident in social relationships, and their academic and school performance may be the root cause of their behaviour.

## Common mistakes

Parents make a variety of mistakes when dealing with an attention-seeking child. For example, parents often:

✔ Assume that their children don't have the skills to do the job, when they really do. For example, parents may think their child won't be able to sit and read her book for five minutes when she can.

✔ Ignore their child's behaviour and fail to listen carefully to what their child is saying.

✔ Make hasty and inconsistent judgements about their child. For example, 'You're always the last one to come out from judo. You're so disorganised all the time.' Perhaps this is the first time they've come out late.

✔ Don't look beneath their child's misbehaviour to find the underlying causes.

✔ Don't give their child any attention.

## Solutions

Because an attention-seeking child is doing everything possible to gain your attention, she may need reassurance that she deserves your attention. Give her some proper time and praise her for every small thing she does right. Most importantly, when you give your attention, give it fully.

Additionally, an attention-seeking child may feel that

✔ **She doesn't fit in with other children.** As a parent, you can help her by talking her through appropriate ways to talk to other children or ways to behave with other children when they are playing or socialising.

✔ **She's not good enough at academic subjects.** As a parent, you need to talk to her about what she can do to improve in school and find practical ways to support her if she finds some subjects difficult. (For example, do five minutes of mental maths in the car on the way to school; or talk with her teachers about other confidence-building activities.) Find ways to turn negative behaviours into positive, supportive experiences for her.

Children who attention seek need to feel successful at something. Look for things to praise your child about – being reliable in feeding the cat, being a great help with her sister, concentrating for ages when she draws, being a good friend, building models from scratch. Keep looking for opportunities to praise her naturally and easily.

Following are some practical solutions to dealing with an attention-seeking child:

✔ Help her take on responsibilities to highlight her leadership abilities. These can be both at home and at school and include tasks such as walking the dog, feeding the hamster, laying the table, being home on time, joining the Guides, and so on.

✔ Take time to really talk to your child about her insecurities. Try to discover what the underlying cause of her anxiety is.

✔ Be kind, caring, calm, and firm in your discipline – and quick to reward positive behaviour.

✔ Be a model for the behaviour you want to see: Speak calmly, softly, and quietly.

✔ Look out for improvement so you can affirm how pleased you are to see a change.

✔ Never exclude your child because doing so exacerbates feelings of not being good enough.

✔ Avoid making your child over-anxious because doing so often worsens behaviour.

You may be breaking habits when you change the way you approach your child. Be patient with yourself. Building up a new tactic or strategy takes time. Stick with your new approaches for a few weeks before you expect to see results.

# Responding to Children who Need Power

The need for power causes misbehaviour. Children with this need argue a lot and refuse to follow rules. These children are sometimes labelled defiant, rule-breakers, or bullies.

Power-needy children truly feel that their lack of power lies behind all their troubles. They believe that more power is the answer to all their problems because they could tell their parents what to do rather than vice versa. Power-needy children usually feel defeated or beaten if they do as they're told; they think they're losing if they do what their parents want them to do.

## Common behaviours

A defiant, power-needy child frequently behaves in the following ways:

- ✔ Openly challenges parents or teachers at almost every opportunity.
- ✔ Talks back.
- ✔ Dares parents to punish her.
- ✔ Appears unaffected by what parents say or do – and may even laugh at parents.
- ✔ May refuse to accept punishment.
- ✔ Is overly critical of a parent's sense of fairness.
- ✔ Is quick to claim injustice, saying things like 'Nobody likes me'.
- ✔ Is extremely conscious and critical of how she is treated by siblings, other children, parents, and teachers.
- ✔ Doesn't appear to feel very good about herself.
- ✔ Loses sight of the fact that her behaviour is actually the reason for what is happening in relationships.
- ✔ Has little self-control.
- ✔ Responds in highly emotional ways.
- ✔ Tries to rationalise or justify what's happening as someone else's fault.
- ✔ Taunts and picks fights with siblings, other children, and even parents over the smallest of incidents.

Effects of this type of behaviour are:

- Parents frequently feel threatened by their child's behaviour and have difficulty knowing how to respond to or handle this child.
- Meals, events, and lessons are disrupted.
- Rules are constantly being challenged.
- Home and classroom are often in daily turmoil and crisis.
- Parents feel a great deal of anguish and stress.
- Parents feel uneasy and may even become ineffective.
- Parents worry about disciplining their other children because they haven't been successful with their defiant child.
- If a defiant child's behaviour is allowed to go unchecked, other siblings may question a parent's fairness when reprimanded.
- Tension becomes an ever-present condition in the home.

## Underlying cause

A defiant, power-needy child wants to be disliked because failure has made her give up trying to get attention in an acceptable way. Interactions with other people have become very negative and the child is feeling a lot of emotional pain, which is being demonstrated by her defiant behaviour.

## Common mistakes

Parents make a variety of mistakes when dealing with a defiant child. For example, parents often:

- Get involved in 'yes, you will' contests.
- Become emotionally involved.
- Lose their dignity, raise their voice, or argue with their child.
- Feel they are the cause of their child's defiance. (This is probably not true unless you shout, argue, or attempt to handle your child with sarcasm in retaliation.)
- Take their child's defiance personally.
- Deal with their child in front of others, rather than on a one-to-one basis in private.

✔ Try to get their other children on their side.

✔ Assign unusually harsh and inappropriate punishments in retaliation.

✔ Issue threats that they're really not prepared to carry out or are capable of carrying out.

✔ Try to appease their child.

✔ Let their child think they're afraid of her.

# Solutions

Parents must do things to demonstrate the worth of a defiant child. This tactic doesn't mean you have to accept defiant behaviour, but you do need to accept your child as a person. Also, a defiant child needs lots of different ways to feel in control of her life, rather than by being defiant.

You are the outlet, not the cause, of your child's defiance (unless you're shouting, arguing, or attempting to handle her with sarcasm). Therefore, do not take the defiance personally.

Two techniques work particularly well with defiant children:

✔ **The third-person technique.** Rather than saying 'Stop yelling at me!' to a defiant child, say 'Lydia, what's the matter? That doesn't sound like you' or 'What's making you so upset?' By using this approach, even if it doesn't reflect your feelings, you place yourself in the position of a third person who can help rather than confront. You can maintain both your dignity and your position of authority. In addition, you emphatically convey to any other children that the defiant child is the problem, not you.

✔ **The delayed parent reaction.** If your child says 'I won't do it', do not say anything for a moment. Rather, look at her in surprise and say 'I don't think I heard you'. This response gives the child a chance to retract the statement – to change unacceptable behaviour into an apology without a reprimand.

If the situation with a defiant child has already deteriorated to the point that you can't really use the delayed parent reaction in front of other children, use it in private. A problem can never be handled past this point publicly. Sometimes, you can only try to quiet the child by saying, 'Let's not talk about it here. Let's have a chat later when you can tell me everything that's on your mind.'

Here are some practical solutions to dealing with a defiant child:

- ✔ Regardless of the situation, never get into a 'yes, you will' contest with a defiant child. Silence is a better response.
- ✔ Whatever you do, don't lose your dignity.
- ✔ Never raise your voice to argue with your child.
- ✔ Speak to your child one-to-one in a quiet, private, neutral place.
- ✔ Be caring but honest. Tell your child exactly what it is that's causing problems as far as you're concerned. Be sure you listen to her as well. In the process, insist upon one rule – that you both be respectful.
- ✔ Avoid power struggles; they get you nowhere.
- ✔ Give your child some responsibilities.
- ✔ Look for various group activities so your child can have positive experiences with peers.
- ✔ Always listen to your child. Let her talk and don't speak until she's finished.
- ✔ Ask if time alone would help, but don't force it on your child prior to talking about it because such surprises only make a defiant child more defiant.
- ✔ Make your child a part of any plan to change behaviour. If you don't, you become the enemy.
- ✔ Be very specific in telling your child what behaviour is unacceptable.
- ✔ Reach an agreement with your child on how you will treat each other.

# *Responding to a Revenge-Seeking Child*

Some children find their places by being disliked. Failure makes them give up trying for attention and power. Unfortunately, these children find personal satisfaction in being mean, vicious, and violent. They seek revenge against parents and other children or siblings in any way possible.

Destructive, revenge-seeking children write on desks in school, beat up other children or siblings, threaten younger children, and vandalise. They're out to get even – although they may not realise why they're behaving in this way or why they feel so angry.

# Common behaviours

A destructive, revenge-seeking child frequently behaves in the following ways:

✔ Exhibits destructive behaviour.

✔ Repeatedly breaks things.

✔ Takes furniture apart.

✔ Writes on walls, desks, or tables.

✔ Writes in or tears pages out of books.

✔ Bangs on furniture and damages walls.

✔ Destroys materials belonging to other people.

✔ Goes to extremes with her own possessions – not taking care of them or being meticulous about them.

✔ May not treat people any better than property.

The effects of this type of behaviour include:

✔ Parents feel fearful, irritated, or angry.

✔ Parents are confused and baffled as to why their child acts in this way.

✔ Sometimes other children are amused, which seems to reinforce the poor behaviour.

✔ School resources are being wasted.

✔ Parents may want to punish – harshly – rather than help.

✔ Parents have difficulty explaining to teachers why the destructive behaviours are occurring.

✔ Parents feel frustrated and don't know what to do to correct the behaviour.

✔ Parents may feel they're being lax or incompetent.

✔ Teachers may appear to dislike a destructive child.

✔ Parents have difficulty disciplining other children for comparatively minor misbehaviours.

✔ Confusion and controversy is created about who is financially responsible for damage.

## Underlying cause

The reason for a destructive child's behaviour is that she feels a great deal of pain and frustration. Destructive children often feel 'on the outside' of everybody and everything. The power they feel from acting out hostility often makes up for their sense of failing at other things in school.

## Common mistakes

Parents make a variety of mistakes when dealing with a destructive child. For example, parents often:

✔ Ignore the situation.

✔ Accuse their child openly and publicly which embarrasses the child and exacerbates the problem.

✔ Insist on rules that are too strict, too numerous, or unrealistic.

✔ Continuously remind their child that they'll never forget her behaviour.

✔ Lose their composure and reveal their frustration and anger in public.

✔ Believe they can't help to change the destructive behaviour.

✔ Fail to see that this behaviour is really a cry for help.

## Solutions

Long lectures about why a child is acting in a destructive way accomplish very little. (Talks about 'why' are necessary, but they happen later on in the process.) Instead, talk about what is happening. Then present your child with a definite plan that includes compensation as well as short-term goals and school involvement.

When you do talk with your child, try to reach to the heart of the matter. Rather than feeling embarrassed or nervous to talk about the issue, be open and talk about the fact that revenge is not the right thing to do. Remember that your child feels a failure or inadequate in some way. Find out what lies at the core of her feelings.

Never ignore acts of destruction. Make sure your child knows that your concern is genuine. Emphasise that you'll always inform the appropriate people of your child's destructive actions. Doing so teaches your child the consequences of her actions.

At the same time, never openly accuse your child unless you have overwhelming proof or witnesses. If your child is only a suspect, discuss the situation without making any accusations. Privately discuss your concern about 'a problem being experienced' with your child. Do so gently, in a quiet, concerned, and serious way. A tough approach only makes your immediate and long-term tasks more difficult.

Here are some practical solutions to dealing with your destructive child:

- ✔ Consider possible alternative causes for the behaviour – your child may just be seeking attention.

- ✔ React objectively to the destructive behaviour – and never take an incident personally.

- ✔ Look at both viewpoints. Always let your child tell you what her problem is.

- ✔ Find a need and fill it. A destructive child is hurting badly in some way.

- ✔ Allow your child to restore what has been destroyed. This is the most appropriate behaviour adjustment.

- ✔ Work with your child's teacher. Help your child find an activity that gets her fully involved in school. Involvement – listening to younger children read in school, playing hockey, or learning the bass guitar – can be the key to helping her turn unacceptable behaviour into acceptable behaviour.

- ✔ Give your child recognition for each positive thought or solution. Don't ignore anything she has to say about the situation. Rather, get her to say what should be done and to be part of the solution.

- ✔ Arrange for your child to experience a trusting relationship with an adult other than yourself. Your child must have someone and must not be abandoned by all the important adults in her life after such incidents.

- ✔ Try to encourage better feelings about school by talking about all the positive and good things about school.

- ✔ Consider taking your child for professional counselling.

Always emphasise to your child that her destructive behaviour – not you – determines what action becomes necessary. This distinction is vital. Don't say, 'I'm going to punish you.' Rather, say 'Your behaviour tells us what we have to do.' This strategy keeps the focus on the behaviour, not you as the parent.

# Responding to a Child Who Can't Concentrate

Most children can sit playing with a toy while the television is on, adults are talking, and the dog is barking, but some children find those things very distracting and difficult to handle because they can't concentrate on it all. Children who can't concentrate get bored quickly. Your child may get into trouble because her schoolwork is messy, her room is scattered with toys, and her things are often broken.

It seems as if your child's mind is elsewhere. She doesn't listen when she's spoken to and halfway through a sentence she may forget what she was going to say.

Children who have difficulty concentrating often exhibit behaviours that are annoying, and as parents you may think the situation is more a social problem than a discipline problem.

## Common behaviours

A child who can't concentrate frequently behaves in the following ways:

- ✔ Talks at inappropriate times and gets others to join in the conversation.
- ✔ Asks questions that are not related to the subject at hand.
- ✔ Interrupts frequently.
- ✔ Is easily distracted.
- ✔ Has a short attention span.
- ✔ Often relates better to younger children because she's not accepted by peers.
- ✔ Seldom becomes absorbed in an activity at hand.
- ✔ Watches others more than she participates with others.
- ✔ Is unable to focus on one activity at a time.

The effects of this type of behaviour include:

- ✔ Learning is constantly being interrupted.
- ✔ Parents, teachers, and peers are always aware of the distracter's presence; this child demands individual attention continuously.

✔ Both adults and other children are annoyed by the behaviour.

✔ At school, classroom tension can be created when efforts to get this child involved fail.

## Underlying cause

A child who can't concentrate may never have learnt how to concentrate or been expected to concentrate for long periods of time. She may find school so difficult that she has to take frequent breaks from assigned tasks.

I remember a child in my Reception class who found the classroom environment with sand, water play, bricks, books, plasticine, and painting pots all too much for him. He seemed over-excited and overwhelmed, flitting from one activity to the next with little real engagement. After I showed him how to play with one thing at a time in a focused way, he gradually built up his concentration.

Sometimes a child is trying to avoid the thought of failure by engaging in distracting behaviour. The child's need to belong and get attention arises from the need for status and self-worth. In these cases, the continuous interruptions are really saying, 'Look at me – I'm somebody.'

## Common mistakes

Parents make a variety of mistakes when dealing with a child who can't concentrate. For example, parents often:

✔ Allow the child to affect them personally rather than maintaining their objectivity.

✔ Fail to take immediate action when problems begin to arise.

✔ Call attention to the behaviour or confront it publicly.

✔ Explosively over-react or lose control.

✔ Fail to give the child positive reinforcement for appropriate behaviour.

✔ Feel that nothing can be done to help the child.

✔ Deprive the child of activities.

✔ Fight the child's need rather than try to meet it.

## Solutions

Distractions are a form of power. Your child's effort needs to be positively directed if you are to remain the one in control.

Additional strategies to respond effectively to a child who can't concentrate include:

✔ Get your child involved by giving her physical tasks or routine responsibilities.

✔ Give your child tasks suitable to her attention span and gradually increase the amount of work involved in each task.

✔ Build up a contract with your child for behaviour expected for her, and offer rewards for appropriate behaviour.

✔ Chat with your child so she's clear about what you expect and why it is important for her to behave in a certain way.

✔ Consider taking your child for a medical check-up. A short attention span and inability to concentrate can be the result of a physical, nutritional, or biological problem.

✔ Stay positive and praise generously and specifically. Little successes may help reduce distracting behaviour.

✔ Use a timer when your child is doing chores or working on homework. Distracting children often like 'competing' against a clock.

# Responding to a Child who Lacks Self-Confidence

Children who lack self-confidence honestly *expect* failure. They don't feel they have the ability to function in the classroom but may feel completely adequate outside school or when they're supposed to be doing something connected with school. They're often labelled bullies. Boys tend to react in a more physical way, whereas girls tend to use a more emotional, verbal way to intimidate and manipulate others.

They frustrate their parents because they're often capable of handling their schoolwork successfully but they don't. These children use inability, real or assumed, to escape participation. When they're supposed to be doing their homework, they play and look for distractions instead. Then they make excuses like they couldn't do it or that they feel stupid. No amount of parental encouragement seems to make a difference to them.

When lack of self-confidence is the cause of the misbehaviour, parents often feel frustrated or angry. They consider their child's behaviour to be a cop-out.

Some parents think that bullying is part of growing up and that it can help children learn to stick up for themselves.

# Common behaviours

A child lacking self-confidence frequently behaves in the following ways:

✔ Pushes people around, verbally and physically.

✔ Threatens others.

✔ Has a bad temper – and often a bad mouth.

✔ Brags about her strengths.

✔ Is extremely negative and has a poor self-concept.

✔ Becomes aggressive with others at the first hint of trouble.

✔ Thinks others are trying to put down or take advantage of her.

✔ Talks back.

✔ Publicly announces what she plans to do.

✔ Has learning problems.

✔ Uses physical aggression (generally only outside the classroom) as well as verbal threats about what she'll do after leaving the classroom.

✔ If articulate, may be verbally aggressive.

✔ Degrades others and humiliates others in public view.

✔ Is generally either a loner, a bully with few friends, or a gang leader.

✔ Has a reputation for being a fighter.

✔ Responds to all interaction negatively and physically.

✔ Looks for trouble.

✔ Often encourages fighting by her attitude to others.

The effects of this type of behaviour include:

✔ Other children are frightened.

✔ Some children watching a bully sometimes think it's funny and laugh out of nerves.

- A negative atmosphere of fear exists in and around the classroom.

- The rights of others are restrained by the bully's behaviour.

- Confrontations take place.

- A bad example is set as other children see the problems being dealt with by violence.

- School time is wasted. A bullying experience in class immediately stops the learning process.

- Some children wish they had the nerve to act the very same way because the bully seems to receive a great deal of attention.

- Other children who are being bullied are threatened and naturally become highly emotional and upset and may be afraid to go to school.

- Physically weak children may follow the bully for protection.

- Teachers may feel that they have lost power in the eyes of the rest of the class.

## Underlying cause

A child who is being a bully and lacking self-confidence is demonstrating her power or ability to physically hurt other children. Bullying gives a sense of being in control and being in charge of her life. This child knows bullying another child is wrong, but being the strongest one in the relationship helps the child feel important. Also, a bullying child is sometimes bullied herself at home and wins approval at home by being 'tough'.

## Common mistakes

Parents make a variety of mistakes when dealing with a child who bullies or lacks self-confidence. For example, parents often:

- Tell their child, 'People won't like you when you act that way.' This is *exactly* what a bullying child wants because it gives her the desired attention.

- Publicly put down the child.

- Publicly show pride or pleasure in the child's physical victories, which only reinforces behaviour.

- Prejudge a situation because of past behaviour.

- Treat the bullying child inconsistently.

✔ React personally and make threats in an attempt to change behaviour.

✔ Try to bribe the bullying child.

✔ Attack the child – and not the behaviour.

✔ Fail to dig out the bullying child's true underlying motives.

✔ Fail to reinforce positive behaviours.

✔ Overlook the child's potential and exclude them from activities.

✔ Protect others, but never protect the bullying child.

✔ Fail to treat *both sides* of a conflict.

## Solutions

Kids who fight authority figures do so only to compensate for insecurity in their own characters, which they may not recognise. Therefore, you as a parent must help a bullying child learn about themselves.

Be gentle rather than tough. A bullying child can handle toughness; it's her defence mechanism. What a bullying child can't fight is gentleness – and this is actually what she's seeking and really wants.

Parents shouldn't assume that a bullying child is tough. If your child is bullying, she may in fact be weak and using her behaviour to cover up feelings of insecurity.

Following are some strategies to respond effectively to a child who is bullying or lacks self-confidence:

✔ Let your child know that bullying is not tolerated – no matter what.

✔ Establish a one-to-one relationship with your child. A child who lacks self-confidence can really benefit from having a strong and successful adult role model (such as yourself) in her life.

✔ Create a safe environment for your child to be vulnerable to others. Help your child to open up to her feelings of anxiety or insecurity; otherwise your child will keep bullying because that behaviour keeps others away and shields her from being exposed as vulnerable.

✔ Help your child to recognise that most people feel worried and insecure at times – and that it's perfectly normal.

✔ Re-channel your child's energies constructively. Find ways to direct her leadership and assertive strengths in a positive way, such as in sports, or helping you around the house.

✔ Continually praise your child for appropriate behaviour. Reinforce appropriate behaviour by calling it 'being strong'.

✔ Show your child that you care about, respect, and trust her. This may surprise your child, but by investing in her you build up loyalty.

✔ Let your child know that you love her, but that you strongly dislike her behaviour.

# Considering Smacking

Some parents claim they cannot cope without smacking. They accept that other more positive discipline methods are valuable, but they believe that some situations require a smack.

The National Society for the Prevention of Cruelty to Children (www.nspcc.org.uk) points out that numerous phrases have evolved to justify smacking children. As its literature notes, 'It almost seems to suggest that smacking is an essential part of a parent's toolkit – that without smacks, children will be uncontrollable and go off the rails – when in fact the opposite is true.'

Some common phrases – and myths – about smacking include:

✔ 'I'll teach you a lesson.'

✔ 'You need a good smack.'

✔ 'Spare the rod and spoil the child.'

✔ 'Smacking never did me any harm.'

✔ 'Don't let her get her own way.'

✔ 'You're making a rod for your own back.'

✔ 'You have to show her who's boss.'

The following are some things parents have said about smacking on my discipline courses:

✔ 'I didn't smack my 13-year-old son, but I did smack my 10-year-daughter because she was so strong willed. One day, when I smacked her, she said, "That didn't hurt!" I knew then that I mustn't smack her again because I was afraid of what might happen, and I never did.' This was a turning point for this mum in her relationship with her daughter because she recognised that things could get out of hand.

✔ 'He bit his baby brother, so I had to smack him.' Sometimes parents feel a behaviour is so outrageous that they want to demonstrate to their child that it is totally unacceptable. Unfortunately, smacking gives a very confusing, contradictory message – that using force or hitting someone when you're angry or want to make a point is okay. This message doesn't teach the child *why* her behaviour is unacceptable.

✔ 'Smacking works faster.' In the short term, smacking may look like it has the quickest desired effect because it stops the behaviour immediately. Your child may cry or seem apologetic. But smacking can have some undesirable long-term consequences such as damaging your loving relationship with your child.

## *Recognising the downsides to smacking*

One of the biggest problems with smacking is that things can very quickly spiral out of control. Sometimes parents find they need to smack harder and harder in order to get a result.

Children may feel emotionally hurt, resentful, or angry when they're smacked because it shows a huge lack of respect for them as human beings. Smacking can even spoil close family relationships because your children may become withdrawn and frightened of you.

Finally, children who are often smacked believe that this is the right way to behave with others. You are your children's role model and they'll copy your example. If you yell at or hit your child, she's more likely to hit or bully other children. Your child's anger is also likely to turn back on you at some point later on.

## *Finding healthier alternatives*

> *When I am feeling really wound-up and tense I just can't help myself smacking my children. It seems to help release my tension, but I feel absolutely awful afterwards.*
>
> —A mum on one of my Communication and Discipline Courses

Research shows that physical punishment can lead to further problems of low self-esteem and violence later on. Previous generations of parents did the best possible with the information available at the time. Ideas on bringing up children have changed because people now know a great deal more about why children behave as they do and about the psychological effects of smacking.

Rather than smacking, make an effort to find healthier, alternative ways to release the tension and stress associated with the instinct to smack a child.

- ✔ **Press your internal pause button.** Step back and take a deep breath. Leave the room and go and shout in the garden. Pound a pillow or have a swear quietly under your breath. But resist your need to lash out.

- ✔ **Find ways to help yourself relax.** Exercise, listen to your favourite music, make a quiet cup of coffee, water the garden, or visualise a beautiful, peaceful scene on a tropical island with gently blowing palm trees – whatever works for you.

- ✔ **Take time for yourself.** Set aside some time (even just 10 minutes to read a book or to take a quick walk around the garden) to do something you enjoy. Make this an everyday occurrence, if possible.

- ✔ **Choose positive discipline techniques.** Modern parents realise that smacking is rapidly becoming outdated. In fact, it is now banned in many countries, as well as in schools and child care settings. Refer to Chapter 8 for more on positive parenting and discipline.

Hitting *does* teach your child a lesson – but not one you really want her to learn and repeat. Positive parenting and discipline works best for everyone.

# Keeping Your Temper under Control

It happens to every parent: One minute you're having a great time and feeling on top of the world. You're calm. You're patient. You're fun to be with. Then suddenly, without warning, you start to change. You feel your heart beating faster and your temper rising and suddenly you explode into the parent from Hell!

Welcome to what I like to call a 'Parent Losing the Plot' moment! The trouble is, the cause probably wasn't even a major incident. You may not even remember why or what exactly made you snap.

Getting angry doesn't make you a bad parent. Everyone feels anger from time to time because it's a perfectly normal emotion. How you handle your anger is what's really important.

Most people think their anger is justified at the time, but often afterwards many realise they have probably over-reacted and said or done regrettable things.

# Analysing your anger

Anger that is expressed in an out of control way can be dangerous and have serious consequences for the whole family. It can damage trust and create an atmosphere of fear. So discovering new ways to manage your anger is a good idea.

Understanding what makes you angry and how you deal with that anger can help you handle it better. By asking yourself these questions you get a clearer idea of how you are behaving, so you can make some changes if you want to:

- ✔ What presses my buttons and makes me throw a wobbly? (The sidebar 'Top parental wind-ups' lists some of the situations that aggravate parents I work with.)

- ✔ How consistent are my boundaries and limits and what makes me angry if my boundaries are ignored or crossed?

- ✔ Am I clear in how I express what I want? If I'm unclear, perhaps my kids don't understand what I want.

- ✔ What is my child learning from the way I respond to them when I'm angry? Am I teaching them that it's OK to lose the plot uncontrollably by my behaviour so they can do the same?

- ✔ When I imagine a perfect situation where everything is going beautifully and I'm in control of my temper, what am I doing, hearing, and feeling?

- ✔ What can I do differently to reach my perfect scenario – and to make an improvement in controlling my anger? And what's stopping me from making these changes?

Stress and anger are closely linked, so think of ways to reduce your stress (having some 'me time' away from your children, finding someone to talk to, taking some form of physical exercise, walking the dog, or going out in the garden) and use these activities to help you cool off your anger as well.

Be patient with yourself as you discover new ways to cope with anger and stress because learning new habits takes time. Celebrate your baby steps towards happier relationships. Reward yourself with little treats to celebrate your successes every day – a bubble bath with candles, a fresh cup of coffee, flowers, or a magazine.

## Top parental wind-ups

Although all parents are different, I've found that the following behaviours bug parents the most:

- Keeping untidy bedrooms.
- Fighting amongst brothers and sisters.
- Not saying 'please' or 'thank you'.
- Not eating food properly or at all.
- Not washing or brushing teeth.
- Not doing chores.
- Shouting at parents and generally acting rudely towards them.

As children get older, parental peeves often expand to include:

- Not getting up in the mornings.
- Leaving the bathroom in a mess – or not leaving at all!
- Not doing homework.
- Playing music loudly.
- Choosing an inappropriate style of dress (or undress).
- Acting irresponsibly with money.
- Staying out late.

## *Identifying top temper tantrum triggers*

A parent tantrum is when a parent loses control and starts to throw their toys out of the pram – figuratively speaking! A parent tantrum is powerful. It is like a tornado. It is destructive. It needs controlling.

The following steps can help you think about what makes you lose the plot and become really angry.

1. **On a sheet of paper or a page of your diary, list the top four things that trigger your anger.**

   Check out the sidebar 'Top parental wind-ups' for some ideas of possible tantrum triggers.

2. **Look over your list and identify which one makes you feel worse than all the others.**

   Try to identify reasons that a particular trigger is most powerful for you.

3. **Think about what you can do differently in that situation if you can feel more grounded, more centred, and more in control.**

4. **Move your attention to or put your hand on the place just below your tummy button – this is the centre of balance in your body.**

   Feel centred, solid, and rooted to the ground – like the roots of a tree going down into the earth.

5. **Imagine a situation that usually winds you up and see it from this calm, centred place where you're rooted and in control.**

   Imagine everything going perfectly and experience how you feel from this great place.

Remember to do this exercise the next time you find yourself losing your temper and notice the difference.

When conflict occurs, you can choose to engage in battle, back off, or negotiate. Your choice depends very much on how secure you feel, how much you hang onto power, and how sure you feel of your own ground. But one thing is for certain, a loss of control may

✔ Stop your relationship from deepening and developing with your child.

✔ Stop your child from facing problems and dealing with them in an effective way.

✔ Encourage your child to manipulate you.

✔ Damage everyone's self-esteem.

## Keeping an anger diary

Keeping a diary gives you a place to identify your anger triggers (see the 'Identifying top temper tantrum triggers' section, earlier in this chapter) and change how you handle those circumstances. A diary also helps you to spot the signs of anger – such as getting a tense neck, going red, or developing a churning stomach. You can download The Positive Parent Confident Kids Anger Diary from my Web site at www.positive-parents.com. This diary helps you to look at what causes you to lose your temper, where it' happens, and helps you to work out things you could do differently.

After you recognise the signs of anger, you can start saying to yourself lines such as, 'I'm getting wound up now, but it's okay, I can handle it' or 'I can feel my temper rising like a volcano, but if I remember to take deep breaths I can stay calm and in control.'

You can use a diary for yourself as a parent or as a tool to help your child or teenager learn how to manage her own anger. Simply adapt your diary to how you want it to fit in with your family.

After a week of using your diary you'll have a clearer idea of what's causing your anger and will be ready to make some small but powerful changes to the triggers and consequences.

Here are some useful questions to ask yourself after using your diary for a week:

- ✔ Where were you when you lost your temper?
- ✔ What happened immediately *before* you lost your temper?
- ✔ What physical signs did you get when you started to feel angry?
- ✔ What were your thoughts at the time?
- ✔ What did you remember to do to stop yourself losing it completely?
- ✔ What could you do differently next time?

## Adopting an 'I' message strategy

Often when parents are angry, they use language that attacks their children as people, rather than addressing specific behaviours. They say things like 'You never . . .', or 'You always . . .', or 'You're so . . .'. These statements damage relationships.

Change your anger-related language to 'I' messages. This tactic may help you to say what you feel without hurting your child's feelings. An 'I' message expresses your anger in a clear, respectful, and assertive way. It also helps you keep a lid on your anger and stops situations from getting worse.

'I' messages contain four elements:

- ✔ **Because . . .** Begin an 'I' message with 'because', saying clearly why something upsets you. For example, 'Because you come in later than the time I set you, I feel you don't listen to me or respect me.'

- ✔ **When you . . .** Next describe in specific detail what happened. An example may be, 'Like last Thursday when you arrived in late laughing and joking.'

- ✔ **I feel . . .** State what specific emotion you're feeling. 'I feel angry, annoyed, or fed up' are all clear emotional statements.

- ✔ **I would like . . .** Conclude your 'I' message by saying what you want to happen or change. For example, 'I would like you to show that you respect our rules by coming home at the agreed time so I can relax and go to bed knowing you're safely home.'

## Establishing family anger rules

Create *anger rules* for your family, which make it clear to your children the ways in which expressing anger is acceptable and unacceptable. Sit everyone down and devise a list of guidelines for acceptable ways to show and deal with anger.

Consider asking your child to design a poster listing your family's rules. Display the poster in a place where everyone can see it.

Following is an example of healthy family anger rules:

> It's okay to feel angry, *but . . .*
>
> Don't hurt anybody.
>
> Don't hurt anybody's feelings.
>
> Don't hurt yourself.
>
> Don't damage property.
>
> Don't cover up the truth.
>
> And let's talk about your anger.

Or with older children, rules can be adapted to:

> Respect yourself.
>
> Respect others.
>
> Respect property.
>
> Talk about your anger openly.

# Helping Your Child Stay Calm

Your environment affects your stress levels, your mood, and how susceptible you are to getting angry. The same is true for your child.

As a parent, you can help your child stay calmer by:

- Having a regular routine and making sure your child gets enough sleep.
- Avoiding violent TV programmes, books, and games.

✔ Helping your child deal with worries and anxieties.

✔ Not yelling or shouting at your child.

✔ Providing a healthy, balanced diet without too many additives.

✔ Keeping the noise levels down in your house.

✔ Avoiding extreme heat.

✔ Talking about what being angry feels like.

Teach your children to use 'I' messages, described in the earlier section 'Adopting an "I" message strategy', so they too can have a structured pattern and strategy to help express their anger in a healthy manner.

Additionally, encourage your children to safely deal with their anger in the following ways:

✔ Punch a pillow.

✔ Do some physical exercise – ride a bike, kick a ball, run round the garden.

✔ Draw a picture of how angry they feel.

✔ Write a letter to get it all out of their system. Even if they never share the letter, writing down their feelings can be a great release.

✔ Find their own space to cool down.

For additional help, consider the following:

✔ Reading *Time Out for Anger Handbook* from Positive Parenting Publications and Programmes, available at `www.parenting.org.uk`.

✔ Visiting the British Association of Anger Management Web site at `www.angermanage.co.uk`.

✔ Chatting to your doctor, health visitor, or a trained counsellor.

# Part IV
# Helping Your Child Cope with Common Problems

The 5th Wave          By Rich Tennant

"Six of Jennifer's goldfish died today, and, well, I just don't think it's worth the three of us keeping our reservations at Takara's Sushi Restaurant tonight."

# In this part . . .

This part is about helping your children cope with school; common problems such as experiencing bad dreams and bullying; and bigger issues such as puberty, parental divorce, step-family life, sibling rivalry, and bereavement.

This part looks at family life from the point of handling change. I share positive and practical ways to help you move through change easily and effortlessly, giving you confidence to handle whatever life throws at your family.

# Chapter 11

# Coping with School

. . . . . . . . . . . . . . . . . . . . . . . . . . . . . . . . . . . . . . . . . . . . . . .

## In This Chapter

▶ Preparing your child for school

▶ Responding to school struggles

▶ Acting like a scholar: Studying, homework, and exams

▶ Moving on to secondary school

▶ Dealing with negative experiences

. . . . . . . . . . . . . . . . . . . . . . . . . . . . . . . . . . . . . . . . . . . . . . .

*E*very child deserves an education. No matter what a child's circumstances or background, I believe that education is a great equaliser,
giving children equal opportunities. Children can transform their destiny
through education. You only have to look at Oprah Winfrey, Cherie Blair,
Margaret Thatcher, or Bill Clinton – powerful and influential people from
humble backgrounds who changed their lives through education.

Teachers have the power to shape and direct young minds. Most people can
point to a teacher who changed their lives. For me it was Mrs Bulger who
said I had a talent for writing, and Sister Eleanor who made me laugh and
believe in myself.

I have taught in a variety of schools in both deprived and privileged areas,
I've seen first-hand that education is a wonderful opportunity to raise
children's expectations, give them tools to cope in life, and set them off with
goals and a future where they can have more work choices and directions.

 John F. Kennedy said, 'Let us think of education as the means of developing
our greatest abilities, because in each of us there is a private hope and dream
which, fulfilled, can be translated into benefit for everyone and greater
strength for our nation.'

This chapter is about helping you guide and encourage your child through
the ups and downs of school life.

# Getting Ready for Primary School

Starting school is a BIG moment in your child's life – and a BIG moment in your life, too. Your child is growing up and becoming independent from you. While this realisation can be both liberating and daunting, the key to handling it successfully is *your* attitude. So be positive and be relaxed.

## Preparing your child

Life is full of new experiences for youngsters. If you, as a parent, relax and handle change in a confident manner, your child sees that change is okay and something to take in his stride.

Start preparing your child for nursery or school as early as you can. Let your child play at friends' or relatives' houses for a couple of hours so he can get used to being away from you for short periods of time. These excursions gradually build a child's self-confidence, self-esteem, and ability to be more independent.

## Getting to know your new school

Look at lots of nurseries and schools so you feel confident in your choice. You're likely to get an intuitive feeling that a place is just right for your child. Then take your child along to the school's open mornings or playgroups to help him become familiarised slowly and naturally with the new surroundings.

Make at least one visit to your new school with your child before his first day. Look round the classroom to see where the coats get hung up and where the toilets are. Identify with your child all the lovely activities going on and have a look around the playground. Talk about the routines, such as having milk and a biscuit before playtime, or story time at the end of the morning, which can help your child feel secure and relaxed in this new environment.

Meet your child's new teacher. Talk to the teacher about the strategies they use to settle the children. Let your child know how comfortable you are around this new adult. Speak positively about your child's teacher often.

For some children, looking around is enough. Children who learn by hearing may benefit and feel reassured if you describe things and give them a chance to listen to happy sounds from the other children or the soothing and confident voice of their new teacher.

## My son's first day at school

I remember taking my son Will to the Mother and Toddler group in the summer holidays at the school where he was supposed to start his Nursery mornings later in the year. The group met in the same lovely and colourful room that his class was to be held in. He got used to the surroundings naturally, with me alongside him. He found out where the toilets were and where to hang up his coat. He got used to the toys and met some of the children who were also starting in September.

I made friends too, which was really reassuring and helped make the whole transition natural, friendly, and relaxed. So on the big day, he walked confidently up the path and left me outside feeling like a blubbering wreck – emotional but also relieved he was so happy.

Let your child join in with the Introduction session and stay if you feel more comfortable. Every child is unique in how he handles a first-day experience, so go with the flow. But always check that your approach is acceptable to the school, as they all have slightly different ways of settling in new children.

After visiting the new classroom, talk to your child openly about what he liked – and what he fears. Don't push your child's fears aside because they are very real. Talk about how you felt when you started your first job or went somewhere new. Name the feelings and acknowledge them and then accept them in a matter of fact way as something to be dealt with and overcome gently.

To help create a feeling of excitement, rather than fear, about starting school:

- ✔ Point out the school whenever you pass it.

- ✔ Tell funny and positive stories about your school experiences.

- ✔ Make a school out of cardboard, play dough, or bricks and act out and talk about some scenarios that may happen. Work with your child to figure out ways to handle these situations easily.

- ✔ Draw or paint pictures of the new school.

- ✔ Ask your child, 'What are you looking forward to most about starting school?'

- ✔ Read some books to your child about starting school, like *Topsy and Tim Start School* by Jean Adamson (Ladybird Books) or *Starting School* by Alan and Janet Ahlberg (Puffin Books).

- ✔ Walk or drive to school together so your child gets to know the route.

One of the main anxieties for children (and parents) is the fear of not knowing anyone or not having anyone to play with. Children are usually very flexible and good at making friends. Most schools make a particular effort to help the children get to know one another in a relaxed environment.

If your school has a parents' evening for new parents, always go along and take some notes. You'll receive a booklet and feel reassured by the professionalism and sympathetic approach of the staff. You also have a chance to meet other parents in the same boat, which makes you feel better too.

One lovely idea before my children started school was a picnic and BBQ in one of the parent's houses for a couple of hours with toys and games. The children had a lovely time with us all together, and I also got to know some of the parents in a relaxed and really enjoyable way before term started.

## Getting ready to learn

The exciting world of school introduces your child to different experiences of the world, new friendships, new technology, stories from the past, different cultures and beliefs, and new physical and emotional experiences through PE, dance, drama, and music.

### Academic skills

You can help prepare your child for classroom activities in a variety of ways. For example, by playing with paints and drawing pictures with colourful pencils and crayons, young children develop dexterity. They can then be ready to trace patterns and write with a pencil.

Make sure from the beginning that your child holds a pencil correctly. If you're unsure of the proper way to hold a pencil, purchase a pencil grip from your local stationery shop. Developing a good habit early on is easier than breaking a bad one later.

Parents often worry that they haven't taught their children to read before they start school. Remember that education isn't a competition. If you read lots of stories to your children, sing nursery rhymes, and talk to them, they'll be ready and curious to learn about books and stories. Reading will naturally flow from their experiences at school.

To develop other specific skills and interests, try the following:

 ✔ **Mathematical concepts.** Try playing with water or sand. Pouring water or sand between different sized jugs helps your child discover the concept of capacity. You can also talk about some jugs holding 'more than' or 'less than' each other.

TIP

## Entering the countdown zone

Regardless of whether your child is starting school for the first or fifth time, you can do several things to help ease his transition:

✔ If your child is on a 'holiday routine' (which in my house means going to bed later and getting up later), change his routine to gradually bring bedtime back to a more suitable one for school nights. Introduce more regular features like bedtime bath and make sure mealtimes are at set times.

✔ Shop for your child's uniform together. Make the experience a special event. Go shopping in plenty of time, so if the shop has run out of anything or the correct size isn't available, you have time to wait without getting anxious.

✔ Get yourself more organised by writing a list of all the things you need to do, such as getting the dinner money ready or lunch boxes prepared. Write yourself notes about reading folders or which days require PE clothes. Stick your reminders on your fridge and tick them off as you do them, all of which helps you feel in control.

✔ Also involve your child in the preparations. Let him help you pack his bag or lunch box and lay out his uniform.

✔ Set your alarm clock early for the first day of school because even the most organised parents need extra time to get ready on the big day. Leave in plenty of time on the first day, so your child can enter school in a relaxed state of mind – not flustered and stressed.

---

✔ **Weight.** Talk with your child about things being 'heavier' or 'lighter' when you pick them up and compare them.

✔ **Size.** Use language like 'bigger than', 'smaller than', and 'the same size' to describe various objects.

✔ **Shapes.** Play with different colourful shapes and match up the same ones. Use correct names, for example 'square', 'circle', and 'triangle'.

### Other skills

As your child's first day approaches, remember to see that your child also has the following skills:

✔ **Toilet-related skills.** Help your child practise going to the toilet by himself. Teach him to flush the toilet and wash his hands. Also make sure the words your child uses for asking to go to the toilet are the same ones the school uses to avoid any confusion or upset.

✔ **Clothing skills.** Make sure your child can do up buttons and put a coat and shoes on. All these things create a sense of independence and self-confidence and also really help the teacher get the children ready for play time quickly and easily.

✔ **Noise.** Make sure your child is comfortable in a noisy environment because a classroom can be a loud place at times.

✔ **Confidence.** Encourage your child to ask for what he needs – for example, going to the toilet, getting a biscuit, or having another piece of paper.

## Controlling your emotions

Saying goodbye at school on your child's first day may be a very emotional moment for you. But try to send your child off with a smile, a wave, and reassurance that you'll be there to pick him up later.

In all my years as a Reception teacher, I found that distressed children settle very quickly after parents have gone. Make your leave-taking loving but brief. I know you'll go off feeling awful thinking your child is sad, but actually he'll be fine within three minutes – probably having forgotten all about you while enjoying the sand or cars! (If you're particularly worried, you can always phone the school to check whether your child is okay.)

Your child is guided by your emotions, so make sure you're feeling relaxed and positive. Do things calmly, in plenty of time, and with compassion and patience. Use positive words and body language, happy facial expressions with lots of smiles, and cuddles.

## At the end of the day

Being there when he comes out is actually the most important thing you can do to help your child settle into school. Being on time helps your child feel secure and safe in the knowledge that, although you go away, you *always* come back. A few minutes late can seem like an eternity to a young child, who may feel tired out.

Don't bombard your child with questions straight away. Let him relax. He may be hungry, so consider bringing a healthy snack when you pick him up or offer him something as soon as you reach home.

Give your child some quiet time with or without you; he'll talk when he's ready. Make listening your key priority, and natural opportunities for talking will just come up. Help your child embrace this wonderful opportunity to discover new things about the world by taking an active interest in what he says to you. Listen attentively and chat openly about your child's day.

Let your child get plenty of early nights because he's likely to be exhausted for the first few weeks of constant new experiences.

If your child still finds settling in particularly difficult after a number of days, chat with his teacher, who can help you all come up with a practical solution. As my old school motto said, 'A happy child learns'.

# Starting Secondary School

Watching your children grow up can be one of the greatest experiences in the world, but not always one of the easiest. You're sure to feel every emotion from love, pride, and joy to despair, fear, rage, grief, and confusion.

Any change to your routine or way of life can be confusing and scary, so starting a new secondary school can be challenging. However, if you provide lots of love, security, and encouragement, your child can adapt to the changes easily and naturally.

The transition period between primary and secondary school can be a very testing and emotional time, as your child moves from a thoroughly familiar and stable situation to a new experience, which may be neither. This transition can have a huge impact on your child's self-esteem, school performance, and emotional well-being.

## Bridging the gap

At primary school, your child may have had responsibility and status, as well as established and positive relationships with friends, teachers, and administration staff. As your child moves on to secondary school, he is suddenly in a situation of uncertainty, with new rules and expectations. Be aware that:

- ✔ Relationships with teachers take longer to build at secondary school, which can also place more strain on your child's peer relationships.

- ✔ Worry abounds. Children may worry about getting lost because the school is much bigger and looks like a maze of endless corridors with thousands of people. Or they may worry about not fitting in or being ridiculed if they don't like the same things as everyone else. They worry about their physical appearance, their spelling, their journey – the list is endless.

✔ Your child must make emotional and cognitive changes, as well as adjustments to a host of body changes with the onset of puberty.

✔ Children who have experienced parents divorcing may be particularly anxious. They may have additional difficulty thinking clearly or performing to the best of their abilities.

This time in your child's life marks a passage into adolescence and requires adjustments from both of you – no wonder you both feel tired out.

## Creating confidence

You need to focus on the bigger picture of supporting and nurturing your child through these changes. Be patient with him and do all that you can to help develop his confidence.

As your child enters secondary school, try asking him these three questions:

✔ What is the best thing about your new school?

✔ What will you miss most about your old school?

✔ What is the scariest thing about your new school?

These three questions address the highs and lows your child is experiencing. Talking through issues and concerns that arise builds your child's confidence and gives him support in coping with the practical and emotional worries he may be experiencing.

Many larger schools have their own Web sites, and you can find answers to many of the questions that come up, including school trips, sports fixtures, homework expectations, and the choice of clubs on offer. A little research can help alleviate the uncertainty.

## Managing new challenges successfully

Moving schools can be a stressful time, so don't be surprised if your child loses his temper or gets irritable more often. Your child may start to argue with you over trivial things like school uniforms, packed lunches, or pencil cases.

For a successful transition from primary to secondary school, your child should:

✔ Get organised. When you're organised, life for everyone is much easier.

✔ Never be afraid to ask for help. Encourage your child to talk to someone he trusts – such as his mum, dad, or a tutor.

✔ Make the first effort to make new friends. Remind your child that everyone is in the same boat. Moving through change is easier if you do it with a friend or two.

✔ Realise that first impressions last a long time. Encourage your child to make sure he makes a good impression in terms of organisation, presentation, and behaviour. Secondary school is a chance to make a fresh start.

✔ Try something new. Secondary school is rich in new opportunities. Encourage your child to try out clubs and activities.

✔ Make notes and write down anything he needs to remember.

✔ Behave in a way that doesn't attract negative attention.

✔ Work out the layout of the school, noting where all classrooms (and toilets) are.

✔ Find out his timetable – and remember it! Your child must know what time to be at school and what time to go home.

✔ Find out what uniform and sport kit he needs.

Try to see your child's experience as something positive. If you are upbeat, your child will be as well.

You can avoid much of the distress of this transitional period by supporting your child through the new routines, specifically:

✔ Reviewing his timetable together.

✔ Helping him pack his kit and school bag the night before.

✔ Ensuring he gets enough sleep.

✔ Making sure he has a healthy breakfast to give him the energy needed to start a new day.

If things don't settle and you're concerned about your child, make an appointment to see his teacher or personal tutor. Don't let the situation escalate or fester so that the whole new school experience is negative – that's not good for your child's transition to a new chapter in his life.

# Staying Involved and Connected

Children live and learn in two worlds – home and school. The way these two domains interact and communicate can make an enormous difference in how your child manages in both places. You, your child, and your child's teacher need to trust each other and listen and talk regularly to each other to get the best out of your child.

Of course, family life is very different today than it was a generation ago. You probably spend far less time together than families in the past. You may face an uphill struggle to balance the demands of your family life and your career. Sometimes these pressures can result perhaps in you not participating fully in your children's school life. However, you must try to find the time to get involved in some way.

Recent studies show that when families are involved in their children's education in positive ways, the children achieve higher grades and test scores, have better attendance at school, complete more homework, and demonstrate more positive attitudes and behaviour. These reports also indicate that families who receive frequent and positive messages from teachers tend to become more involved in their children's education, which benefits the children's attitude and approach to learning.

Although you may feel uncomfortable when you have to contact your child's school, your involvement tells your child that education is important and valued by you. Children really benefit from having you show an interest in their school work, regardless of whether you're divorced, separated, or happily married.

The best way to encourage your child's education is to get actively involved with his school. Go to parents' evenings, sign your child's homework diary, or help in some way at social functions. By sharing responsibility with your child's teacher for creating a working relationship, you help your child succeed academically.

# Struggling at School

All children have problems at school at some time, so don't panic or feel bad when a problem occurs.

Talk to your child's teacher to find out exactly what's happening. If you still feel the problem isn't being addressed, ask for another meeting with the head of department, deputy head, or head teacher. Usually the problem can be sorted out easily and quickly, but if the issue is more serious, then you can either go to the school governors or your local education authority.

Children can't learn when they're anxious, stressed, worried, or unhappy – either at home or in school. Inform your child's teacher about major changes or unusual events happening at home, such as the arrival of a new baby, a divorce, the death of a grandparent, or if someone has been made redundant. The school also needs to be able to tell you if your child is experiencing a change in attitude, behaviour, or academic achievement. A two-way, respectful interaction should occur between you and the school.

Children develop at different rates. Most children are more advanced in some areas and slower in others. However, when you feel that your child is truly struggling at school, remember the following:

- ✔ **Don't assume anything.** Always meet with your child's teacher to get his insights before deciding that your child is at risk academically.

- ✔ **Define the problem.** Clarify what you think the problem is *before* you initiate a meeting with your child's teacher. He may not realise that your child is having a problem. Also, take time to research the problem and come up with possible solutions *before* you meet with the teacher.

- ✔ **Be positive.** When negotiating with your child's school and teacher, show a willingness to co-operate and do your part to help. But remember you're the expert on your child and his best supporter. Some gentle and persistent pushing may be necessary.

- ✔ **Follow your instincts.** If you have faith in the school and your child's teacher, trust them to find the best solution for your child. But if your intuition tells you they're not doing enough, seek further advice.

- ✔ **Consider testing, when appropriate.** Insist on testing if it is needed and educate yourself on the meaning of the results. You can either talk to your Special Needs Co-ordinator at your child's school or the Head Teacher to get the ball rolling. Alternatively you can pay to have a test done by an Educational Psychologist.

- ✔ **Visit your child's classroom.** Ask to be present for a time in the classroom, perhaps for half an hour in the morning. Offer help, pay attention, notice, and always monitor your child's progress or lack thereof.

- ✔ **Look outside the school, too.** If you reach a stalemate and the school is unable to help your child adequately, don't settle for this outcome. Find the help your child needs outside of the school by contacting your Local Education Authority or have a chat with an Educational Psychologist. If possible, try to integrate this help and advice into the regular school day.

✔ **Be prepared for anything.** Your child possesses the ability to learn but he may simply learn differently. Children are either *visual*, *auditory*, or *kinaesthic* learners in the way that they process information.

Visual learners learn best by seeing information; auditory learners learn best through listening; and kinaestic learners learn best by doing things hands on. Schools are very aware of these different learning styles and provide many different ways to teach children. Things may not work out the way you anticipated, but as long as you're there for your child, he'll be okay.

✔ **Extra help is okay.** Try to avoid feeling embarrassed or guilty if your child needs extra help in a subject. Helping your child does not take away resources from the other children. Your child is perfectly entitled to get the extra support he needs.

The preceding strategies are for any child struggling over a short period of time or in a particular subject. For children who have more long-term learning problems, see Chapter 14.

# Structuring Studying

During the school year, studying is an everyday activity for your child, regardless of whether he's doing homework, preparing for a minor quiz, or revising for a major exam. This section covers the skills and strategies your child needs to succeed as a student.

## Developing study skills

Study skills sometimes get lost amidst all the subject-specific details your child encounters on a daily basis. From early on in your child's education, help him develop study skills that can benefit him throughout life by utilising these six essential techniques:

✔ **Note-taking.** Show your child ways to abbreviate and condense information because fitting notes onto one side of paper makes things easier to remember. Encourage your child to rewrite and reduce while working through assignments.

✔ **Highlighting.** Buy your child a highlighter pen and show him how to target key areas of text using different colours and symbols. If he's a visual learner, highlighting helps him remember critical facts. (Creating diagrams, charts, and maps can help him learn new information, too.)

✔ **Recitation and recording.** Recite important information out loud several times to aid in remembering it. Have your child record notes onto an iPod or other device. Speaking and listening to notes is especially effective for auditory learners.

✔ **Movement.** Get your child to move around while reading new material or reciting information, particularly if he's a kinaesthetic learner.

✔ **Create mind maps.** Mind maps involve writing down a central idea and thinking up new and related ideas that radiate out from the centre. By focusing on key ideas written down in your child's own words, and then looking for branches out and connections between the ideas, your child is mapping knowledge in a way that helps him understand and remember new information.

✔ **Self-testing.** Encourage your child to test himself. See what he can remember without notes. Avoid self-testing on subjects your child already knows – it's a waste of precious time.

✔ **Timed tests.** Get your child to time himself. For example, completing past exam papers against the clock is an excellent way of getting up to speed.

For more tips to help your child study effectively, check out *Rev Up for Revision Mind Maps for Kids* by Tony Buzan (HarperCollins) or *Taking the Sting Out of Study* by Frank McGinty (Pembroke).

## Handling the horrible homework

Often parents are unsure about how long homework time should be. The UK government provides guidelines that offer a broad indication of how much time pupils may reasonably be expected to spend on homework. So, a reasonable time is

✔ **Years 1 and 2:** 1 hour per week

✔ **Years 3 and 4:** 1.5 hours per week

✔ **Years 5 and 6:** 30 minutes per day

✔ **Years 7 and 8:** 45 to 90 minutes per day

✔ **Year 9:** 1 to 2 hours per day

✔ **Years 10 and 11:** 1.5 to 2.5 hours per day

For more information, visit www.parentscentre.gov.uk/education
andlearning/whatchildrenlearn/learningathomeoutsideschool/
homework/

The guidelines encourage schools to plan homework carefully alongside the work that your children do at school, and to make sure that all activities are appropriate for individual children. The purpose of these guidelines is to emphasise the importance of homework and how it helps your child to learn, rather than focusing on whether his homework always takes a certain amount of time.

Special needs children need to work with their school's special educational needs co-ordinator (SENCO) to make sure their level and amount of home-work is right and appropriate for their needs.

Here are some ideas to help with homework:

✔ **Discuss homework.** Give your child a chance to talk about his school work if he wants to. Even if you know nothing about a particular subject, you can still help just by talking, listening, and helping him find his own answers.

✔ **Encourage your child.** Help him take responsibility for organising and doing his homework. Never forget to praise your child for his hard work, improved concentration, handwriting, or presentation.

✔ **Use available tools.** Many schools have homework diaries or daybooks for parents to sign each day. Show your interest in, commitment to, and respect for your child by signing his diary regularly. Doing so helps you and your child know that his homework is being monitored and also builds up goodwill between you and your child's school.

✔ **Help your child keep to a routine.** Some children prefer to do home-work straight after school, whereas others prefer to unwind first or have a meal and then do homework. Let your child decide.

✔ **Establish a study zone.** Create a suitable place where your child can do homework, ideally somewhere with a clear work surface, good lighting, and no interruptions. Teach younger brothers and sisters not to get jam on books or to interrupt when homework is being done. If there isn't space in your home, try a local library. Some schools offer homework clubs.

Some children like to work with music on and actually study better with some extra sound to keep them company.

✔ **Allow for differences.** Children are all different and have different learn-ing styles. Some prefer to study alone, whereas others like to study with friends or family. Help and support your child in creating the type of study situation he prefers.

✔ **Use resources.** Visit the local library with your child and encourage him to use it. He can access the Internet on library computers if you don't have access at home.

## Celebrate reading

One practical way to help your child is to read together. Reading together is particularly useful when your child first starts school, but even as children get older, they still love to be read to. Keep the following reading-related tips in mind:

✔ Be sure to share reading responsibilities between both parents – dads are powerful role models and can strongly influence their sons' attitudes toward reading.

✔ Let your child see you and older children read.

✔ Listen to your child read often and regularly. You're likely to notice a huge improvement in your child's reading ability and confidence.

✔ Take your child to the library to get a library card and help him find books to suit his interests and hobbies. Libraries are very keen to help you find suitable books, and during the summer holidays they often run exciting competitions and reading events to encourage your child to enjoy reading.

✔ **Get tech savvy.** The Internet is great for research. Encourage your child to become an independent learner and to go the extra mile with their studies by utilising online resources.

✔ **Offer rewards.** Make homework rewarding by setting up some treats such as staying up 10 minutes later, enjoying 10 minutes extra on the computer, having a friend round, or playing a game with you.

The National Charity Parentline Plus (www.parentlineplus.org.uk) provides useful support and information on getting your child to settle down to homework.

## *Studying for exams*

Exams are one of the most stressful things in any child's life. Help your child to pace themselves and to get a healthy balance between work and play by using the following practical strategies for planning and revision:

✔ **Make a plan.** The odd hour here and there isn't enough to make a real difference in passing exams. Your child needs to make a revision plan that is realistic and that he can stick to. He needs a daily outline that includes times for breaks and meals. Getting the balance right is vital to success.

✔ **Mix it up.** Spend some time studying weak subjects, then some time with stronger subjects. Don't encourage your child to tackle all the difficult topics at once because he may lose confidence and get more anxious.

# The seven secrets of successful revision

Help your child to prepare for exams – and effectively combat test-day nerves – with the following strategies to take the mystery and fear out of studying:

✔ **Use relaxation techniques to encourage your child to be calm, curious, and confident before they start revising.** A relaxed, focused, and positive frame of mind is essential for successful revision and enhances brain chemistry for better learning.

Encourage your child to take three deep breaths and centre himself. Or get him to remember a time when he was doing something really easily and well. Ask him to mentally step into that memory. Get your child to visualise learning key points each time he sits down to revise, and to practise stepping into that picture physically or mentally. Encourage your child to focus on feeling the success, hearing the positive things people say, and seeing the exam paper with a wonderful grade on it.

✔ **Teach your child to always make his own revision notes.** Your child learns as he writes things down. After he has notes in his own style, he's halfway there.

✔ **Encourage your child to be brief.** Check the syllabus or have your child ask his teacher to make sure key areas are covered succinctly.

✔ **Make sure your child rewards himself.** Encourage him to pat himself on the back for planning revision because doing so motivates him to keep going.

✔ **Don't let your child overdo it.** Concentration lapses after a couple of hours, so encourage him to take regular breaks. Go for a walk, do something physical, or listen to some music. Changing your environment and thought processes gives your eyes and hands a complete break from reading and writing. Your child will come back more refreshed and raring to go.

✔ **Encourage your child to experiment with different revision techniques.** Variety beats boredom every time.

✔ **Build confidence through review.** Help your child look over past exam papers and see how questions could be asked. This review provides practical experience and also gives him confidence in answering questions in the style of the exam.

✔ **Set goals.** Help your child set targets that he knows are achievable. Write down these goals and encourage your child to tick them off as he accomplishes them. This tactic provides a sense of going forward and makes your child feel he's achieving something each day.

✔ **Get help.** Always encourage your child to ask you, siblings, teachers, or friends for help when needed. Doing so helps him feel supported.

✔ **Keep a simpler schedule.** During this stressful time, don't overload your child with too many after-school activities or responsibilities.

✔ **Work with others – or don't.** Your child may enjoy working with other people when revising but, if he can't concentrate, encourage him to save getting together for weekends when he can really relax and take a well-deserved break from the books.

✔ **Think bigger.** Help your child keep a wider perspective on life. Although exams are important, they're only one aspect of his life.

✔ **Be alert.** Make sure your child gets professional help if you think he's in danger from too much stress or feeling overwhelmed. Don't let him bottle up anxieties and worries.

# Forging Friendships

Friendships are important in helping children develop emotionally and socially. Through interacting with friends, children are able to discover the joy of sharing, laughter, support, loyalty, and great happiness to name only a few emotions. They also:

✔ Experience the give and take of social behaviour.

✔ Set up rules, weigh up alternatives, and make decisions when they're faced with dilemmas.

✔ Experience a wide range of normal emotions such as fear, anger, and aggression.

✔ Discover what's appropriate and what's not.

✔ Figure out social standing and social power – who's in, who's out, how to lead and how to follow, what's fair and what's not.

✔ Encounter different people, viewpoints, and situations, all of which call for different behaviours and reactions.

✔ Belong to groups, thus improving their sense of self-esteem.

✔ Find comfort and support to help cope with troubling, transitional times (moving up to a new school, entering adolescence, dealing with family stresses, facing disappointments, and so on).

Friendships aren't just a luxury; they're a necessity for healthy psychological development. They can be a wonderful source of emotional strength that helps your child develop lasting self-confidence. Research shows that children with friends have a greater sense of well-being, better self-esteem, and fewer social problems when they become adults.

Developmentally, friendships often follow patterns:

✔ Between the ages of 5 and 9, friendships usually begin forming quite casually and often change very rapidly. You know the pattern – your child may be great friends with someone one day, then best pals with somebody else the next.

✔ After the age of 9 years or so, children are more likely to have a 'best friend' and form more intense, longer-lasting friendships on the basis of a variety of shared interests and things in common.

## Making friends

Your child may be happy with just one friend or be extremely popular with a large circle of friends. Alternatively, your child may seem perfectly content alone – sometimes because he has different interests from other children his age.

Worrying if your child seems upset by a constant lack of friends is perfectly normal. This situation can mean he's more vulnerable to loneliness, low self-esteem, and even lower academic achievement, eating disorders, and depression. But if your child is happy with his own company, that's fine. Not overreacting is important. While the vast majority of children rely heavily on friendships, some do not and they're quite happy with that situation. Many grow into resourceful, creative adults. You only need to worry if your child seems upset about feeling left out or rejected by friends.

For some children, however, making friends causes enormous anxiety. Your child may be so shy that he has great difficulty reaching out. Alternatively, your child may have bullying or aggressive tendencies, which lead other children to avoid him.

Help your child surround himself with all the friends he needs by using the following tips:

✔ **Talk about friendship.** Share your own memories about your childhood friends and ask your child about his thoughts and feelings about current friendships.

✔ **Teach social skills and sociable behaviour.** Take the time to show your child how to make eye contact, smile, and show he's friendly. Be sure to cover basic social rules as well – not to grab things or hit others and how to share and co-operate. Or have your child practise saying something like: 'Hello, I am Sam, would you like to play?'

Sometimes children need help understanding non-verbal cues (for example, when someone's smiling at them) as well as verbal cues (when someone's making a joke or funny remark). Your child may be misinterpreting these and missing great opportunities to make friends. Or your child may overreact to teasing or pressure others to play. Take the time to explain some of these skills adults take for granted.

✔ **Develop ways to negotiate and handle conflict.** Talk to your child about how to listen to others and compromise. Teach him how to put across his point of view assertively but not aggressively.

✔ **Make your child's friends welcome in your home.** Don't judge your child's choices too harshly or force him to play with children you choose. Never show up your child or tell him off in front of friends. Doing so sets you apart from your child and damages your relationship.

For my 16th birthday party, my parents left my cousin in charge while they popped next door for a drink with the neighbours. They came back only an hour later and discovered the music whacked up, lights dimmed, and food everywhere. The amazing thing I remember about the incident is that my parents handled it with grace in front of my friends. (Of course, I got a rocket when they'd all gone home and had to clear up the mess!)

✔ **Make an effort to talk to other parents at school.** You're setting a good example for your child to follow, plus your friendliness encourages your children to get to know each other too.

✔ **Find local activities where your child can make friends outside of school.** Look to Cubs, sports, a drama group, or swimming lessons as ways to broaden your child's circle of friends and meet a range of children from different cultures and backgrounds. Having non-school friends can help your child feel at ease in many different situations.

✔ **Show your love and affection.** Your love for your child is invaluable in bolstering his confidence, even if he does experience occasional friendship difficulties.

Try not to interfere too much in matters connected with your child's friendships and social life. Give him the chance to sort things out in his own way, whenever possible. Of course, if you think your child is falling prey to negative, harmful influences, that's another matter – one I address in the section 'Dealing with bad company', later in this chapter.

I remember the parents of two 10-year-old children in one of my classes getting over-involved in their daughters' friendship tangles and taking it all too personally. The adults ended up shouting at each other at Open Day in front of lots of other parents who were trying to enjoy the school choir and the lovely displays on the wall. Their children had made up by then and felt really embarrassed by their parents' behaviour.

## Dealing with bad company

You may worry about your child getting in with a 'bad' crowd or making what you feel are unsuitable friends. These types of situation can be quite difficult because any attempts you make to ban such friendships usually only make your child more determined to carry on with them!

You're better off allowing the friendship to run its course and keeping an eye on things – especially when the children are playing in your home. Stick to your house rules and insist that there is no fighting, violent computer games, or swearing.

Keep your child safe with the following tactics:

- ✔ Don't let your child go off alone unsupervised – especially with a friend you feel uncomfortable about.

- ✔ Be wary of groups that you don't feel happy about. Boys especially can be led on into much worse behaviour when a gang is egging them on.

- ✔ Make sure you always know where your child is. Have clear rules that he must come and tell you before moving on somewhere else or use his mobile phone to tell you of any change of plan.

## Combating cliques

All children experience feeling left out by their friends once in a while because children can be notoriously fickle. The hard part for you is that you can't always protect your child from the hurt feelings.

I've seen children fall out and make up within the same playtime. But sometimes kids form groups that they won't let other kids belong to, and that is called a *clique*. Not all groups of friends are cliques. The thing that makes the difference is that the group leaves some children out *on purpose*.

Both girls and boys have cliques, though some research claims that girls are often more hurtful and spiteful in the way they treat and ostracise the girls who aren't in the group.

In a clique, usually one or two popular children control who gets to be in the group and who's left out. During my teaching days, I remember a girl bursting into tears when her friends suddenly voted her off their lunch table. This rejection can be very painful for a child who can't understand what they've done wrong.

Probably the hardest part of dealing with a clique is how awful it feels when a friend of your child's suddenly becomes part of the clique and starts treating your child differently. Often the problem starts with an argument between the two, but other times there appears to be nothing to trigger it.

The children who get into cliques want to be popular and 'cool' and think that being in a clique will stop them from being left out and guarantee their friendships. Clique members gain confidence in knowing they're part of the 'in' group.

Children in cliques often start to act differently than they do outside the group and they may suddenly go along with what the others are doing or saying, even if it means leaving their friend out. They often feel bad about new behaviour, but they can't work out how to be cool and be nice at the same time. (However, other children manage to be consistent and loyal to their friends while being part of a clique, so self-confidence may be the real issue.)

Fortunately, children usually grow out of this phase.

Being in a clique (or being excluded from a clique) is not the same as bullying, but clique behaviour needs to be addressed because it's not a pleasant experience for children on the outside of the group. If your child finds himself excluded from a clique:

✔ Tell him to talk to a teacher who can help him find ways to handle the situation. Teachers can help children learn to play together, mend hurt feelings, and repair broken relationships. They can also do Circle Time (where children explore their feelings, and learn about emotional literacy, sitting in a circle) or a PSHE (Personal, Social, and Health Education) session to help children address the clique situation and develop respect and kindness towards each other.

✔ Help your child focus on other children, outside the clique or perhaps from non-school clubs, who are more open and receptive.

✔ Encourage your child to speak up and say what's happened.

✔ Invite children round to your home so they learn to see your child from a different perspective.

✔ Encourage your child to make friends everywhere and to be friendly and open to everyone.

# Dealing with Tough Times

During one of my PSHE lessons, I filled a glass half-way with coloured water and then asked the children whether the glass was half full or half empty. The point was to teach the children that the answer could be either, depending on their point of view or perspective.

Having a balanced perspective is really important in all areas of life, and it is an interesting part of my work as a Parent Coach. I work with parents who can't see the wood for the trees and help them to change their perspective and see things from the point of view of their child, partner, other family member, and a detached observer. The process can be really enlightening and can help families make changes in their relationships.

Shifting your own perspective – as well as your child's – is critical to responding to each of the following difficult experiences: Disappointment, failure, and embarrassment.

# Handling disappointment

Disappointment is a feeling of sadness or frustration because something wasn't as good or as satisfactory as you expected, or because something you hoped for didn't happen. You feel disappointed when someone lets you down and it can be hard to deal with when you're a child. Often, circumstances intervene – it's no one's fault. Some of my clients get frustrated with their ex-partners who say they're coming to take the kids out but fail to show up. The children feel let down and hugely disappointed.

You are a role model to your children at all times. How you handle life's ups and downs sends a message to your children about how they should handle them, too.

Here are some suggestions for helping your child handle disappointment:

- ✔ **Stop the pity party as soon as you can.** Don't allow that reaction to take a hold just because something didn't turn out well. Make it very clear to your child that a defeat or a loss isn't the end of the world and doesn't mean that he's no good.

- ✔ **Acknowledge disappointment.** If your child goes through a disappointment, talk about it and help him to learn from the experience so he can gain something of value from the situation and learn not to do the same thing again.

- ✔ **Focus on the positive things that can come from the experience.** Not feeling like a total failure from just one setback is important. Remind your child of another time when he felt disappointed and how things turned out fine in the end – or even better!

- ✔ **Share examples.** Talk about a time when you or another member of the family suffered a setback and how you or they handled it.

- ✔ **Get physical.** For some children, particularly boys, rigorous activity such as kicking a ball, hitting a tennis ball, or walking the dog helps them to chew over situations and disappointments. If physical activity works for your child, then the need to chat and analyse feelings, while still useful, is not always essential. Be guided by knowing your own child best.

# *Handling failure*

Failure can occur in many situations: Sports, exams, or in relationships, to name a few. Some children handle failure easily and in their stride. Some sulk for half an hour and then move on. But others take things more to heart and find failure more difficult to cope with.

Here are some ideas for your kids to handle failure:

- ✔ **Step back and reflect.** Stop, calm down, and take some deep breaths. Encourage your child to get some breathing space and spend time taking stock. Things may not seem so bad tomorrow.

- ✔ **Get your feelings out.** Help your child express his feelings in ways that don't hurt him or anyone else. Suggest he hits a pillow, throws a ball against a wall, walks the dog, calls a friend on the phone, or has a good cry.

- ✔ **Talk about the situation.** Let your child discuss things with anyone he respects – a parent, grandparent, or another adult.

- ✔ **Get perspective.** Have your child consider whether the situation is really worth getting angry and upset about. Ask your child to think about what he can learn from the experience and how he can do better next time.

People often judge themselves too harshly. Remind your child that failing at something doesn't mean that you're a failure at everything. Some of the most successful people in the world have made loads of mistakes. Thomas Edison invented more than 10,000 electric light bulbs before he arrived at a design that actually worked. J.K. Rowling, author of the Harry Potter books, was rejected dozens of times by publishers before achieving success. Colonel Sanders, of Kentucky Fried Chicken fame, was rejected hundreds of times by restaurateurs who thought his idea was silly.

Help your child to dust himself off to fight another day. It's not how far you fall, but how high you bounce back that counts!

# *Handling embarrassment*

All children feel embarrassed at some time, but this emotion can be particularly relevant for children going through adolescence when they feel more self-conscious than usual at school.

Help your child handle those red-faced moments by pointing out the following:

- ✔ The situation is only temporary – it will go away.

- ✔ Things are probably a lot worse inside his head. Most people don't even notice.

- ✔ Keep moving forward – and just let the embarrassing moment go.

- ✔ Laugh at himself. Okay, it was a really cringey moment but make a story out of it and laugh at it.

Consider how some American presidents have handled their embarrassing moments:

- ✔ When President George W. Bush choked on a pretzel and passed out, he was making jokes about it before anybody else. The first time he faced the news cameras after his embarrassing moment, he joked that he should have listened to his mum when she told him to chew his food.

- ✔ When President George H.W. Bush (his dad) was visiting Japan, he threw up at the dinner table, right in front of the Japanese Prime Minister. Later he smiled for the cameras and cracked jokes about his dry cleaning bills.

Both of these men took their embarrassing moments and turned them into harmless jokes by laughing about them and showing everyone that they weren't bothered or upset. Your child may not think he's as smooth or quick, but he may find that if he relaxes and turns his mortifying moments into jokes, the cruel people who want to make fun of him don't have the opportunity. After all, why would they bother to poke fun at him when he's already laughed about it himself?

# Chapter 12

# Helping Your Child Cope with Individual Problems

Children are all unique and special and have their own set of troubles or worries that may include bedwetting, bad dreams, phobias, or bullying. This chapter takes a look at ways to help and support you and your child if you experience any of these problems within your family.

## Coping with Bad Dreams

Everyone gets a bad dream or a nightmare from time to time, so if your child has a nightmare it's perfectly normal. Bad dreams may be frightening but they are quite usual.

### Understanding dreams and nightmares

Dreams happen during the REM or Rapid Eye Movement stage of sleep when your eyes move very quickly back and forth. If your child wakes up during the REM stage, he or she is likely to remember a bad dream and feel very scared or upset.

The stressful things that happen during the day can turn your child's dream into a nightmare – this is nature's way of relieving the pressure of a busy day. Pressures usually include dealing with the normal problems of school, homework, friendships, or new situations. Major changes in a child's life, such as a divorce, a house move, or a death in the family, can trigger an increase in bad dreams. Other reasons for bad dreams include watching scary, violent, or inappropriate films or reading scary books just before bedtime. Also, a high temperature, new medicine, or food allergy can all have the same effect.

## Preventing nightmares

Parents can help minimise nightmares, particularly with younger children, by making going to bed a happy event.

Make time to settle your child down, read her a happy story, relax and chat together, tuck your child in, and leave her with a happy thought to think about while falling asleep.

If you use your child's bedroom as a place of punishment – a place she is sent every time she does something naughty – your child is unlikely to feel relaxed about going to bed at night. Think of another place to sit for 'time out' instead of in her bedroom.

Make sure older children have a regular bedtime and relaxing routines without too much stimulation from computer games, loud exciting DVDs, or the Playstation last thing at night. Also make sure they don't watch inappropriate TV in their rooms or listen to adult radio stations after the watershed, because this can lead to nightmares.

## Dealing with night terrors

Sometimes toddlers experience *night terrors*, which are partial wakenings from deep sleep usually early in the night. Don't panic; night terrors are fairly common. In fact, they are more frightening for you than they are for children because they usually remember nothing the next day. Night terrors tend to run in families, and boys seem to be more prone to them than girls. Sometimes night terrors can last until the early teens, but they seem to just stop on their own.

During a night terror, your child won't recognise you or respond to you, even if she has her eyes open. She may scream, shake, lash out and even run around. You need to stay calm. Settle your child back in bed and stay quietly with her until she quiets down. Never wake your child from a night terror, shout, or shake her; doing so can frighten your child. Also, be aware that a night terror can last up to an hour, so be patient.

Although she may seem too young, your child may be suffering from stress. Find out what is worrying your child gently because continual night terrors can be a sign of illness, so seek medical advice, especially if you notice drooling, jerking, or stiffening during the terror.

Following are practical tips for responding to night terrors.

- ✔ Provide your toddler with a safe place to sleep. Pick up toys, lock or bar the windows, and use a stair gate.

- ✔ Never put a child who has night terrors on the top bunk.

- ✔ Warn babysitters and other people who may be with your child at night, so they don't overreact.

- ✔ Sleeping with a cuddly toy or a favourite blanket helps some children feel more secure.

- ✔ Get into a regular bedtime routine, so your child feels relaxed and comfortable by the familiarity.

- ✔ Use a nightlight. Even if your child has given up on having a nightlight, re-introduce it. If your child wakes up from a nightmare, being able to see familiar things is reassuring.

- ✔ Keep your door open. Your child will feel secure knowing that you are close by and can be reached easily.

- ✔ Let your child climb into bed with a brother or sister or yourself to help reassure her.

I remember having my bedroom quite a distance from my Mum and Dad's when I was 9 years old, and it made me feel very nervous sometimes going to bed knowing that I had to walk through a corridor, sitting room, and another corridor to reach them if I had a bad dream. So bear that in mind when you are deciding which rooms are best for your children. Keep them near you and make your room easily accessible.

## *What if the nightmares won't go away?*

Most of the time nightmares aren't a big problem, and your child benefits just from knowing that you are around to reassure and give a hug. But in some cases the bad dreams go on for too long. Here are some ideas to help:

- ✔ Keep a Dream Diary. Have your child write down her dreams – good and bad – so you both can track them. Look for patterns before going to sleep. If you notice a pattern, you can change some things around to try to find a solution.

- ✔ Get your child to rewrite her dream, giving it a happier ending.

- ✔ Encourage your child to draw a picture of the bad dream and rip it up.

- ✔ If you are worried by your child's recurrent bad dreams, talk to your doctor who can help by possibly recommending a sleep clinic.

Everyone has nightmares sometimes. Teach your child that nightmares are not real and can't hurt her. Reassure her that dreaming about something doesn't mean that it will happen in real life, nor does it mean that she is a bad person who wants to do bad or scary things.

# *Beating Bedwetting*

Research on bedwetting (or *nocturnal enuresis*, as it is technically known) suggests that most children achieve dry nights by the age of 4 – but the age at which children achieve consistent dry nights is variable.

## *Knowing the facts*

For the vast majority of children, wetting the bed is simply an indication that their bladder control is slower to develop.

One in seven 7-year olds is a regular bedwetter. Fortunately, 90 per cent of children who wet the bed at 7 years have stopped by their early teens. Additionally, research shows:

- ✔ Bedwetting often runs in families.

- ✔ Boys are twice as likely as girls to wet their beds.

- ✔ Bedwetting is not usually an indication of an emotional problem.

✔ Bedwetting is associated with physical problems in only 1 per cent of cases.

✔ By puberty, the vast majority of children who wet their beds have grown out of it.

Although bedwetting is not usually related to any emotional factors, some events are often associated with bedwetting, including:

✔ Any major change in your family due to death, separation, or divorce.

✔ Any major trauma the child may have suffered or witnessed.

✔ A temporary separation from either parent for one or more months.

✔ The arrival of a new sibling in the family.

✔ Moving to a new house.

✔ Repeated admissions to hospital due to illness.

✔ Excessive pressure from parents to have dry nights and negative reactions when the child wets the bed.

✔ Teasing from siblings over wet nights.

## *Understanding the situation*

You must handle bedwetting sensitively and compassionately – it really doesn't respond to negative reactions from you. Disapproving or punishing your child for being wet can make the problem much worse and can, in the long term, damage your child's self-esteem. So praise and encouragement is very important in dealing with this problem.

For the majority of children who wet the bed, no major treatment is necessary, but a practical and supportive attitude from you helps your child while she naturally outgrows this problem.

Children who are slow to achieve dry nights are acutely aware of the problem, especially older children. Always be sympathetic and understanding, which can be really difficult as you wash the bed for the fourth time in a week.

Try putting the situation in perspective: Try to see the world from the eyes of your child. How does your child feel? What does she hear when she has a wet bed? What does your child see from the look on your face to the way your body moves when you come into her room? What does it feel like to be an older child waking up in a wet, cold bed?

Many children admit that bedwetting makes their lives miserable and are very keen and motivated to get help. If your child is suffering a crisis of confidence and is depressed or fed up about her bedwetting, consider discussing the problem with your doctor.

Your child may be too embarrassed to attend the doctor's appointment, so don't force her to go. Instead, talk things over with your doctor or health visitor who can advise you on the best approach to take with your child.

Older children with this problem are often reluctant to discuss it, even with you. They need reassurance that none of their friends will be told about the situation. Often, older children who wet the bed feel they are the only ones in the world with this problem.

Find a good time when you are both relaxed and have a positive talk about how you and your child can go through this phase together. Reassure your child that you understand, aren't judging or thinking she is 'babyish.' Explain to your child that her bladder isn't quite developed and strong just yet.

## Using practical approaches to stop bedwetting

A number of methods have been developed that can help bedwetting children, which I cover in this section.

Whichever approach you try, consider using plastic mattresses and pillows to aid in clean up and help keep your child's room smelling fresh. You can also buy mattress protectors to pop on top of the mattress.

### Bladder training

Night-time wetting can be helped by exercises to strengthen and increase the capacity of your child's bladder.

Some children who wet the bed have been found to have small bladder capacity, so training your child to resist the immediate urge to go to the toilet and gradually increase the time between visits to the bathroom can help to increase her bladder size. Stopping urine in midstream can help strengthen the bladder muscles. (This reminds me of the similar advice I received when I was pregnant!)

Bladder training exercises should be done under the guidance of your doctor.

### *Food/drink modification*

Changing eating and drinking habits can also have a positive effect. Avoid the foods and drinks that contain caffeine before bedtime (chocolate and fizzy drinks) because caffeine is a diuretic that causes the body to eliminate water through urinating, which may contribute to wetting the bed at night.

Limiting the amount of any fluids in the few hours before bedtime is also a good idea.

### *Night lifting*

*Night lifting* involves you bringing your child to the bathroom sometime during the night.

This technique helps some children but doesn't help others. Some professionals argue that children can become dependent on parents waking them and that it doesn't encourage children to take responsibility for waking themselves up. It has also been suggested that, rather than teaching the child to reduce urinating at night, it encourages them to urinate.

But for those children who sleep very deeply, night lifting may help. Try it and make up your own mind.

### *Enuresis alarms*

Enuresis alarms usually consist of two pads of wire mesh that are placed on a child's bed between two sheets. The pads are attached to an alarm and when a child wets during the night, the circuit is connected, which activates the alarm. Upon hearing the alarm, the child gets up, goes to the bathroom, and then remakes the bed with a parent's help before going back to sleep.

The rationale behind this method is that eventually the child will come to associate the sensation of urinating with waking up. But it does take a lot of patience on a parent's part to get up in the middle of the night on a regular basis to help change the bed. Also, if a child is a deep sleeper, the parents wake up before the child.

Smaller alarms have come on the market recently. These portable alarms are placed in a child's underwear, or, if preferred, sandwiched between two pairs of underwear, and are attached by wire to a unit clipped to the neck of a child's pyjamas or nightdress.

Before using the alarm, make sure your child gets to hear the alarm, so she isn't frightened the first time it goes off during the night.

Alarms are useful with children aged 6 and older and have a good success rate and fewer relapses than medication. However, the child and parents need to be motivated and patient because alarms can take months to work.

### Medication

Sometimes your doctor can give you a prescription of tablets for a short time if your child is going away on a school trip or has a birthday party sleepover at a friend's house. Although medication is useful to give you and your child a break, using medication isn't an appropriate long-term solution. Many children relapse after stopping taking medication.

### Star charts

Star charts can be a fun way to help focus younger children on their successes.

Make (or purchase) a special chart that shows the days of the week. Make your child either colour in or put a sticker on each dry night she achieves. Really praise your child for each dry night. Perhaps after a short time – for example, three nights in a row – give your child a reward like an extra 10 minutes watching a favourite television programme, inviting a friend over for a day, or whatever feels like a treat to your child.

Star charts can be really effective because they emphasise your child's achievements rather than her failures and provide a record of progress for both of you to celebrate.

### Hypnotherapy

Hypnotherapy involves the use of hypnosis for the treatment and relief of a variety of physiological, emotional, habitual, and psychological problems. Children prove to be excellent subjects for treatments involving hypnosis because they are so adept at using their imaginations.

Some of the most frequent problems where hypnotherapy can help are bedwetting, nail biting, thumb sucking, anxiety, panic, lack of concentration, behavioural problems at home or at school, test and exam nerves, sleeping difficulties, lack of confidence, and fears and phobias.

Hypnotherapy works well for bedwetting that involves anxiety and stress. A remarkable number of children respond well to specially written CDs.

The advantage of hypnotherapy is it is natural and safe. No drugs are involved, and children enjoy listening to the CDs as they drift off to sleep.

If you're interested in exploring this method, visit `www.firstwayforward cds.com` for CDs targeted for children aged 6 to 9 years and 10 to 15 years.

# Defeating Bullying

Bullying is an age-old problem that is still rife in its various forms throughout schools today. The good news is that the government, headteachers, and school governors are increasingly aware of it. Schools are now legally obliged to implement anti-bullying strategies called 'Don't Suffer in Silence'.

I feel very strongly about this issue because I was bullied in my first year at secondary school and developed alopecia (hair loss) as a result. I thought the bullying must be my fault and didn't want to bother anyone with my 'little problem'. After I told my parents, they went to the school and the issue was dealt with appropriately. I felt an enormous sense of relief.

Don't assume your child isn't the sort who gets bullied. No typical victim of bullying exists. Also, you sadly can't assume that your child will confide in you if she's being bullied. Many kids (myself included) don't want to tell anyone at first because they feel embarrassed and ashamed and hope that the problem will just go away.

If you're a parent of a child who bullies, refer to Chapter 10, where I provide some specific tips for raising and disciplining these children.

## Identifying the telltale signs of bullying tactics

Last year, 31,000 children called Childline (`www.childline.org.uk`), a free helpline for children in trouble or danger, to report bullying incidences – making bullying the service's most common problem. Of the thousands of bullying cases that get reported, 49 per cent involve girls, and 51 per cent involve boys. Forty per cent involve physical violence. Sometimes the consequences of bullying can be tragic – as many as 16 children a year in the UK commit suicide. As a parent, you must address bullying immediately because you can do positive and practical things to help solve the problem.

Bullying can be verbal, physical, or relationship based. (*Relationship-based bullying* involves being left out or having nasty gossip passed around about you; young teenagers can suffer especially from this type of bullying.)

Bullying can take the forms of pushing, shoving, spreading bad and malicious rumours, keeping certain people 'out on a limb,' teasing in a mean way, sending unkind or threatening e-mails or text messages, posting nasty pictures or messages on other people's blogs or Web sites, or using someone else's username to spread rumours or lies.

### Who gets bullied?

Bullies pick on anyone who is different from them in some way. The differences may be as simple as:

✔ Wearing the wrong trainers, having a 'naff' haircut, or dressing differently.

✔ Being from an ethnic minority.

✔ Having a different accent or talking in a 'posh' accent.

✔ Being a high achiever and being considered 'clever' – or the opposite, being seen as 'thick' and a low achiever.

✔ Being different in height, weight, or any other appearance aspect.

### Behaviour of the bullied

If your child is being bullied, her behaviour can change in some way. These changes may include:

✔ Altering appearance in some way to try to blend in.

✔ Nervous and anxious behaviour.

✔ Nightmares.

✔ Signs and symptoms of low self-esteem and even depression (refer to Chapter 6).

✔ Frequent mystery illnesses and other ploys to stay off school.

✔ Changing usual ways to or from school.

✔ Noticeable deterioration or change in school work.

✔ Loss of appetite.

✔ Unexplained loss of pocket money (which may have been stolen or used to pay off bullies).

✔ Truancy from school.

# Dispelling myths about bullying

Because most people have been bullied at some point in their lives, many people have easy – and unfortunately ineffective or outright harmful – responses to bullying. Following are some myths about bullying:

✔ **'I was bullied at school, and it didn't do me any harm.'** Interestingly, this statement is often said quite aggressively, as if the person is still ashamed. They may have forgotten how much pain they really suffered, but it is often still there.

✔ **'You just have to learn to stand up for yourself.'** This does not practically support your child. Asking for help is not a sign of weakness. Before children often say anything, they have reached the end of their tethers.

✔ **'Hit him or her back even harder.'** Bullies are often bigger than the people they pick on, so hitting back can result in a serious injury. Also this sends out the message that hitting and violence are acceptable ways to behave.

✔ **'Sticks and stones may break your bones, but names can never hurt you.'** Name calling lasts forever in people's memories, even when it is innocent teasing. So scars from bullying go even deeper and remain even longer.

✔ **'It's character building.'** Bullying damages your child's self-esteem and can make your child distrustful, reserved, and shy – not the sort of character you want to build in your child.

✔ **'That's not bullying – that sounds like teasing to me.'** Taunting is not teasing. After it gets beyond the stage of 'a bit of fun', it should be stopped.

Relatives, siblings, and friends may mean well but some of the things they say are wrong! Bullying is *never* a good thing because it damages both the victim and the bully.

If you're worried that your child is being bullied, ask her directly. Children are often afraid to open up and admit they are being bullied, so be prepared that your child may deny it the first time you raise it. Encourage your child to talk to you when she is relaxed or when you're doing something casual together like driving somewhere in the car. Always take whatever your child says seriously – that way you can find out exactly what has been going on.

## Responding to bullying

Don't ignore bullying – it won't go away by itself. Children need to know that bullying is *not* their faults and that *no one* deserves to be bullied.

Children who have been bullied and have kept it a secret feel a terrible sense of being alone. After your child confides in you, the first thing you must do is to *reassure* her that from now on she is *not* alone. Tell your child that you, family, and friends are on her side completely. Remind her that the school is completely on her side, too.

Here are some practical ways to help your child respond to bullying:

- **Don't promise to keep the bullying a secret.** Reassure your child that you will help her sort out the problem calmly, but sometimes you must intervene at school.

- **Don't ring up the bully's parents.** Doing so only inflames the situation.

- **Always build up your child's self-esteem.** Bullied children need your reassurance and rock solid support because bullying can be a very traumatic experience. Tell your child that you love her very much and that you are 100 per cent on her side. Reassure your child that the situation is not her fault.

- **Help your child develop better social skills.** Consider whether your child is doing anything that might lend itself to being a victim of bullying and try to remedy the situation. The solution may be as simple as helping your child play more appropriately with other children.

- **Develop effective responses and actions to use when being bullied.** Some ideas include:

    - **Ignoring taunts:** The bully has nothing to respond to and will eventually give up.

    - **Role playing:** Work through scenarios at home with your child to get used to practising her response.

    - **Body language:** Develop more assertive and confident ways to stand or walk – work on being able to look the bully in the eyes.

    - **Quick retorts:** Think up and practise quick responses to taunts that are funny, or at least show that your child has an answer for them.

For example, a good plan for responding to bullying in an assertive way might be: Stand in a strong but not threatening way, look the bully in the eye, count silently to five, say something like: 'I don't like that and I want you to stop', and then walk away.

If these responses don't come easily to your child, teach her to fake it till she makes it.

## Handling hurtful comments

Kids say some terrible things to one another. Here are some strategies to deal with these comments in a healthy, effective manner. Encourage your child to:

✔ Pretend not to hear the comments.

✔ Use positive self-talk, which is a repeated silent message such as 'That's their problem not mine' or 'I'm OK,' to distract herself from negative emotions.

✔ Imagine an invisible shield or a snuggly sleeping bag surrounding her. Imagine all the negative remarks just bouncing off.

✔ Use 'distraction' responses, such as 'maybe' or 'if you say so,' which can confuse the bully.

Practise these techniques with your child.

✔ **Minimise opportunities for bullying.** Encourage your child not to take anything of value into school and not to hang around the toilets or changing rooms alone. Teach your child to stay in groups of friends and give the bully the money or item if she is truly being threatened. (Better to be safe than badly injured.)

✔ **Invite friends round.** Children who have been bullied lose their confidence around other children and don't trust them as easily. Finding like-minded children helps your child feel normal in her interests, thus building her self-confidence. Encourage your child to go out of her usual circle to make new friends – drama classes, swimming, Judo, or whatever your child seems interested in.

✔ **Don't let your child mope.** Give your child plenty of things to occupy her mind. Help your child develop a hobby or new skill. Encourage something that your son or daughter is already good at and develop it further.

✔ **Encourage your child to tell someone she trusts.** A teacher, parent, or adult friend can help listen to and help your child when you're not around.

✔ **Encourage your child to keep a record of what happens.** See the section 'Keeping a bullying diary' for ideas on keeping track of bullying behaviours. Also, remind your child to keep nasty texts or e-mails to show as proof of bullying.

## Bullying-related resources

Most children find it really useful to realise that they're not the only ones being bullied. Some wonderful Web sites and helplines support children. Some great books with bullying as the theme are available as well to help your kid come to terms with what has happened to her.

Some useful online resources about bullying include:

- ✔ **Kidscape** (www.kidscape.org.uk; 020 7730 3300; open Monday to Friday between 10am and 4pm) offers information and support to young people and parents, including action steps to take.

- ✔ **Parentline Plus** (www.parentlineplus.org.uk; 0808 800 2222) provides advice for parents on supporting a child who is being bullied.

- ✔ **Bullying** (www.bullying.co.uk) offers good advice for children on how to recognise bullying and what to do if you are a victim or know of someone who is. For those desiring confidentiality, help is available on the site via e-mail.

- ✔ **Don't Suffer in Silence** (www.dfes.gov.uk/bullying) has produced a video and case studies to aid the teaching of anti-bullying policies. Celebrities such as Patsy Palmer describe their experiences of being bullied.

- ✔ **Childline** (www.childline.org.uk; 0800 11 11) has helped hundreds of thousands of children in trouble or danger. If you can't face ringing them, check out the Web site with fact sheets on many subjects including bullying.

- ✔ **Victim Support** (www.victimsupport.org.uk; 0845 30 30 900) helps people cope with the effects of crime. There are separate advice sections for people living in England and Wales, Scotland, and Northern Ireland.

Fiction for younger readers:

- ✔ *The Willow Street Kids Beat the Bullies* by Michele Elliott (Macmillan)

- ✔ *Hope and the Bullies* by Louise Alexander (Young Voice)

- ✔ *Willy the Champ* by Anthony Browne (Walker Books)

Fiction for older readers:

- ✔ *Fat Boy Swim* by Catherine Forde (Egmont)

- ✔ *Blubber* by Judy Blume (Macmillan)

- ✔ *Ganging Up* by Alan Gibbons (Orion)

- ✔ *Whose Side Are You On?* by Alan Gibbons (Collins)

## Keeping a bullying diary

Keeping an accurate, detailed account of the incidents of bullying helps both your child and the school or the police because having concrete evidence of the times, places, and witnesses ensures something is done about the bullying.

For a bullying diary to be effective, your child needs to write down as much detail as she can about what happened, including:

- ✔ The date and time of the incident.
- ✔ What exactly happened? List and clearly describe what was said or done.
- ✔ Who was involved in the bullying? List all known names – or a description of clothes, faces, height, or size.
- ✔ Where did the bullying take place? In school, on the playground, on the way home, in the toilets, and so on.
- ✔ Was anything taken, damaged, or broken?
- ✔ Where were you hurt?
- ✔ Was anyone else with you or did someone else see what happened?

A free, downloadable version of a Bullying Diary is available at my Web site, www.positive-parents.com.

Teach your children to report bullying if they see it happening to others because they can help put a stop to it. Remind them that they needn't feel afraid of doing the right thing. They are not being 'snitches' or 'grasses.' Explain that even though just standing by may be easier, everyone needs a little help from time to time. Ask them to imagine how they would feel if it were them.

Teach your children to be discrete in how they tell appropriate adults, including teachers, school counsellors, school nurses, a parent, or anyone they trust and feel safe with.

# Dealing with Phobias

*Phobias* are fears, but they are not the same as the usual fears that children have, like passing a barking dog in the street, passing exams, or being afraid of thunder and lightning. A phobia is different because it is an extremely strong fear of a situation or thing that doesn't go away.

Phobias can start in childhood for no apparent reason, or they emerge after traumatic events like bereavement or divorce. Sometimes a phobia develops from a bad experience as an attempt to make sense of the unexpected and intense anxiety or panic.

# Defining different kinds of phobias

One of the most common phobias is *social phobia*, where your child is scared of being embarrassed in front of other people. This is not the same as just being shy because a child with a social phobia is scared to talk to a teacher, or is afraid to walk across the classroom if she needs to go to the toilet. Children with social phobia want to make friends but they can't control or overcome their fear of being with others.

Other common phobias that a lot of people suffer from include:

- Fear of spiders (arachnophobia)
- Fear of thunder and lightning (astraphobia)
- Fear of heights (acrophobia)
- Fear of the dentist (dental phobia)
- Fear of swimming (hydrophobia)

More unusual and complex phobias include:

- Fear of leaving home or entering open spaces (agoraphobia)
- Fear of enclosed or crowded places (claustrophobia)
- Fear of social gatherings or attracting attention (social phobia)

With some phobias there may be frightening thoughts that trigger the response like 'This plane might crash, I'm trapped, I must get out.' However, with other phobias, identifying the thoughts associated with the anxiety is much harder. (For example, it is unlikely that a child frightened of spiders is afraid of making a fool of themselves in front of the spider.) With these phobias, the cause seems to be explained more as a learned anxiety response which has become associated with the feared object.

If children are forced into the situation that frightens them, they can have panic attacks, which can be distressing for everyone. Panic attacks can involve sweating, shaking, rapid breathing, chest pains, and dizziness. A panic attack can make a child feel that something awful is going to happen – or that the child can't escape or may lose control. Panic attacks usually only last a short time but can seem to last much longer.

# Treating phobias

You only need to do something about your child's phobia if it is severe or is interfering with her life and distressing her. Often, simply avoiding the object of a fear is fine.

If you feel the phobia is interfering with your child's normal life, see your doctor first. In many cases, your doctor can suggest a visit to a psychologist, psychiatrist, or therapist.

The following sections cover some common approaches to helping children respond to phobias.

### Hypnotherapy

Like bedwetting, hypnotherapy can be an effective way to help a child overcome her fears. See 'Hypnotherapy' in the preceding section on bedwetting.

### Cognitive behavioural therapy

*Cognitive behavioural therapy* (CBT) can be a practical form of treatment to help children develop problem-solving techniques for themselves. The term cognitive behavioural therapy sounds daunting, but put simply, CBT looks at the two components in treating a phobia effectively:

- ✔ Confronting the feared situation.
- ✔ Dealing with any frightening thoughts that are associated with the anxiety.

These two parts are linked because the way children think and feel affects how they behave and vice versa.

CBT is a talking therapy. The main focus is on getting a child to learn to talk through her experiences, feelings, and typical behaviour. A therapist identifies problem areas and helps a child develop more positive ways of dealing with tricky issues, feelings, or situations. CBT is practical and hands-on – but it requires commitment because the patient must be prepared to carry out the suggestions between sessions. Parents can usually attend CBT sessions with their child.

Often, children are asked to keep a diary of their thoughts, feelings, and behaviours, in particular in relation to situations they find stressful. Their entries are then discussed in detail with the therapist, and the therapist will teach ways of turning the scary thoughts into more positive, helpful ones.

CBT can effectively help some children, but, like other approaches, it's not a guaranteed successful treatment for everyone. CBT doesn't provide a quick solution; it takes time, commitment, and a lot of hard work to learn new patterns of thinking and acting. Children who are extremely impulsive and can't cope with thinking through a situation before they react may find the therapy quite difficult. Some research suggests that CBT is more effective when used in conjunction with medication.

# Surviving Puberty

Puberty is the bridge between being a kid and becoming an adult. As your child crosses this bridge, her body and feelings change a lot. Puberty means major changes physically and emotionally – and these many changes are perfectly normal! Your child also may feel differently about you, your family, friends, and classmates – she may start to view life in a completely new or different way.

Talk about the issues of puberty with your child in a relaxed, informed, and matter of fact manner. Not all of your child's information comes from reliable sources. Information doesn't just come from round the back of the bike sheds today; children are now far more exposed to information about sex and relationships through TV, the Internet, films, and radio. By the time your child approaches puberty, she may be familiar with some advanced ideas, but not really be emotionally equipped to handle the information.

Timing is everything. Just as it helps adults to know what to expect with changes, your child should know about puberty beforehand. Your child can have a much smoother experience if she knows about the changes that puberty causes *before* they happen. If you and your child talk ahead of time, your son or daughter knows what to expect and is less likely to be embarrassed or frightened by changes in physical appearance or emotional outbursts due to hormones. If you're really not comfortable talking about these issues, find a friend or other family member who is and ask them to get involved.

# Physical changes

Usually, puberty starts between ages 8 and 13 in girls and ages 10 and 15 in boys. Some children begin a bit earlier or later than these figures and can experience puberty-related changes at any point during those years. (In fact, one in six girls now reaches puberty before the age of 8.) All this may help explain why some children still look like young kids whereas others look more like adults.

Puberty is a very confusing and awkward time for all teenagers. Your child may feel weird and different. Explain to her that the way she is feeling is perfectly normal.

Expect some of the following physical changes for both boys and girls:

- They gain weight and grow taller.
- They grow more body hair.
- They speak with deeper, stronger voices.
- They often develop acne or spots.

## Emotional changes

Along with the many physical changes, your child will also experience many emotional changes. Most of these emotional changes are a result of all the physical changes and trying to adjust to them.

Both boys and girls experience the following during puberty:

- Moodiness. Changes in hormone levels (oestrogen for girls and testosterone for boys) can cause mood swings.
- Concern about physical appearances. Boys and girls compare their bodies to other people and want to know what others think about them in general.
- Feelings of awkwardness or embarrassment, especially in times of change.
- Feelings of sexual attraction and arousal very easily.
- Sexual curiosity. Boys and girls feel attraction towards people of the opposite or same sex.
- Intense, emotional reactions to situations.
- Seeking to gain more independence from parents.

# What to expect – for boys

Puberty is a very confusing and awkward time for boys. Early bloomers may feel awkward or shy being the subject of stares and jibes from their class-mates. So be understanding and careful with your words or family teasing.

Boys commonly experience the following changes:

- ✔ A growth spurt between 13 and 14 years old (on average)
- ✔ Ears, hands, and feet grow larger
- ✔ Penises and scrotums get larger (around 12 years old, on average)
- ✔ Very sensitive testicles
- ✔ More frequent erections
- ✔ Ejaculations and 'wet dreams'
- ✔ Larger muscles and broader shoulders

For boys, ejaculation is the first sign that they are going through puberty. *Ejaculation* is the release of semen (or cum) through the penis. Ejaculation may occur because of masturbation (self-stimulation, when someone becomes aroused by touching him or herself). Ejaculation also can occur involuntarily while a boy is sleeping. This is called a *wet dream*. It is very normal for this to happen.

# What to expect – for girls

Puberty is also a very confusing and awkward time for girls. Girls may begin puberty as early as 9, and it can be upsetting if your daughter is the first one to get a bra, for example. She may feel alone and awkward or like all eyes are on her in the school changing room, on the other hand she may be delighted to be the first one.

Girls commonly experience the following changes:

- ✔ A growth spurt around age 11 (on average)
- ✔ Breasts grow larger, around age 11
- ✔ Development of rounder, wider hips and narrower waists
- ✔ Start menstruation (periods) around age 13 (sometimes sooner, some-times later) or an irregular and inconsistent vaginal discharge (later becoming regular and consistent)

For girls, their first menstruation, or period, is a sign that they have reached puberty. This is a normal sign that occurs in *all* healthy girls. Menstruation lets you know you have a normal, functioning reproductive system.

Parents should talk to their daughters (and sons) about what to expect related to menstruation. Be sure to cover the following topics:

- Menstruation is a monthly discharge of blood and tissue from the uterus through the vagina.

- Depending on individual body development and hormone levels, a girl's first menstrual cycle may begin at any time.

- The first menstrual period is called *menarche* (meh-NAR-key).

- The first few cycles are irregular but become regular over time, usually occurring every 28 days or so.

- One menstrual period may last between two and seven days.

- During one menstrual period, it's typical for one-half to one cup of blood and tissue to be discharged from start to finish.

- Some girls get *premenstrual syndrome* (PMS) right before their period. Symptoms of PMS include cramps and irritability and are also driven by hormones.

Girls need tampons or sanitary pads to absorb the blood flow. Buy extra tampons or pads so they are on hand whenever needed. Have some at home, but don't forget to remind your daughter to take some with her to school in a purse or book bag, and to keep them anywhere else that she may need them. If your daughter's menstrual period comes on suddenly or when she's not home, encourage her to always have something available to absorb the flow. Thinking ahead and being prepared can really save your daughter a lot of potential embarrassment.

Celebrate the beginnings of having a period with your daughter. She will eventually appreciate it as a symbol of her womanhood. This is also an *excellent* time to discuss the responsibilities involved from now on regarding contraception.

## *Knowing what to say*

Most children receive some sex education at school, but in some schools the lessons are segregated. The girls mainly hear about periods and bras, while the boys hear about erections and changing voices. Girls need to know about the changes boys go through, just as boys must learn about the changes affecting girls.

Check with your child's teacher about his or her lesson plans so you know what gaps need to be filled. It may help you ease into a conversation if you co-ordinate your talks with your child with these school lessons.

When talking to your child about puberty, offer reassurance that all the changes are normal. Puberty brings about so many changes that your child can easily feel insecure. Many adolescents express insecurity about their appearance as they go through puberty, but they need to know that everyone goes through the same things and that there's a huge amount of normal variation in the timing of these events. Acne, mood changes, growth spurts, and hormonal changes are all part of growing up.

Reassure your child that puberty is not a race. Everyone goes through it, but not always at the same pace.

Your child, whether a boy or a girl, needs to know the following about puberty:

- ✔ Girls and boys get pubic hair and underarm hair, and their leg hair becomes thicker and darker.
- ✔ Girls become more rounded, especially in the hips and legs.
- ✔ Girls' breasts begin to swell and then grow.
- ✔ When a girl begins menstruating, once a month her uterine lining fills with blood in preparation for a fertilized egg. If the egg isn't fertilized, she has a period. If it is fertilized, she becomes pregnant.
- ✔ A girl's period may last 3 days to a week, and she can use sanitary napkins (pads) or tampons to absorb the blood.
- ✔ Boys' penises and testicles grow larger.
- ✔ Boys' voices change and become deeper.
- ✔ Boys sometimes have wet dreams, which means they ejaculate in their sleep.

## Answering common questions

Not surprisingly, kids usually have lots of questions as they learn about puberty. Ensure you give your child the time and opportunity to ask questions – and answer her questions as honestly and thoroughly as possible.

Make time to talk and let your child know that you're available any time – even if you've just settled down to eat or want to ring a friend. Try to address issues in a relaxed and matter of fact way. Just as it can be embarrassing or difficult for you to talk about these sensitive topics, your child may hesitate to come to you. As a parent, your job is to discuss puberty – and the feelings associated with these changes – as openly as possible with your child. Tell your child that you're really glad she came to you to ask questions, to make it easier for her to come to you for further answers. Be aware that the question, 'Am I normal?' is often hiding behind questions about sexual development and sexual feelings. Reassure your children as often as possible.

You make these discussions easier if *you* are confident that you know the subject matter. Before you answer your child's questions, make sure your own questions about puberty have been answered. If you're not entirely comfortable having a conversation about puberty with your child, practise what you want to say first or ask your child's teacher for advice. Let your child know that it's a little uncomfortable for you, but it's an important talk to have.

Don't wait until your children ask questions because they may never ask. You need to decide what is important for them to know and then tell them before a crisis occurs. You are the primary sexuality educator of your children, but talking about sexual matters is often hard. Find quiet moments to chat and even make use of television shows and magazines. Say something like, 'I think that programme sends the right/wrong message. Let me tell you what I believe.'

Some of the most common questions (and some possible responses) include:

- ✔ **What is masturbation?** Many parents are particularly embarrassed and uncomfortable talking about masturbation. It may have been a taboo subject when you were growing up and, because of religious or moral beliefs, you may think it's wrong. Even if you have objections to masturbation, let your teen know that it is normal and natural to be interested in exploring her own body. Then you can go on to explain your own values. Try not to use shame or guilt, however, which are far more likely to produce fear and confusion in your teen than to change her behaviour.

- ✔ **What do I need to know about contraception and 'safer' sex?** Most parents want their teens to postpone sexual involvement until they're older and more mature, and some parents feel that by talking about contraception, they're actively encouraging their child to have sex. In fact, teens who are informed tend to delay sexual involvement longer than those who aren't. Your teen may decide to try sexual intercourse, whatever you say. A sexually active teen needs to know the risks and benefits of different contraceptive techniques and how to reduce the risk of getting pregnant, AIDS, and other STDs.

A combination of talking and providing printed material is the best strategy. Ask your local sexual health clinic or your GP's practice for leaflets, and see *The Parentalk Guide to Your Child and Sex* by Steve Chalke (Hodder and Stoughton). But don't simply give them to your teen. Read them yourself and be ready for questions and a discussion as your child makes sense of how she feels about this important issue.

✔ **What is this hard lump in my breast?** Girls (and boys) sometimes notice small, sometimes tender, lumps under their nipples as their breasts are beginning to develop. This is perfectly normal. The firmness and tenderness goes away in time as girls' breasts continue to enlarge.

✔ **Why are my breasts so small (or so large)?** Breast size is hereditary, and your daughter needs to be reassured that, big or small, all breasts are beautiful. Size doesn't affect your daughter's attractiveness or her ability to breast-feed if she becomes a mother.

✔ **Why is my penis so small (or so large)?** Reassure your son that the size of the penis when erect has nothing to do with the size of the penis when it's not.

✔ **Why don't I have pubic hair yet?** Everyone develops pubic hair, but some teens are naturally hairier than others, and some get hair later than others. Just as with breast size or height, the amount depends on each individual.

If your child continues to have questions or concerns about her development that you can't answer, a visit to your child's doctor may help provide reassurance. The following Web sites can help as well:

✔ www.kidshealth.org

✔ www.iwannaknow.org

✔ www.coolnurse.com/puberty.htm

# Chapter 13

# Helping Your Child Cope with Bigger Issues

*B*ringing up children isn't an exact science. Many parents do encounter common themes such as finding effective ways to discipline their children or helping build their self-esteem, but other, more specific issues, have a great impact on family life, such as getting divorced, becoming a stepfamily, or coping with sibling rivalry. In this chapter I help you develop your confidence and skills when dealing with these more specific experiences.

## Navigating through Divorce

A bad marriage can make parenting – and life in general – stressful. The loss of the family structure can be very upsetting and distressing for everyone involved in the major change.

Despite divorce being on the increase around the world, parents often feel at a loss when searching for practical support. They also feel overwhelmed, confused, afraid, resentful, or completely frozen in panic about how to handle the changes in their family's way of life.

Sometimes this fear manifests itself as animosity, which turns the whole divorce process into a battle, with children trapped in the middle and feeling powerless.

Divorce needn't be like this. Parents can make positive, healthy choices during this very emotional time and make the transition less painful for everyone.

Divorce isn't about winners and losers. It's about working out a way to handle the separation with dignity and compassion and minimising the disruption to your children emotionally. This section offers numerous approaches and strategies for making the experience of divorce as positive and healthy as possible.

## Presenting a united front: Telling the kids

I've worked with many parents going through divorce and one of the main worries is how to tell their children about what is going to happen and what to actually say to them.

Children naturally fear that they'll lose one of their parents in divorce or that their parents will abandon them. They also fear the changes and disruptions that divorce inevitably brings to their family. Children often blame themselves.

When a marriage becomes troubled, a couple often relies on old habits of interacting, which lead to fights rather than solutions. If those old habits didn't lead to constructive solutions during the marriage, they'll surely reap no better results during the divorce. You may not have been a united front while married, but you and your partner must take this opportunity – for the good of your children – to work together.

The following sections cover various activities I lead parents through to help them and their children cope with divorce.

### Critical question

One of the key things I ask parents to do is to work out together the answer to this critical question: What are the key messages you want to convey to your children? Consider:

- ✔ Your child's need to feel reassured that you will both always be his parents and be there to support, nurture, guide, and love him.

- ✔ Your child's need to express himself and his feelings – this may include anger, silence, denial, bravado, or pleading.

- ✔ You need to weigh up whether each parent tells each child separately, or all together. If you can manage to speak to them together, this gives an opportunity for them to see that you're not blaming each other, that they don't have to take sides, and that you're both still there for them.

✔ Think about the sort of questions your children are likely to ask. 'Will we still see you and spend time with you?' 'Who will take us to football training?' 'Who will we live with and where will we live?' 'Will we have to change school?' 'Will we still see Grandma?' You need to explain that at the moment you don't have all the answers but reassure them that you'll have more clarity and answers soon and they don't need to worry.

### From your child's perspective

I ask parents to place a piece of paper on the floor, step onto it, and imagine they're looking at the situation from the eyes of their child. I then ask them to answer the following questions as if they were their child:

✔ What do you see and hear around you at the moment?

✔ How do you feel?

✔ How could Mum and Dad make you feel better? What could they do or say?

### Reassurances and guarantees

I ask the parents to write seven reassurances and guarantees that they can honestly give to their child in a graphic wheel. (Refer to Chapter 1 for an example of a blank wheel form.) The reassurances and guarantees are things that will help their child cope with the enormous changes that are coming.

Be honest – don't hedge around the difficulties. Don't give false promises that you can't keep because you destroy their confidence and belief in you at a critical time in your relationship. Give them information but not too much – give details of things in the not-too-distant future.

### Working together

I also help divorcing parents develop some co-parenting strategies. For example:

✔ Plan and agree on what both parents will say *before* they talk to their children. This helps to avoid mixed messages, which can confuse and really distress children.

✔ Look at the benefits of telling the children together or individually.

✔ Work on overcoming the 'blame' mentality and the feeling that the divorce must be someone's fault.

✔ Look for ways to avoid making children feel that they must take sides.

> ✔ Try to take the emotional charge out of telling the children.
>
> ✔ Help each parent gain more control over his or her distressing feelings and emotions during this difficult moment.

Divorce changes – but it does not end – a family. Your children are now members of two families.

## Managing your emotions

Like most things in life, divorce is a process not an event. How *you* view the process is very important. If you see divorce as a negative, painful, angry, aggressive, guilt-laden time, then it will be exactly that. If you see it as a major life crisis that can be handled in a positive way with dignity and a step towards a new life with new opportunities, then it will be so.

If you appear calm and in control most of the time, your children feel more secure. Be realistic and honest with your children, but also find a safe outlet for you to let off steam, cry, rant, and vent your frustrations – just don't do it in front of your children. You are a role model and how you handle this major event is a blueprint for how they handle stressful situations in their lives.

---

## Honesty is the key

Getting your child to talk openly about a divorce or separation is rarely easy. As a parent, you must create opportunities to find time to hear about how your child feels. Children have their own views about what is happening to them, and bottling up their feelings may cause problems in the future. Their moodiness and angry outbursts may be cries to be heard.

Find some quiet, uninterrupted time to talk through your child's feelings and explain, in terms appropriate to his age and maturity, what is actually happening. Keeping children in the picture helps them feel secure and safe.

Don't hide the truth from your child because you feel you should protect him. When children feel they don't matter, they start to imagine the worst. They often then start to blame themselves for what's happening.

I remember one year when I was teaching a group of 8 to 9-year-olds, five families in my class were going through divorce. I set up with my colleague Val Weir, a trained counsellor, a 'Drop in and Chat' facility where kids could call into my classroom at break time or lunch time to just talk about their feelings, air their concerns, and feel heard. I remember one little girl saying she felt no one was listening to her at home and she felt invisible. The drop in and chat took many different forms: Sometimes children drew pictures of how they felt; other times they played with clay and talked if they felt like it about the changes going on in their lives; some just talked or cried but felt released from tension.

You are teaching your children respect, dignity, and compassion in stressful situations. They haven't fallen out of love with the other parent, you have.

Ending your marriage isn't just a legal matter; you must also work through numerous personal stages. The following sections cover many of the typical emotional hurdles that you need to clear as you progress through a divorce.

### Grief and sorrow

Elisabeth Kübler-Ross, a pioneer in the hospice movement, first described the five stages of grieving more than three decades ago. Although her work is often applied to the handling of death and dying, her stages can serve as a good map for recovering from a major trauma such as divorce. Kübler-Ross's stages can be described as follows:

- **Denial**: 'This divorce isn't happening to me. It's all a misunderstanding. It's just a midlife crisis. We can work it out.'

- **Anger and resentment**: 'How can he/she do this to me? What did I ever do to deserve this? This is not fair!'

- **Bargaining**: 'If you'll stay, I'll change' or 'If I agree to do it [money, childrearing, sex, whatever] your way, can we get back together?'

- **Depression**: 'This is really happening. I can't do anything about it. I don't think I can bear it.'

- **Acceptance**: 'Okay, this is how it is. I'd rather accept it and move on than wallow in the past.'

When you're in the early stages of the grief and recovery process, thinking clearly and making decisions can be especially difficult. So take a few minutes and ask yourself: 'Where am I now emotionally?'

Understanding and identifying these stages can be very helpful when you're talking about divorce and deciding how to nurture your children through this difficult time. Identifying your present stage of grief and being aware of it is an important step toward ensuring that you make the best choices you can.

### Guilt and shame

Experiencing guilt and shame is a normal reaction to the end of a marriage. These feelings arise when you feel a sense of failure – of not fulfilling your own, your family's, or your community's expectations. In the case of divorce, people often feel guilt and/or shame because they have failed to stay married for life.

To begin addressing your guilt and shame, ask yourself:

- What role am I playing in this divorce?
- In what role have I cast my partner?
- What am I teaching my children through my actions, words, and body language?
- When our children look back on this period in ten years' time, what will they say about it?
- What can I do differently to make sure when we all look back on this time, we feel it was handled well?

### Fear and anxiety

Fear and anxiety are common reactions to divorce because everyone has a fight-or-flight instinct. Human bodies react to stresses (such as angry phone calls from a spouse) by using physical alarm mechanisms dating back millennia, to times when humans had to react instantly to avoid being eaten by wild boars. Your heart speeding up and adrenaline pouring into your bloodstream are meant to save your life, but these reactions can definitely limit your ability to take in new information and think through situations rationally.

When you find your adrenaline pumping and heart beating, step back for a moment to regain control. Refer to Chapter 2 for tips on effectively regaining control.

## Talking, listening – and not taking sides

Your children, regardless of their ages, will find that their lives have been turned upside down because your divorce is their divorce, too. Life will never be the same again, so you are responsible for helping your children cope with the profound changes that are happening.

Your children may want something that's not possible, like getting back together with your ex-partner. You must gently explain to them why this won't happen and then listen, *without interrupting*, to their feelings. Your children must feel heard not ignored; being deprived of a voice can seriously damage their ability to cope and their self-esteem.

Children may react differently to the news about your divorce. Some may express anger, fear, or tremendous grief, while others may appear indifferent. Some children may feel shame and hide the news from their friends or pretend it's not happening. Some may even seem relieved if they've experienced constant fighting in the home. Each child is unique and no set ways to handle change exist. Whatever your children's reaction, divorce is a big change.

You may be surprised by the intensity of your children's feelings about the divorce, but try not to undermine them. Resentment and anger, for example, can be particularly hard to deal with when expressed by your children.

Anger is a completely natural response to loss. Although it may seem difficult, you can help your children through their anger by:

- Giving them opportunities to express their anger openly – without judgement.
- Listening carefully and attentively to them.
- Trying not to react to their anger with displays of your own anger or by taking the anger personally.
- Resisting the urge to fix situations that are not fixable.
- Easing your children into new routines and living situations.
- Being extra patient and loving with them.

Anger is often closely tied to anxiety. To help your children cope with anxiety, you can:

- Listen patiently as they express their fears and worries, even if they repeat them over and over again.
- Respond honestly and supportively to their concerns. If their worries are well founded and may occur, acknowledge that fact as gently as possible.
- Provide as much stability, security, and consistency as possible. An anxious child often appreciates a consistent routine, seeing familiar people, and going to regularly visited places.

## Dealing with changes

You and your children will experience many emotional, financial, and physical changes during a divorce, but you must make their lives as stable and predictable as possible. Treat your kids like children, not adults, and don't burden them with your problems whilst going through this transition and change. Your children need your reassurance.

Never make your children feel stuck in the middle or feel that they have to take sides. Make it okay for your children to still love both you and your former spouse.

Never make negative or derogatory comments about your former spouse in front of your children. Doing so is unhelpful and immature and only upsets your children because they still love and respect both their parents.

Grandparents may also feel confused about the role they now play in your family – and your children may feel confused about whether their grandparents are still available and interested in their lives. Your children need to know that just because you and your spouse are splitting up their other relatives and friends still love them and are there for them.

## Coping with the fear of being rejected

Your children may feel they've been forgotten if they have less contact with either parent during separation and after a divorce.

Whether you live with your children or not, make sure you make an effort to see them regularly, talk to them on the phone, text them when they are playing in a school match, or e-mail them often so that they still feel valued, supported, and loved. Make your children feel you're still really interested in their lives even though you are living separately from them.

What works for one family in terms of keeping connected may not work for you, so decide on your own how you want to do things. Be clear and practical and work out positive solutions that suit your own family's needs.

## Creating a parenting plan

Although doing so can be very difficult, you need to put your children's best interests first. Of course, all parents disagree from time to time, even parents who are happily married, but to help you and your partner through the divorce, here are some practical things to keep in your mind when you are working out custody, education, holiday access, and so on:

- ✔ **Focus on your children's needs to help them through this time.** Talk with your children, listen to them, hold them, and reassure them.

- ✔ **Keep your routines the same, as much as possible.** Doing so gives your children consistency and stability. Children thrive on the familiar during times of major change.

- ✔ **Encourage your children to spend as much time as they can with your ex-partner.** Be understanding and flexible about not unneccessarily setting strict limits for the amount of time your children spend with your ex.

> ✔ **Make the transition between homes as smooth as possible.** For exam-
> ple, have school uniforms, familiar toys, and games in both houses.
> Create a new bedroom if you're establishing yourself in a new space. A
> special room or area helps your children feel that they are properly part
> of your new life.

> ✔ **Communicate directly with your ex-partner.** Don't use your children as
> go-betweens; doing so places too much responsibility on them.

Stephen R. Covey, author of *The 7 Habits of Highly Effective Families*, suggests
that successful parents have a purpose that is bigger than the problem. I
think bearing this notion in mind while you're going through a divorce can
help you focus on the bigger picture of your parenting. Chapter 4 offers more
ideas for focusing on the big picture as a parent.

## Dealing with money worries

As you begin to take care of yourself emotionally and physically, you now
have to spend at least as much time taking care of your financial future.

Try to keep your emotional and financial issues separate. When you and your
former spouse are talking about emotional issues related to your children, try
to save financial or legal matters for another discussion time. (And when you
do talk about financial and legal concerns, prepare yourself for a business
meeting and aim to act in a business-like manner.)

Never make your children feel responsible for your change in finances. They
don't understand your concerns over child support or worry about how the
next phone bill will be paid. Don't involve your children in blaming the other
parent for the change that may have occurred in your financial circumstances
either – doing so only creates resentment.

## Keeping discipline steady

Children thrive on predictability. During a divorce, parents often over-
compensate when disciplining their children because they feel guilty
about what has happened.

All parents wonder if they're too strict or not strict enough. You may not
have felt comfortable disciplining your children before your divorce. But
maintaining your boundaries is even more important while your children are
discovering new ways of living.

Refer to Chapter 8 for a more complete look at disciplining your child, and remember, you learn a lot more by listening to your child than you ever do by talking.

## Juggling new and old routines

Keeping to regular routines is important while you're going through the emotional rollercoaster of divorce because it gives your children the stability and security they need to handle the change well. Knowing what to expect from the routines helps you, as well as your children, feel more confident and relaxed.

Try to have one meal together each day as a family. Plan regular mealtimes together and serve the meals at the same time each evening, if possible.

Consistent nightly rituals are also soothing for children. A gentle winding down time before bed helps children feel secure and relaxed before falling asleep. Feeling secure at bedtime can also prevent the nightmares that often occur during the transition of adapting to your separation.

## Encouraging personal growth

Feeling good about yourself is an important part of being a successful parent. This feeling won't happen overnight, but you can work toward being your best during and after divorce by:

- ✔ Finding out what you enjoy
- ✔ Identifying your strengths
- ✔ Learning there are things in life you can't control

### Developing your goals

Begin feeling better about yourself in one area of your life and then extend this success to others. Develop goals and a plan to build your skills in one or more areas. Consider the following examples:

- ✔ **Parenting-related goal:** To increase parenting knowledge and spend time with the children.

  **Plan:** Read to the children at least once a day. Attend a parenting class within the next three months. Hold family meetings with your children each week to discuss problems and schedules.

✔ **Personal goal:** To make time for yourself.

**Plan:** Do one thing each week you enjoy. Spend at least 10 minutes a day in the garden. Get up 20 minutes earlier each morning so you can watch the morning news on television before you wake the children.

✔ **Household-related goal:** To make household jobs less stressful.

**Plan:** Try one new recipe every couple of weeks and get the kids involved in making it. Break large tasks into small ones – for example, clean the downstairs rooms on a Saturday rather than trying to clean all the rooms at one time.

### Working on control issues

At times you probably feel that fate decides your future. While there are things in life you can't control, you can manage some. Think carefully about what you can – and can't – control.

1. **Write down some of the frustrations and difficulties you face each day.**

2. **Categorise and organise your frustrations into three categories:**

   - **I have control:** For example, showing my children I love them through hugs, kisses, and words.

   - **I have some control:** Making sure my children eat nutritious food.

   - **I have little or no control:** What sort of relationship my ex-partner has with his new girlfriend.

3. **Review your categorised list.**

   Do you spend time and energy worrying about things you can't control?

   Take control of things you *can* change and let go of the things you can't.

I am a great believer that if you are in a good place emotionally, your kids are too. Invest time in getting yourself sorted out first so you can guide, manage, and support your children through this time of change.

# Focusing on the future

After divorce, the most important thing you can do is to move forward logically. Here are some ideas to help you on your way back to a fulfilling life:

✔ **Accept that the relationship is over.** When you're living alone and your partner has moved on, accepting that your marriage is over ought to be easy, but realistically it's not. Forgive yourself for struggling to move on.

Healing is a process. Healing after divorce isn't like fixing a broken arm – it takes as long as it takes. However, accepting that you and your former partner now lead separate lives is helpful. The sooner you accept this, the quicker you can find happiness again.

✔ **Don't live in the past.** Naturally you'll have some special memories from the time you and your former spouse shared – but don't dwell on these thoughts.

If you find yourself wishing that everything could be 'like that' again, give yourself a mental jolt and remind yourself that some fantastic moments await you in the future.

✔ **Don't try to get even.** No matter how angry you are at your partner – even if they've been unfaithful to you – don't try to get your own back. You'll just end up exhausting yourself and wasting your energy on something that isn't going to be productive. Getting even won't get your partner back, but the resentment will stop you from moving on. Don't do it!

✔ **Don't drench yourself in guilt.** You've probably said a few things that you didn't mean and now regret. You can't change that, so forgive yourself and learn from your mistakes. Take a deep breath, focus on all the things that you have done right, and pat yourself on the back.

✔ **Re-discover yourself.** How much of yourself did you give up during your relationship? Did you find yourself bending over backwards to satisfy your partner? Now is the time to start living for you!

Doing the things that make *you* happy increases your self-confidence. Re-arrange your bathroom, enrol on a course, and go and do a parachute jump. Do anything you like, but do it for *you*. It's time to explore who you are and what you like.

## Resources for dads

Following are some useful resources for divorced dads:

✔ www.dads-uk.co.uk is a helpline for single fathers.

✔ www.equalparenting.org discusses joint custody and shared parenting info.

✔ www.fathersdirect.com is an online information centre for fathers.

✔ www.fatherville.com offers lots of good reading material for dads.

✔ *Always Dad: Being a Great Father During and After Divorce* by Paul Mandelstein (Nolo) is packed with great ideas.

# Building Healthy Stepfamilies

Even though fairy tales end with 'And they all lived happily ever after', stepfamilies have a bad image. Think of Snow White's jealous stepmother or Cinderella's ugly sisters. At the other end of the spectrum, picture unrealistically positive stepfamilies, such as the Brady Bunch.

But real life is more complicated than either stepfamily model. Stepchildren have to come to terms with their new family, their parent's new partner, and a whole new way of life. The whole experience can leave children feeling isolated, confused, or resentful.

## Exploring stepfamily myths – Cinderella doesn't live here anymore

Following are some stepfamily myths that need looking at:

- **Myth 1:** Marriages are easier the second time around.

    **Fact:** All marriages are different. Of course, both parents learn things from their first marriage, but each relationship is different, unique, and special.

- **Myth 2:** All stepfamilies learn to love each other eventually.

    **Fact:** Some do, some don't. Some family members will grow to love one another; others merely tolerate each other. But *respect* is a vital key energy that helps families work and bond together.

- **Myth 3:** Stepfamilies work the same way as first-time families.

    **Fact:** Families develop individually and have their own styles. Blending a family takes time and patience.

- **Myth 4:** Children are so adaptable – they'll quickly and easily accept the situation.

    **Fact:** Adaptability depends on the child. Some children whose lives change dramatically find accepting others difficult, while others don't. You cannot predict how your child will come to terms with the new situation that he is placed in.

- **Myth 5:** If I'm kind and loving to my partner's children, everything will be okay.

    **Fact:** Nice sentiment, but it only looks at a relationship from one side – yours. A child needs to grieve and come to terms with the loss of the family he knew. So no matter how nice you are to your stepchild, he may still be unhappy.

✔ **Myth 6:** Relating to stepchildren is just the same as relating to my own kids.

**Fact:** Stepchildren and natural children are different. Expecting to feel exactly the same way towards stepchildren as your natural children is unrealistic – and remember the feeling is mutual. If you've ever heard 'You're not my Dad – you can't tell me what to do,' you understand that stepparenting takes patience, skill, and self-control.

## Blending together

Ron L. Deal, in his book *The Smart Stepfamily: Seven Steps to a Healthy Family*, uses a very interesting analogy when talking about stepfamilies. He suggests that rather than 'blending a family', 'cooking up a stepfamily' is a better description. *Blending* suggests that everyone merges together easily, whereas in reality, families integrate slowly – just like in a casserole!

To continue the cooking analogy a step further: As a parent, you must understand that *time* and *low heat* make a healthier family combination.

Let your stepchild dictate the pace of the relationship. Accept that being 'Daddy' to your own child, 'James' to your stepson, and 'Mr McLoughlin' to your new teenage stepdaughter is okay. Be flexible and adaptable in your relationships.

## Dealing with the disruption

Going through any change is difficult, so expect to experience a series of stepfamily stages:

1. **Fantasy stage:** Family members are on their best behaviour. During this period everyone imagines they'll love one another and create one big jolly family living happily ever after.

2. **Confusion stage:** Tension grows, happiness begins to slip away, and differences emerge. The romance seems to disappear.

3. **Conflict stage:** Anger can start to erupt as family members realise that their needs are not being met. Arguments can begin, and true feelings start to appear. Hopefully, if you're prepared, negotiations and honest communication can also begin.

4. **Comfort stage:** Family members start to relax and begin to look forward to their future together. Communication is deeper and bonds solidify.

Here are some guidelines for making an easy transition through the various stages of becoming a healthy stepfamily.

- ✔ **Start out in a home that's new for all, if possible.** Doing so makes for less territory squabbles and hurt feelings and can help to get rid of your ghosts from the past. If moving house isn't an option, get a 'new home' feel to your existing home by moving the furniture around, buying some new bits and pieces, and redecorating the walls.

- ✔ **Develop new traditions.** Developing new rituals and special celebrations speeds up the sense of belonging and connectedness. This deceptively simple tip represents a key part of successful stepfamily life. It doesn't matter what your rituals are – pizza on Wednesday night or bike rides on Sunday afternoon can be effective rituals.

- ✔ **Celebrate every member of your new family.** For example, if you keep family pictures on your desk, be sure to include photos of your stepkids, too.

- ✔ **Nurture your new couple bond.** When couples have a good relationship, they're able to work together on meeting the needs of their children. A good marriage also reduces your feelings of being caught in the middle between the children and your new partner.

- ✔ **Be prepared to adjust visitation and custody timetables.** Particularly as your children enter adolescence, you may need to let go of some time with your children, which can be a painful experience. Remember that your teenager's needs are the overarching concern here. Teens want to spend a significant amount of time with peers and it's important they have it.

- ✔ **Love generously.** As one stepmother said on a course of mine about divorce and stepfamilies, 'The children taught us there's enough love to go round and we don't have to ration love!'

- ✔ **See life through a different perspective.** Trying for a different perspective can be an especially effective tool in creating a loving stepfamily. Check out the exercise in Chapter 4 for how to see life from your children's point of view.

- ✔ **Communicate, communicate, and communicate.** Doing so isn't always easy! If you find you cannot listen well to one another, get someone outside the family to help you: A minister, a rabbi, a counsellor, a family friend – anyone who understands stepfamily life and can help you adjust to your new circumstances.

## Welcoming a new baby

For most stepfamilies, 'How exciting, a new baby is on the way' is quickly followed by 'Oh my goodness, how are we going to prepare the kids?'

Bringing a new baby into a stepfamily is exciting but can add considerable stress and strain because it affects a number of people in your family and different people react in different ways – particularly if your family relationships are a bit fragile to start with.

A new baby can trigger unpredictable feelings and responses from your children. Existing children may feel that you won't love them anymore or that the new baby will take their place. On the positive side, some children look forward very much to a new half brother or sister, and the new half sibling can help bond everyone together, with the whole family getting involved in looking after a new baby.

Here are some practical ideas for preparing for your new addition to the family:

- ✔ Tell your children about the new expected baby yourselves. Don't leave this important message to another parent, relative, or friend, or your children will feel left out.

- ✔ Spend time with your children/stepchildren and reassure them that your love for them hasn't changed.

- ✔ Share your news with grandparents, who often feel confused about their role when a new baby joins the family. Phone calls and photos are simple but effective ways to help grandparents feel involved. Encourage grandparents to treat all the children the same. Try sitting down and having a chat with them because gauging their role after a son or daughter has a new partner can be hard for grandparents.

# Working and Parenting

While some people seem to effortlessly put in a full working day and still manage to achieve an idyllic family lifestyle, for most, juggling and keeping all the plates spinning at the same time is an overwhelming challenge.

Here are some of the *big* questions I ask working parents to get them thinking:

- ✔ Do you feel in complete control of your life?

- ✔ Are you constantly tired, fed up, and stressed?

- ✔ Are you actually too busy to really enjoy your life?

- ✔ Do you find yourself thinking, 'There has to be a better way?'

If you find yourself answering yes to one or more of these questions, then you need to take time to make some changes and begin *balancing* your life – which is exactly what the following sections are about.

# Looking at stress, guilt, and pressure

You may feel that you don't have enough hours in a day to be a parent, manage a job, maintain a home, and have some sort of social life. Balancing work and home is never easy, but it is important.

Of course, pros and cons exist in every situation, whether you work full time, part time, or are a stay-at-home parent. Having a better standard of living or being able to afford a holiday or those new trainers may be important to you. Having your own independence may help you to feel more confident. Or having friends and stimulus outside the home may also be essential to you.

You may be overwhelmed with things to do, and feel that you're missing out on family life or that you're not 'there' for your children or your partner. You may resent the housework if it isn't shared equally, or you may feel constantly tired, stressed, or guilty. The secret to overcoming these feelings is gaining control.

The following parent-coaching suggestions can help you achieve some sort of balance between home and work.

## Think it through

What's important to you? Ask yourself the following questions:

- What do you *really* want?
- What are your priorities and goals at the moment?
- How would you like all the different aspects of your life to feel?

Write your answers in your journal to crystallise and clarify your thoughts.

## Colour co-ordinate

Odd question, but if each part of your life were a colour, what colours would they be? Think about work, fun and recreation, health and exercise, friends and family, finances, personal development – what colours would represent these areas of your life? In your journal, use different coloured pens to explore what you want to achieve in different areas of your life.

## Prioritise

You really can't do everything. Unlike Mary Poppins or Mrs Doubtfire, sometimes some things have to go by the board. Letting go of routines can be hard. Choose the things you have to do and leave those that can be left. Ask yourself which is more important – that the washing up is done immediately or that you enjoy reading your children a bedtime story?

I remember a mum who came on one of my Work–Life Balance workshops saying, 'The time I saved on eating ready-cooked meals during the week allowed me to help the boys with their homework. So I stopped beating myself up about being an earth mother and enjoyed the time with the kids more.'

Finding time is often a question of priorities.

## Making friends with the juggler: Practical ideas for balancing your life

Everyone defines 'ideal balance' differently. Your balance is likely to change with time, circumstances, and stage of life. The important thing is that *you* know what you mean and are very clear about what your priorities are in each area of your life.

Working out what you most want from your life may take you some time, especially if you've never stopped and thought about it before. Be patient with yourself and let the answers come to you gradually over time.

Here are some ideas for striking a better balance between work and home:

- ✔ **Stop feeling guilty that you're a working parent.** Turn down that inner voice that says 'Good mums stay at home and always put their children first' and replace it with a kinder, soothing voice that says, 'I'm doing my best and I love my kids.'

- ✔ **Don't allow other people to make you feel guilty – especially those at work.** You may have to leave work at 5.15 because you're a parent and have to pick up your child from his nursery – not because you're shirking your work responsibilities.

- ✔ **Get good quality childcare.** Doing so gives you peace of mind, stability, and reassurance. You don't want to spend time at work worrying about your child, so visit a range of different nurseries and childminders to find the one that really feels intuitively right for you and your child.

- ✔ **Get the support of your partner.** When your child is sick, you don't want to waste time arguing about whose job is more important. Make sure that you always have a fall-back position with a friend or relative in case of an emergency or an unexpected event.

- ✔ **Let your standards slip.** Even if you find it really hard, acknowledge that you can't be a working parent and have a perfect home. If you aim for this, you'll burn yourself out. Get help with the ironing or cleaning if you can afford it.

✔ **Help each other.** What's stopping you getting everyone in your home taking some responsibility, too? Get your children and your partner to help with chores such as washing up, keeping rooms tidy, making beds, and preparing meals.

✔ **Reduce morning stress.** Get everything ready the night before. Make the packed lunch, iron the school uniform, polish the shoes, and leave the trainers by the door. Leave an extra supply of nappies or clothes with your childminder, relative, or nursery if you have very young children. Don't waste valuable time hunting for things at the last minute.

✔ **Focus on the positive.** When you've had a bad day, make a list of all the positive reasons you go to work and think of a different or good day. When everything goes well, write down what you like best about those days; doing so gives you a sense of balance and a different and wider perspective.

✔ **Look at your options.** Try talking to your employer about different ways to work. Some employers now consider flexible working hours, job sharing, or working from home some days a week.

I spend a lot of time working with stressed and guilty working parents looking at their time management. After they get that aspect of their lives under control, everything else seems to fall into place: Homework gets done easily, mealtimes are less fraught, kids seem more obliging and accommodating, and parents start enjoying their parenting again.

Stay centred in where you are. If you're at work, be there 100 per cent in your attitude, energy, and commitment. Don't start worrying about the ironing at home. If you're at home, don't start worrying about the list of to-do things waiting for you on Monday morning – enjoy the game of Cluedo and relax with your kids.

# Tempering Sibling Rivalry

Sibling rivalry has always had a bad press. Consider Cain slaying Abel and Joseph's brothers throwing him down a well and selling him because they were jealous of his multi-coloured coat.

*Siblings* are any children who are related to the same parent and are living in the same family. *Sibling rivalry* is the jealousy, competition, and fighting that goes on between brothers and sisters. Sibling rivalry generally means that one child is vying for your attention. Many factors can create this situation.

If children feel that they're getting unequal amounts of your attention, they will fight for it. Children don't always know positive ways to get you to respond, so they pick arguments with siblings.

If you've ever experienced the age-old conflict of your young child whining 'It's not fair. Why can't I stay up until 9.30 like Pete?' you know that fairness has got nothing to do with it. You know your son George is younger, needs more sleep, and is a nightmare to get up in the morning if he doesn't have enough rest. Never give in to the old 'it's not fair' strategy. Besides, when George is finally allowed to stay up until 9.30, it will seem a real privilege to him.

Many parents I work with feel that in order to be fair they must try to treat their children *equally*. Equality is a good goal to aim for, but it can become ridiculous. (If you hug one child, must you stop what you're doing and hug all your children equally?) Acknowledging that if it's your son's birthday or he's ill, he's the one who merits the special attention and presents is more practical. All children understand and recognise the inherent fairness of these normal situations.

## Growing respect and building bonds

If you help your children build bonds with each other from the beginning, those bonds can last a lifetime. You can then be reassured to know that in a crisis, if you're not available, your child can turn to his brother or sister first.

Build bonds between siblings by teaching social skills, including:

- ✔ **Sharing.** Sharing is the art of give and take and the skill of negotiating. To encourage sharing, put your children in charge of the sharing. For example, you might say, 'I've bought some chocolate chip ice-cream. What's the best way to share it out fairly?'

- ✔ **Fairness.** Siblings compare *all* the time, and the root of jealousy is when one of your children feels that the other gets special treatment or more attention or is loved more. Be fair in your dealings with them and make sure they know you value them equally and explain your thought processes.

  As one dad on a course told me he said to his kids: 'It's not fair that some people thump their kids or that there are kids in the world starving to death. Life isn't fair all the time, so arguing about who gets the last Jellytot in the packet doesn't seem very important to me. Get over it!'

- ✔ **Unity.** Develop a 'united we stand, divided we fall' mentality. Children work out the power of sticking together when they want something special for Christmas and pester together! Families work best when they stick together. Look out for one another and recognise your responsibility for each other. Even very young children can learn that 'we all pull together and pitch in when things get difficult'.

✔ **Celebrating uniqueness.** Teach your children the importance of recognising and celebrating different strengths, talents, and skills without feeling jealous or inferior. If each of your children is made to feel special for his own talents, each child can have a well of self-esteem to draw on and feel secure in his individuality.

The idea of 'your success is my success' can be helpful in recognising differences. When my daughter won the Player of the Week netball award, my son was thrilled for her and very effusive in his praise. He likes to celebrate her successes just as she likes to celebrate his.

✔ **Respect.** Teach your children how to treat each other respectfully, even when conflicts arise. Show them how to express their anger without name-calling or ridicule. Help them recognise and acknowledge their feelings with words and then teach them how to channel their angry feelings into ways that are acceptable, such as kicking a ball, running in the garden, or punching a pillow.

To build strong bonds, don't be afraid to tell your children that blood is thicker than water and that brothers and sisters are important to each other. If they speak disrespectfully to each other, remind them that they wouldn't speak to a complete stranger like that so they mustn't speak like that to each other either.

Try getting your kids working together on jobs round the house. Chores can become an opportunity to spend time together: They can stick on the radio, do the washing up, and have a laugh at the same time.

In our family, we all sit down in the winter after Sunday lunch, light a fire, and watch a family film together. Yes, this takes a little bit of negotiating to please everyone, but that's the whole point really – helping the kids negotiate a compromise that pleases everyone.

## Eating together

If you want to deepen the bonds between siblings, try increasing the amount of time your family spends together – particularly *eating together*.

Mealtimes are a good place to share more than just the food because sitting round the table encourages your family to take time to chat, share experiences, and talk about their feelings or worries. Recent research from the National Centre on Addiction and Substance Abuse at Columbia University suggests that children who eat together with their family do better in school and avoid problems like smoking, drinking, and drug abuse.

If you think your family may need some conversation starters – rather than just 'Pass the broccoli' and 'Don't chew with your mouth open' – following are a few ideas that are hopefully a bit more inspiring:

- ✔ What surprised you today?
- ✔ What made you smile today?
- ✔ If you were going to be an animal, what would you want to be?
- ✔ If you could sit down to dinner with five people from any period in history, who would they be?

## Facing the green-eyed monster

Not recognising the fighting, bickering, pinching, pushing, teasing, tale-telling, and tormenting that goes on in most households is foolish and naive. Sometimes you must acknowledge that healthy competition has turned into deadly rivalry, or that an older child's bossy attitude is turning into bullying.

*Jealousy* – the persistent feelings of unfairness, competitiveness, and one-upmanship – is the main emotion behind most issues causing conflict between siblings.

If you start to experience some jealousy-based conflicts in your home, try keeping a diary for a week. Jot down a few notes to remember what you see and help you think about what to do properly afterwards. Note things such as:

- ✔ What are the children fighting about?
- ✔ What happens when they argue?
- ✔ Do they both start it, or is one child more demanding?
- ✔ Which child do you hold accountable for the fights – the one who's the loudest? The one who comes to you first?
- ✔ Do problems happen at certain times of the day?
- ✔ Are they hungry, bored, or tired when the fights happen?

# Building bridges

The following are a few practical tactics to improve sibling relations:

- **Consider whether you are treating your children differently.** Have a look at the types of things that set off your kids and how you react.

- ***Never* compare your children.** This one is a biggie. Don't typecast, label, or pigeonhole them – just let each child be who he is, unique and special in his own way.

- **Make sure each child has enough time and space of his own.** Kids need chances to do their own thing, play with their own friends without their sibling, and have their space and property protected.

- **Set aside 'alone time' for each child.** Spend some one-to-one time with each child on a regular basis. Try to get in at least a few minutes each day. Just 10 minutes of uninterrupted time with a parent can mean so much to your child. (Driving my son to his football practice on a Thursday evening was when we used to chat about 'stuff' for half an hour alone together.)

- **Listen – *really listen*.** Find out how your children feel about what's going on in the family. They may not be so demanding if they know you at least care how they feel.

# Resolving conflicts

Research shows that while you should pay attention to your kids' conflicts, so that no one gets hurt and you can notice abuse if it occurs, not intervening is best. Jumping into sibling squabbles to protect one child (usually the younger child against the older child) escalates the conflict because the older child resents the younger child and the younger child often feels that he can get away with more because the parent is 'on his side'.

Instead, encourage your children to create win-win negotiations, where each side gains something. Teach them how to compromise, respect one another, divide things fairly, and so on. Give them the tools and then express your confidence that they can work it out by telling them, 'I'm sure you two can figure out a solution.' Don't get drawn in.

If you are constantly angry at your kids, no wonder they are angry at each other! Anger feeds on itself. Develop ways to manage your anger so you can teach your children how to manage theirs. Refer to Chapter 10 for more on how to control your anger.

Here are some suggestions:

- **Consider simple solutions first.** You may be able to sort things out by just feeding them earlier or getting them to let off steam after school by riding their bikes in the garden.

- **Set rules together.** Involve your children in setting clear and consistent ground rules because doing so can help prevent many squabbles. Get them to draw, paint, or print out a set of rules.

- **Use family meetings.** Sit down at the same time each week and discuss issues. The purpose of the family meeting is to recognise that everyone's opinion makes a difference. Family meetings help to build co-operation and responsibility and make anger and arguments less likely.

- **Give your kids reminders.** When they start picking on each other, help them remember how to state their feelings to each other. Don't solve the problem for them, just help them remember *how* to problem solve.

- **Give warnings.** Give your children a warning that if they don't play together peacefully, you'll stop their game or whatever activity they're participating in. Use the football metaphor of a 'yellow card' as a graphic way to issue a warning (this works particularly well with boys) and then the threat of a 'red card'. A 'sending off' may be all you need to stop the bickering.

- **Change the battlefield.** Bickering and squabbling often bothers you more than it bothers the kids. As long as you're sure things won't get out of hand, try moving the argument to somewhere where you can't hear it – upstairs, out in the garden, and so on.

- **Separate the parties.** Playing alone isn't as much fun, and a bit of physical space is often enough to cool tempers.

Dangerous fights need to be stopped immediately. No hurting, hitting, kicking, pinching, name-calling, yelling, or telling tales is allowed. When they have calmed down, talk about what happened and make it very clear that no violence is ever allowed.

I know it can be stressful if your children are competing between themselves but if you openly discuss ways to help solve the issues and feelings that arise, you give your children some wonderful resources that can serve them well later in life. Siblings learn how to share, confront jealousy, and accept individual strengths and weaknesses through growing up together.

## Useful books on sibling rivalry

Following are some favourite books that deal with the topic of sibling rivalry.

✔ *Siblings Without Rivalry: How to Help Your Children Live Together So You Can Live Too* by Adele Faber and Elaine Mazlish (Harper Collins) is an excellent resource for parents.

✔ *I'd Rather Have an Iguana* by Heidi Stetson Mario (Charlesbridge Publishing) is a great

book for children aged 4 to 6 having to cope with a new baby in the family.

✔ *Brothers and Sisters: Born to Bicker?* by Pamela Shires Sneddon (Enslow Publishers) is an intriguing entry in the Teen Issues series that focuses on the interaction between siblings.

# Responding to Death and Dying

Children experiencing loss – whether the death of a pet or a loved one – need information, companionship, emotional expression, and time to remember.

When my dad died two years ago, someone gave me great advice. They said, 'How you handle death and grief provides a blueprint for how your children handle death and grief in their own emotional lives.' As a parent, I know that I'm a real-life role model for my children, but I hadn't considered this fact regarding grief and bereavement until it was pointed out to me.

## The death of a pet

For many children their first real experience with loss happens when a pet dies. When a much-loved pet dies, children need consolation, love, support, and affection more than complicated medical explanations. They need to have their feelings understood and validated. Their reactions depend on their age and stage of maturity, but realise that children don't fully understand that death is permanent and final until around age 9.

Children often have questions such as:

✔ Why did my pet die?

✔ Is it my fault?

✔ Where does my pet's body go to?

✔ Will I ever see my pet again?

✔ If I wish hard enough and am really good can I make my pet come back?

Answer these questions simply but honestly. Let your child know missing a pet after it dies is perfectly normal and encourage him to come to you with questions or for reassurance and comfort whenever he feels sad or overwhelmed.

Mourning a pet has to be done in a child's own way. Children need to be given time to remember their pet, and talking about the animal with friends and family or even at school may help.

## Beginning the grieving process

When a beloved person dies, it is a distressing event and people react differently. Some people may be shocked, some seem numb, while others get very upset and tearful. Anger is often a common reaction to grief, and because grieving is a process for you, as well as for your child, it isn't linear.

Coping with your own feelings can be especially difficult when you're trying to support your children, too. You may be feeling shocked, sad, angry, guilty, anxious, relieved, lonely, orphaned, irritable, or a mixture of the whole lot. No such thing as a perfect parent exists, so just be a real one.

Crying in front of your children is perfectly natural – if you explain what you're feeling. A record, a photograph, an everyday memory, or a family occasion can trigger emotions. Talking and crying together helps heal the grief and unites you as a family as you come to terms with the loss and changes.

Once, during circle time, something came up about the death of one of the children's hamsters, which naturally led onto talking about the death of another child's grandparent. It was a really moving but healing lesson that caught me by surprise. Because I felt comfortable talking about these issues, the children all joined in and supported each other and learnt that healing from grief can be painful and slow but something everyone experiences.

Parents often try to protect children by not talking about illness or death. Of course, doing so is understandable because not everyone is comfortable talking about their emotions or knows what to say. Still, the situation and the emotions need to be addressed honestly and openly.

When my mum was very ill with emphysema and was always being rushed to hospital, it took a toll on me emotionally. My kids often found me tired, overwhelmed, and tearful. Finally, we all sat down one day and chatted openly about how difficult it all was juggling full-time working and caring for her. I just tried to be honest and direct. The kids felt included in the process. By the end of our talk, they understood the situation and were better able to cope themselves.

## Bereavement resources

Many wonderful resources are available to support you and your child through the loss of a pet or loved one.

Remember that resources are only tools that you can use to help the situation – no handbook on death and grief exists. Be guided by your intuition, be flexible, and seek professional help from your doctor or other professional bodies if you feel the process is too overwhelming and you need support.

Some useful books for children include:

✔ *Weep Not for Me* by C. Jenkins (Souvenir Press)

✔ *Goodbye Mog* by Judith Kerr (HarperCollins)

✔ *The Fall of Freddie the Leaf* by Leo Buscaglia (Slack Publishing)

Helpful organisations for bereavement and grief counselling assistance include:

✔ The Blue Cross, Britain's pet charity, has a helpful leaflet on pet bereavement available to download. (www.bluecross.org.uk)

✔ Winston's Wish offers support for bereaved children and their parents or care givers. (Tel: 01242 515157; helpline: 0845 203 0405 Monday to Friday, 9–5 pm; www.winstons wish.org.uk)

✔ Childline (Tel: 020 7239 1000 or 24-hour helpline 0800 1111; www.childline. org.uk)

✔ Childhood Bereavement Network (Tel: 0115 911 8070; www.ncb.org.uk/cbn)

✔ Child Bereavement Trust (Tel: 01494 446648; support line: 0845 357 1000; www.child bereavement.org.uk).

I remember arriving at school one Monday morning to see a little boy of 8 crying at his desk – his dad had died the night before from a sudden brain haemorrhage. His mum just did what she thought was right to keep things 'normal' but obviously he was in shock and couldn't cope. I took him outside and we went for a gentle walk. We started to talk about the great things he'd done with his dad and he started to laugh about funny things he'd said or done. We talked about life never being quite the same again and how change can be painful, but how it does heal when each of us feels ready. It was a great honour to spend time with this little boy as he was going through such a difficult time. I didn't have a 'bereavement policy' in place until after that day. I just made it up as I went along. But I know we helped each other through just listening and being together.

## *Appreciating the importance of rituals*

A funeral is a special family occasion, which marks the end of someone's life and gives children an opportunity to be involved with a ritual and celebrate life.

Prepare your children in advance for funerals so they know what to expect and can choose whether they want to attend or not. No evidence suggests that children who go to funerals are harmed; in fact, the opposite is true. If they choose not to go, a trusted adult should be with them to support them while the funeral takes place.

Simply talk to your child and find out what he prefers in terms of attending the funeral. I remember hearing a story about a child who wasn't allowed to attend her mum's funeral but saw it go by outside her school through the railings. Of course, the adults involved made that choice from the highest of intentions, but the child felt isolated and distanced from the grieving event.

Many parents feel that childhood is a time free from difficulties and challenging events. In reality this just isn't the case. How you *handle* the challenges is what makes your children grow up well balanced, resilient, and strong – able to handle the blows life deals them.

# Part V
# Being Different

"How can you not feel confident? You're wearing Versace sunglasses, a Tommy Hilfiger sweater, Calvin Klein jeans, and Michael Jordan gym shoes. Now go on out there and just be yourself."

## In this part . . .

This part of the book explores dealing with a diagnosis that your child is different; ways to get the best advice, support, and expertise; and practical tips to move forward positively. Children who are unique need your parenting approach to be individual, flexible, and creative because they have different needs to other children.

This part also looks at having more than one child at the same time, and practical and common sense ways to cope with the high demands that multiple births can have on your own energy and time.

Raising happy children is all about treating your children as individuals and doing your very best for them.

# Chapter 14

# Raising Children with Unique and Special Needs

*T*he term 'special needs' is like an umbrella that shelters (and often hides) a huge collection of diagnoses underneath. Children with 'special' or 'different' needs may have trouble paying attention, profound mental retardation, be gifted, have a food allergy, be terminally ill, or have a stammer. The vastness of the term can be confusing and bewildering.

The designation 'special needs' is commonly defined by what a child *can't* do – by milestones unmet, foods banned, activities avoided, and experiences denied. These minuses can hit families hard and may make 'special needs' seem like a tragic designation or a millstone around everyone's neck.

Giving any child a label can limit her. I see every child as a way to find an opportunity to explore her potential in a new or different way that hasn't yet been tried. This chapter covers the characteristics of various 'special' diagnoses that parents encounter, including dyslexia, ADHD/ADD, dyspraxia, Asperger's syndrome, giftedness, and more.

# Understanding Your Child's Diagnosis

Your child's *diagnosis* – the identification of her disorder – is useful for getting the support or services your child needs in school and elsewhere in life. A diagnosis can help you set appropriate goals and gain understanding that your child has a unique talent or unique need.

After finding out their child's diagnosis, some parents focus on the difficulties and grieve for their child's lost potential compared to others. I challenge you to see beyond the diagnosis – to become a family who sees your child's challenges as making her triumphs even sweeter. Your child's apparent 'weaknesses' are always balanced by amazing strengths.

Don't crumple in despair if your child is diagnosed as being different. See the diagnosis as an opportunity to learn how to help your child discover more about herself.

## Responding initially to a diagnosis

Your child's diagnosis may come as a shock or a relief. But whatever your reaction, it is perfectly normal.

Your child's diagnosis may affect you and your partner differently. While one of you may be able to accept the diagnosis, the other may feel that it is not correct and continue searching for alternative explanations for your child's difficulty. Always give yourself time to discuss any decision you make about your child.

Your family and friends are likely to experience a range of reactions to the news of the diagnosis – some may be supportive; some may be hurtful and even distressing.

Here are some tips that you may find useful in the weeks and months after receiving your child's diagnosis:

- ✔ Give yourself time to come to terms with and to develop an understanding of what the diagnosis means for you, your child, and your family.
- ✔ Avoid making any rash or major decisions in the weeks following the diagnosis.
- ✔ If needed, seek another appointment with the professional who gave you the diagnosis so you can ask more questions.

Feeling grief after hearing a diagnosis is perfectly normal. Most parents experience a reaction similar to a feeling of bereavement following a diagnosis. While you love your child regardless, you can acknowledge that you have suffered the loss of a child who may have followed a more customary developmental path.

Yes, the presence of a child with special needs in a family alters the way that family functions, including the closeness of parents and other siblings, the family's decision-making processes, and its patterns of communication. However, these changes may be positive as well as negative.

## Going forward after a diagnosis

While working through your feelings, take the time to educate yourself about the condition affecting your child. Use all the sources of information available to you – the library, Internet, other parents, and organisations. Knowledge is power.

Many parents I work with appreciate the help of organisations and support groups that represent children and families with similar special needs. Making the initial contact can be a very big and frightening step but remember these groups can be a source of fantastic ongoing help and support. When you're ready, make contact. (I include contact information for organisations related to specific diagnoses throughout this chapter.) Remember: You are not alone.

Your child is an individual and her condition affects her in a unique way. While you may find many similarities between your child and another who has the same condition, differences in how the condition affects both children will exist.

Schedule follow-up meetings with professionals or consider getting a second opinion if you feel the first one you have received is flawed. To get the most from any subsequent consultations:

- Decide *before* any meeting what you want from the meeting. Jot down any questions you have.
- If you and your partner can't go to meetings together, take a friend or relative for support and to serve as another pair of ears.
- Keep notes of all your meetings with the professionals you work with. If a professional is compiling a report on your child, ask for a copy for your records.

Try to build relationships with the professionals in your area: Who are they? Where are they based? Do they work as a team or individually?

Having a child with special needs means that you will meet many health and childcare professionals in the course of your child's life. While this situation can be frustrating, it can also be an enriching experience, depending on your relationships with them. Stay focused on the positive and you're likely to get the positive in return.

Even though you may come across many experts, remember that you are the *real* expert on your child. You know her better than anybody else in the world, and you are your child's main champion in seeking the service and care that best suit her needs.

---

## Four stages of dealing with a diagnosis

The feelings and emotions that parents may go through following a diagnosis can be divided into four stages.

You don't necessarily go through all these stages, and the time scale – a few months to several years – is completely individual to you. You may even go back and forth between stages. Also, you and your partner may not pass through the stages at the same time or pace. (Research suggests that dads are more likely to spend time in denial and anger while mums are more likely to suffer prolonged periods of guilt or sadness.)

The four stages are:

- **Shock:** Immediately following the diagnosis, you may feel numb and experience a sense of unreality and anxiety. You may have difficulty absorbing information.

- **Denial:** During this stage, you find yourself questioning the seriousness of your child's condition or wondering whether the doctors have made an awful mistake. You may fantasise about your child being 'cured'.

- **Sadness/Anger:** This stage is characterised by depressive, sad emotions and feelings of guilt. You may also rage against fate, your partner, your child, or the professionals involved. You and those around you may find this stage very difficult to cope with, but in the process of coming to terms with your child's diagnosis, it is important that you do experience these emotions and find your way through them.

- **Adaptation:** You begin reorganising your life in practical ways to accommodate the diagnosis. You can see your child and her future in more realistic ways. Some parents never reach the adaptation stage; they feel that if they accept a diagnosis, they're somehow letting their child down.

If you find yourself stuck at any stage, seek professional help to move forward and to help you put things into a more balanced perspective.

# *Getting good information*

Some parents never get a clear diagnosis regarding the underlying cause of their child's special needs. In fact, sometimes professionals themselves may be unclear about what those causes are.

The lack of clear answers is unbelievably frustrating and can be caused by a number of reasons:

- ✔ The problem is very subtle and difficult to assess.
- ✔ Your child is very young and a clear picture of her special needs is yet to emerge.
- ✔ The problem is rare and unusual.
- ✔ The professional assessing your child may be unfamiliar with your child's condition.
- ✔ Your child may have a mixture of problems, which makes a clear diagnosis difficult.

Many professionals, especially in the case of younger children, are slow to give a clear diagnosis. A particular diagnosis can act as a very powerful label, which may remain with your child for the rest of her life, impacting almost all aspects of your lives. Therefore, if any uncertainty exists, professionals are often unwilling to make a clear diagnosis because they know the implications of labelling a child with a specific condition.

Lack of clear diagnosis can be frustrating. (You want to know what exactly is wrong with your child so you can go about helping her!) But even without a clear diagnosis, you can do a number of useful, important things for your child:

- ✔ If you suspect your child has a specific condition but are unable to get an assessment, seek out and arrange a consultation with experts in a particular area.
- ✔ Ask the professionals dealing with your child to compile a report on her strengths and weaknesses. Use this report to plan interventions to help your child achieve her full potential. Make sure you're involved in this planning so that the issues specific to your family are taken into account.
- ✔ If your child is very young, try to be patient. Young children can change dramatically in their early years, so allow professionals to take their time and gather as much information as possible about your child and

her behaviour and development before coming to a diagnosis. (Of course, don't wait to seek specialist help at an early stage, because often early interventions can have significant, positive results.)

✔ If you're unhappy with how an assessment is going or do not understand why you are being asked any questions, share your concerns with the professionals you are dealing with. They should be able to explain why they're working in a particular way and why they're asking particular questions. Keep asking – don't be intimidated.

# Dyslexia

The word *dyslexia* comes from the Greek language and means 'difficulty with words'. Dyslexia is a difference in the brain area that deals with language. It affects the underlying skills that are needed for learning to read, write, and spell.

For centuries dyslexia has been wrongly equated with a lack of intelligence, but we now know it's more a problem of perception. Modern brain-imaging techniques show that dyslexic people simply process information differently; this is not necessarily a bad thing. I prefer to think of dyslexia as a perceptual talent – a gift!

## Common characteristics

In addition to a family history of dyslexia and/or reading difficulties, the following are some indications of dyslexia (from the British Dyslexia Society):

✔ **Persisting factors**, which appear at an early age and are often still noticeable when a dyslexic child leaves school, include:

   • Has obvious 'good' and 'bad' days, for no apparent reason

   • Is confused between directional words (up/down, in/out)

   • Has difficulty with sequences (for example, coloured bead sequences, days of the week, or numbers)

✔ **Pre-school language-related indicators** include:

   • Consistently jumbles phrases (for example, 'cobbler's club' for 'toddler's club')

   • Substitutes words ('lampshade' for 'lamppost')

   • Can't remember the labels for known objects

- Has difficulty learning nursery rhymes and rhyming words
- Develops speech later than expected

**Non-language indicators** include:

- Walked early but did not crawl – or was a 'bottom shuffler' or 'tummy wriggler'
- Has difficulties getting dressed efficiently and putting shoes on the correct feet
- Enjoys being read to but shows no interest in letters or words
- Is often accused of not listening or paying attention
- Trips excessively, bumps into things, and falls over
- Has difficulty catching, kicking, or throwing a ball, and with hopping and/or skipping
- Has difficulty clapping a simple rhythm

✔ **Primary school-age language-related indicators** include:

- Has difficulty with reading and spelling
- Writes letters and figures the wrong way round
- Has difficulty remembering tables, the alphabet, and formulae
- Leaves letters out of words or puts letters in the wrong order
- Still occasionally confuses 'b' and 'd' and words such as 'no' and 'on'
- Needs to use fingers or marks on paper to make simple calculations
- Has poor concentration
- Has problems understanding what she reads
- Takes longer than average to do written work
- Has difficulties processing language quickly

**Non-language indicators** include:

- Has difficulty dressing and tying shoe laces and ties
- Has difficulty telling left from right, order of days of the week, months of the year, and so on
- Is surprisingly bright and alert in other ways
- Has a poor sense of direction
- Lacks confidence and has a poor self-image

✔ **Senior school and beyond indicators** include all primary school indicators, plus:

- Still reads inaccurately

- Still has difficulties with spelling

- Needs to have instructions and telephone numbers repeated

- Gets tied up using long words such as 'preliminary' or 'philosophical'

- Confuses places, times, dates

- Has difficulty with planning and writing essays

- Has difficulty processing complex language or long series of instructions at speed

**Non-language indicators** include:

- Has poor confidence and self-esteem

- Has an area of strength

## *Working with a child with dyslexia*

The following are some positive, practical ideas for helping a child with dyslexia learn better:

✔ **Teach your child to write in a continuous cursive style.** Typically, when first learning to write, children print their letters then move on to cursive writing. For children with dyslexia, learning two styles of handwriting can add an extra layer of difficulty and cause confusion. Young children are often better off learning a single handwriting system, such as continuous cursive.

Continuous cursive features letters that are formed without taking the pencil off the paper, so words are formed in one, flowing movement. Key advantages to this system are:

- By making each letter in one movement, a child's hand develops a physical memory of the letter, which makes producing the correct letter shape easier.

- Because letters and words flow from left to right, a child is less likely to reverse letters, like b and d or p and q.

- Capital and lower case are more clearly defined.

- The continuous flow of writing ultimately improves speed and spelling.

If you want to practise handwriting with your child, use a recommended teaching resource, which shows exactly how to form letters and to practise writing. Contact the British Dyslexia Association (Tel: 0118 966 2677; helpline: 0118 966 8271; www.bdadyslexia.org.uk).

✔ **Use lined paper.** At the earliest stages, use double lines to show the correct size of *ascenders* (b and d, for example) and *descenders* (p and q). Lines should be well spaced to start with (10 mm), gradually reducing to single lines about 5 mm apart.

✔ **Encourage proper posture.** Make sure that your child's chair and desk are at a correct height. Your child's back should be straight and her feet resting on the floor. A right-handed child should have her book slanted to the left; a left-handed child, to the right.

✔ **Use appropriate writing implements.** Choose a standard HB pencil, well sharpened. With youngest children, you can use a chunky triangular pencil to aid the grip. As children get older and more confident, move on to a fountain pen or a special handwriting pen. Avoid using ballpoint pens for handwriting exercises.

✔ **Play rhyming games.** Playing rhyming games is a brilliant way to help children develop reading skills, because they get used to the spelling and sound of words. You can find great tools on the Internet. Take a look at www.enchantedlearning.com/rhymes/matching/.

✔ **Emphasise letter sounds.** Help your child listen for letter sounds, which will help your child learn to read and write. Say a word, and then get your child to say a word that starts with the sound your word ends with. Speak distinctly and emphasise the ending sound. See how long your chain can be. For example, bed-dog-goat-table-elephant-tiger.

✔ **Read the words all around you.** Read out the names of places you pass as you drive or walk around with your child. Your child probably already knows lots of words and symbols from the signs and billboards that she passes every day. It's a great step towards reading when your child knows that the big, red sign at the end of the street means 'stop', that a green traffic light means 'go', and can recognise a word on a billboard!

✔ **Label everyday objects.** Sticky notes are a great way to get children reading wherever they go. Use sticky notes to label everyday objects around your home such as the table, chair, bed, television, door, wall, window, doll, teddy bear. Read them with your child. Remove several and see if your child can stick the labels back on the right objects. Change the things you label every couple of weeks to hold their interest.

---

## Dyslexia resources

Books about dyslexia include:

- *The Gift of Dyslexia* (Souvenir Press Ltd) by Ronald D. Davis with Eldon M. Braun is a breakthrough book by the authors of *The Gift of Learning* with real answers for dyslexic children and adults.

- *Dyslexia: Practical and Easy-to-follow Advice* (Vega Books) by Robin Temple is a guide for parents in helping their dyslexic child – at home and with school.

- *In the Mind's Eye* (Prometheus Books) by Thomas West offers an in-depth look at how creativity and imagination combine to create both genius and dyslexia.

Useful Web sites abound, but here are just a few:

- `www.empowering-solutions.co.uk`

- `www.dyslexia.com`

- `www.lesblind.is/dislexic1/index.cfm`

---

# ADD/ADHD

*Attention deficit hyperactivity disorder* (ADHD) has been described as 'one of the most prevalent and intensively studied syndromes in child psychiatry and possibly the most controversial' (Tannock, 1998).

*Attention deficit disorder* (ADD) and ADHD have their basis in the same perceptual differences as dyslexia (see the 'Dyslexia' section earlier in this chapter). The difference is that ADD/ADHD aren't a reaction to words and letters, but rather a confusion in a child's environment. So when ADD/ADHD distortions happen as an automatic and compulsive response, a learning difference manifests itself.

A child with ADD/ADHD experiences difficulty

- Controlling her impulses
- Focusing her attention
- Controlling her *motor activities* (movements)

## Common characteristics

The three types of ADHD are predominantly inattentive, predominantly hyperactive-impulsive, and combination type.

✔ **ADHD predominantly inattentive type children** have some difficulty in paying attention, are very easily distracted, but may not display hyperactive behaviour. They often have problems:

- Sustaining attention during lessons or play activities

- Starting and finishing school work and other activities

- Following instructions (sometimes they may seem to ignore instructions)

- Remembering details and getting organised

✔ **ADHD predominantly hyperactive-impulsive type children** need to be constantly on the go. They seem to move continuously and are unable to sit still for any length of time, which naturally hampers their ability to concentrate. They often have problems:

- Fidgeting and/or moving inappropriately in classroom situations

- Running around and being on the go

- Being very noisy and over-talkative

- Being very impatient when involved in taking turns

✔ **ADHD combined type children** combine hyperactivity with inattention and are easily distracted. They show many of the preceding traits of both types.

As babies, children with ADHD often cry a lot and have trouble sleeping. They often find physical contact distressing or uncomfortable. As these children get older, they may experience problems in understanding the feelings of other people or may seem cruel or aggressive. These behaviours are not their fault because the children are not intentionally unfeeling towards others. The result of their aloofness is that they're sometimes ignored or shunned by other children and this can be upsetting for a parent to witness.

Many parents of children with ADHD also find that their children are of average to high intellectual ability – but their achievements are often below their apparent level of ability. This discrepancy can be very frustrating and disheartening for both parent and child.

Often, because children with ADHD look perfectly normal, other people have high expectations of them, not understanding their limitations. These people may react with hostility to a child's inability to follow instructions or behave like other children in her age group. A child with ADHD may feel bewildered and demoralised a lot of the time.

I remember a lovely boy called Christopher who threw a stone at another child just to see what would happen. He clearly didn't understand the response he got from the teacher on playground duty. I think part of the difficulty arose because Chris was 8, and in the eyes of the other staff and children he 'should have known better'. Fortunately, I was his class teacher and happened to be on the scene and was able to explain to the other teacher. Chris and I were then able to chat about appropriate ways to behave in the playground and the consequences of his actions.

## Working with a child with ADD/ADHD

If your child is diagnosed with ADD or ADHD, don't despair, feel isolated, or to blame. Children with ADD or ADHD grow, develop, explore, and have productive, enjoyable, and successful lives.

ADHD affects many areas of a child's life. It can make family life difficult, tiring, frustrating, and stressful and can lead to many difficulties in relationships both within families and with other children. ADHD can damage a child's self-confidence and self-esteem if not handled carefully.

Children with ADD or ADHD first must become aware of what is happening to them. Only then can they be shown how to consciously and unconsciously control their behaviours and disorientations (through neuro-linguistic programming (refer to Chapter 6), cognitive behavioural therapy (refer to Chapter 12), or other techniques). Through training and practice, children with ADD/ADHD can learn to switch off their sense of disorientation and achieve a clearer, calmer view of their environment. For example, if your child can hear accurately what other people are saying to her, she can sit still and listen for longer; in the process, your child can feel more confident socially and join in with a group in a more relaxed frame of mind, thus increasing her self-esteem.

Pharmaceuticals are another option some parents and children pursue. Strong drugs like anti-depressants, methylphenidate, dextroamphetamines, and others have their place – and associated risks. Always consult your doctor and do your own research about treatment options.

The following are some positive, practical ideas for helping a child with ADD/ADHD learn better:

✓ **Get an ADD/ADHD diagnosis.** After ADD/ADHD is diagnosed, you, your family, your child, and the school can react to your child's differences with understanding and compassion. This understanding helps your child find solutions to many of the circumstances in which she finds herself.

✔ **Keep a diary of your child's behaviour.** Doing so enables you to identify patterns – particular places, people, or circumstances that exacerbate your child's behaviour. A diary provides you with something tangible to go forward from.

✔ **Don't give up.** Many parents I've worked with have been told that their child's behaviour is due to a lack of parental control, even in families where other children behave appropriately. Some parents have even been told that they must change the way they deal with their child.

Parenting a child with ADHD is very different to parenting a child of a similar age that doesn't have the condition. So trust your instinct and be confident in your parenting. You know your child best, but if you feel you need some support, don't be shy in going forward to find it either.

---

# ADD/ADHD resources

The following organisations can help connect you and your child with support groups:

✔ ADDISS: Attention Deficit Information Services (Tel: 0208 906 9069; www.addiss.co.uk)

✔ www.addsuccess.co.uk

✔ www.adhdsupport.com

✔ www.livingwithadhd.co.uk

ADD/ADHD helplines include:

✔ Adders helpline: 01843 851145

✔ Contact a family: 0808 808 3555

✔ Parentline Plus: 0808 800 2222

✔ YoungMinds: 0800 018 2138

Books about ADD/ADHD include:

✔ *1-2-3 MAGIC: Effective Discipline for Children 2–12* by Thomas W. Phelan (Child Management Inc) includes steps for disciplining ADD/ADHD children without yelling, arguing, or smacking.

✔ *Understanding ADHD* by Dr Christopher Green (Vermillion) is a new guide to ADD in children by the author of the widely acclaimed book *Toddler Taming*.

✔ *Understanding Girls with AD/HD* by Kathleen Nadeau, Ellen Littman, and Patricia Quinn (Advantage Books) focuses on the specific needs and issues of girls with attentional problems.

✔ *ADD: Helping Your Child* by Warren Umansky and Barbara Steinberg Smalley (Warner Books) is a comprehensive programme to help children with ADHD at home and at school.

✔ *ADD Success Stories: A Guide to Fulfillment for Families with Attention Deficit Disorder* by Thom Hartmann (Underwood Books) focuses on practical coping strategies for teenagers and adults with ADD.

# Dyspraxia: The Clumsy Child

*Dyspraxia* is an immaturity in the way the brain processes information, which results in messages not being properly or fully transmitted. Estimates put the number of children experiencing the condition at between 2 and 10 per cent of the population. Boys are four times more likely to have this condition than girls.

## Common characteristics

People who have dyspraxia tend to have poor understanding of the messages that their senses communicate to their brains and have difficulty in relating those messages into physical actions. They may also have difficulty in planning and organising their thoughts. Dyspraxia also affects language, perception, and thought processes.

In some cases, dyspraxia isn't identified until a child reaches secondary school. Some children manage their earlier school experiences with only minor difficulties, but the structure and organisational demands of secondary schools prove to be too difficult. If dyspraxia isn't identified and a child enters secondary education, she can experience low self-esteem and alienation; her behaviour starts to suffer and can become a cause for concern.

The following are some indications of dyspraxia at various ages:

- ✔ **By 3 years old,** children with dyspraxia are already showing indications. Babies are usually irritable from birth and may exhibit significant feeding problems. They are slow to achieve expected developmental milestones (for example, by the age of 8 months, they still may not sit independently).

  Many children with dyspraxia fail to go through the crawling stages, preferring to 'bottom shuffle' and then walk. They usually avoid tasks which require good manual dexterity.

  Dyspraxia can be difficult to diagnose at an early age, so be careful you don't read too much into a situation. Wait and let your child develop.

- ✔ **During pre-school (3 to 5 years old),** children with dyspraxia often:

  - Exhibit very high levels of motor activity, including feet swinging and tapping when seated, hand-clapping or twisting

  - Are highly excitable, with loud/shrill voices

  - Are easily distressed and prone to temper tantrums

- Constantly bump into objects and fall over
- Flap hands when running
- Have difficulty pedalling a tricycle or similar toy
- Lack any sense of danger
- Are messy eaters, may prefer to eat with fingers, and frequently spill drinks
- Avoid constructional toys, such as jigsaws or building blocks
- Have poor fine motor skills, such as holding a pencil or using scissors
- Produce immature drawings
- Lack imaginative play and show little interest in dressing up or playing in a home corner or Wendy house
- Isolate themselves within the peer group and are rejected by peers; they may prefer adult company
- Are not yet clearly left- or right-handed
- Experience persistent language difficulties
- Are sensitive to stimulation, including high levels of noise, tactile defensiveness, wearing new clothes
- Have limited response to verbal instruction and may be slow to respond or have problems with comprehension
- Have limited concentration and often leave tasks unfinished

✔ **By 7 years old**, children with dyspraxia often:

- Continue to exhibit high levels of motor activity
- Have difficulties adapting to structured school routines
- Have difficulties in Physical Education lessons
- Are slow at dressing and are unable to tie shoe laces
- Have barely legible handwriting
- Have limited copying and concentration skills, as well as poor listening skills
- Use language literally
- Cannot remember more than two or three instructions at once
- Are slow to complete class work
- Tend to become easily distressed and emotional

- Have problems co-ordinating a knife and fork
- Are unable to form relationships with other children
- Have sleeping difficulties, including wakefulness at night and nightmares
- Report physical symptoms, such as migraine, headaches, and feeling sick

✔ **By 8 to 9 years old**, children with dyspraxia may have become disaffected with the education system because they've experienced some or all of the preceding problems and feel disillusioned and fed up trying.

## Working with a child with dyspraxia

Having a child who has dyspraxia affects the whole family. You may find that you gear all your family life around the needs of that child and brothers and sisters can often feel neglected. Avoid this situation by

✔ Pursuing activities which involve the whole family equally, and which don't exacerbate your child's different ability (such as swimming or bike riding can do). Try playing board games, cards, or playing the dexterity game Operation. The Shrek edition (produced by Hasbro) is great fun and it can also help your child improve her dexterity and pencil grip, too.

✔ Encourage each child to develop her own hobbies and interests so that comparisons are irrelevant.

✔ Talk to your partner about the problems and be open about how you both feel.

✔ Try to arrange time each week to concentrate on each child, and your partner.

✔ Take time for yourself and keep in touch with friends.

✔ Join a local support group. (Some groups run events which include siblings, too.)

The basics of everyday life can be a tremendous struggle for people who have dyspraxia. The following simple adjustments can make a huge difference to their quality of life.

✔ **Clothing-related tips:**

- Lay out clothing layer by layer with underwear on top to help.
- Buy baggy clothes that are easy and comfy to wear.

- Buy trousers with elasticated waists, which saves fiddling with difficult buttons and zips. Pleated trousers can also help children identify the front of them more easily.

- Avoid tight neck-holes.

- Buy shirt collars one size larger than really fits because they're easier to fasten.

✔ **Eating-related tips:**

- Use a flexible straw with a drink to prevent spilling.

- Don't fill cups too full.

- Use a damp towel under plates to stop them moving.

- Sit down to eat where possible.

✔ **Tips for getting organised:**

- Keep to a daily routine.

- Put sticky notes around the house at eye level to remind your child about things and events.

- Use transparent cases and storage containers that allow your child to see the contents easily.

- Keep keys and purses on a long chain which clips to your child's clothing.

Poor handwriting is one of the most common symptoms of dyspraxia. Children who have poor handwriting don't need their parent or teacher to tell them about it. Every time they write, they can see that they're not as good as their friends.

## Dyspraxia resources

As I point out throughout this book, don't feel alone, isolated, anxious, or terrified. Go out and get some virtual or real support. Find out as much as you can about your child's diagnosis and explore the new and developing resources to help you as a family relax, feel in control, and enjoy life together.

The following organisations can help:

✔ www.dyspraxiafoundation.org.uk/index.php

✔ web.ukonline.co.uk/members/madeleine.portwood/dysprax.htm

As a child progresses through the educational system, the requirement for written work increases. *Take Time* (Robinswood Press) by Mary Nash-Wortham and Jean Hunt provides exercises that can help with handwriting. *Write from the Start* (LDA) by Ion Teodorescu and Lois Addy features the Teodorescu Perceptuo-Motor Programme, which helps develop the fine motor and perceptual skills needed for effective handwriting.

# Asperger's Syndrome

As soon as you meet a person, you make judgements. Just by looking, you can guess age or status. By the expression on the person's face or the tone of her voice, you can tell immediately if the individual is happy, angry, or sad. From these judgements, you can respond accordingly.

Not everyone has this natural ability to recognise these details about people. Children with Asperger's syndrome find it more difficult to read the signals which most take for granted. As a result, they find it more difficult to communicate and interact with others.

*Asperger's syndrome* is a form of autism, a condition that affects the way a person communicates and relates to others. A number of traits of autism are common to Asperger's syndrome, including:

- ✔ Difficulty in communicating
- ✔ Difficulty in social relationships
- ✔ A lack of imagination and creative play

However, children with Asperger's syndrome usually have fewer problems with language than those with autism. They often speak fluently, though their words can sometimes sound a bit formal or stilted. Children with Asperger's syndrome don't usually have the accompanying learning disabilities associated with autism; in fact, these children are often of average or above average intelligence.

Because they generally don't have learning difficulties, many children with Asperger's syndrome enter mainstream school. With the right support and encouragement, they can make good progress and go on to further education and employment.

## Common characteristics

Asperger's syndrome shares many of the same characteristics as autism. The following are the main features of the condition, but because every person is an individual, these characteristics vary greatly, and some may be more pronounced than others.

Because the symptoms of Asperger's syndrome are not as marked as those of classic autism, your child may not be diagnosed for a long time, which means her particular needs may go unrecognised. You may blame yourself – or worse, blame your child – for unusual behaviour, so you must get an early diagnosis to help all of you understand what's happening.

Key characteristics of Asperger's syndrome are:

- **Difficulty with social relationships.** Unlike the person with classic autism, who often appears withdrawn and uninterested in the world, many children with Asperger's syndrome want to be sociable and enjoy human contact. They have difficulty understanding non-verbal signals, including facial expressions, which makes forming and maintaining social relationships with other children and adults challenging.

- **Difficulty with communication.** Children with Asperger's syndrome may speak fluently. but they don't take much notice of the reaction of the people listening to them. They may talk on and on, regardless of the listener's interest, or they may appear insensitive to their feelings. They find it hard to gauge rapport with other people.

  Often, children with Asperger's syndrome have good language skills but sound over-precise or over-literal. They find jokes, exaggerated language, turns of phrase, and metaphors difficult, which can lead to misunderstandings at school. For example, a child with Asperger's syndrome may be confused or frightened by a statement like 'she bit my head off' because she may take it literally.

- **Lack of imagination.** A child with Asperger's syndrome may excel at learning facts and figures but find it hard to think in abstract ways. This situation can cause problems for some children in school because they may have difficulty with certain subjects like creative writing or religious studies, but be really good at other subjects like maths and science.

- **Special interests.** Children with Asperger's syndrome often develop almost obsessive interests in hobbies such as plane spotting or collecting something, such as fossils. Usually their interest involves arranging and memorising lots of facts about a special subject, such as football statistics. If you work with, and not against, this passion and gift, then studying at school and working isn't a problem for a child with Asperger's syndrome.

- ✔ **Love of routines.** Children with Asperger's syndrome find change upsetting. Young children may insist that they always walk or drive the same route to school. At school, they may get upset by sudden changes such as an alteration to the timetable.

Your child may prefer to order her day according to a set pattern. If she goes to school or work at set hours, any unexpected delay, such as a traffic jam or a late train, can make her anxious or upset.

## Working with a child with Asperger's syndrome

The causes of autism and Asperger's syndrome are still being investigated. Many experts believe that the pattern of behaviour from which Asperger's syndrome is diagnosed may not result from a single cause. Strong evidence suggests that the syndrome can be caused by a variety of physical factors, all of which affect brain development. Whatever the cause, you must know that Asperger's syndrome isn't due to any emotional deprivation or the way you brought up your child.

As a developmental condition affecting the way the brain processes information, no 'cure' for Asperger's syndrome exists. But so much can be achieved to make life less challenging for you as a family if you embrace the challenges and look for new and innovative ways to support your child.

---

## Autism and Asperger's syndrome resources

For more information on Asperger's syndrome and autism, try the following resources:

- ✔ National Autistic Society (Tel: 020 7833 2299; www.nas.org.uk)
- ✔ www.udel.edu/bkirby/asperger
- ✔ www.tonyattwood.com.au
- ✔ www.asquarterly.com

I recommend these books:

- ✔ *The Complete Guide to Asperger's Syndrome* by Tony Attwood (Jessica Kingsley Publishers)
- ✔ *All Cats Have Asperger's Syndrome* by Kathy Hoopmann (Jessica Kingsley Publishers)

With time and patience, children with Asperger's syndrome can be taught to develop the basic skills needed for everyday life, such as how to communicate appropriately with people, manage changes, and find their place in the world.

The following are some positive, practical ideas for helping a child with Asperger's syndrome learn better:

- **Share your child's diagnosis.** Because Asperger's syndrome is often less obvious than autism, your child can be more vulnerable and become an easy target for teasing or bullying at school. Make sure your child's teacher is aware of her diagnosis so she can prepare the rest of the class and build the tolerance and understanding that is needed.

- **Communicate clearly.** Because children with Asperger's syndrome struggle with the nuances of language, keep your sentences short – be clear and concise. Discuss your child's communication needs with siblings, other family members, and her school.

- **Write down changes.** Because children with Asperger's syndrome often thrive on organisation and structure, changes to a daily schedule or process can be unsettling. Writing down changes (on a memo board, sticky notes, and so on) can help.

I remember a girl in my class who hated the relaxed routines at Christmas when the class was winding down and making decorations. She felt unsettled and anxious. By writing the changes on the board, in order, she felt more in control and learnt to relax just by seeing the changes visually displayed.

Children with Asperger's syndrome often go on to gain academic success and have really rewarding jobs because they're punctual, reliable, and dedicated. They have remarkable concentration and tenacity and love doing meticulous work. They can be very logical and make exceptional programmers and computer scientists.

# Gifted and Talented

*Giftedness* is a blend of intelligence, personal characteristics, and interpersonal skills. Most parents meet the discovery that their child is gifted with a combination of pride, excitement, and fear. They may worry that they can't keep up with their child or adequately stimulate her. They may fear that their child will become a geek or nerd. In fact (from personal experience), parents may even keep their child's giftedness a secret for fear friends may think they are showing off.

Most people think that gifted children are advantaged children who receive lots of press coverage and attention and who are well supported in school. Well, this situation may be true for the precocious musician, the potential chess grandmaster, or the exceptional athlete but in my experience, these examples form only a tiny minority of gifted children. Many, many more remain unrecognised and unsupported because schools really don't seem to know what to do with them.

Schools are becoming more aware of the need to identify gifted children and provide provision for them in schools. However, ultimately it's your responsibility to seek out the relevant support for your child if you think she is displaying gifted or talented skills.

## Common characteristics

Highly gifted children have the same basic needs as other children, but they are also very different. You can't ignore or gloss over a gifted child's differences without doing serious damage. The differences don't go away; a gifted child doesn't suddenly grow out of her giftedness. These abilities naturally affect every aspect of the child's intellectual and emotional life.

The author Stephanie S. Tolan's microscope analogy can be a useful way of understanding a gifted child's view of the world:

> *'If we say that all people look at the world through a lens, with some lenses cloudy or distorted, some clear, and some magnified, we might say that gifted children view the world through a microscope lens and the highly gifted view it through an electron microscope. They see ordinary things in very different ways and often see what others simply cannot see. Although there are advantages to this heightened perception, there are also disadvantages as well.'*

Because many children eventually become aware of being different, prepare yourself and your child for different reactions to being identified as gifted. Let your child know that unusual gifts – just like hair, eye colour, and shoe size – aren't earned; a gifted child is born that way. What matters is what a gifted person *does* with her abilities. (You may want to use the microscope analogy with your child to help make sure she doesn't become arrogant or over-confident.)

Often, parents first recognise that their child is bright for her age. Many checklists of gifted characteristics exist, but in general they contain several common elements (the following are taken from the National Association for Gifted Children):

A gifted child often:

- ✔ Has a wide vocabulary and talks early

- ✔ Asks lots of questions and learns more quickly than others

- ✔ Has a very retentive memory

- ✔ Is extremely curious and can concentrate for long periods on subjects of interest

- ✔ Has a wide general knowledge and interest in the world

- ✔ Enjoys problem-solving, often missing out the intermediate stages in an argument and making original connections

- ✔ Has an unusual and vivid imagination

- ✔ Can read from an early age

- ✔ Shows strong feelings and opinions

- ✔ Has an odd sense of humour

- ✔ Sets high standards and is a perfectionist

- ✔ Loses interest when asked to do more of the same

Not all gifted children show all these behaviours, but very bright children typically fit a significant number of them.

In classes with inadequate provision or a real lack of differentiation, a gifted child may become bored because not enough is being demanded of her. Gifted children sometimes switch off – daydream, avoid school, clown around, or become disruptive or argumentative. Your child's switching off is all the more reason to find out whether she's really gifted to clarify the situation for everyone.

The best way to find out whether your child is gifted is to have her IQ (Intelligence Quotient) assessed by a psychologist. This can be rather expensive (£325), but the assessment results are something tangible to take to your child's school to make sure she is being served and stretched in the right way.

## *Working with a gifted child*

Exceptionally gifted children have two primary needs:

- ✔ They need to feel comfortable with themselves and with their differences compared to other children of the same age.

- ✔ They need to develop their potential.

Your long-term goal as a parent of a gifted child is not to seek fame, money, or the Nobel Prize, but to bring up a happy, confident, well-balanced child and adult – one who enjoys life and fulfils her true potential, whatever that may be.

As a former teacher in both the private and state sectors of education in England, I have come across many pushy parents who try to live out *their* expectations or frustrations through their children. Nothing saddened me more than to see young children pushed, cajoled, and driven to numerous classes to fulfil their parents' dreams. The greatest gift you can give your child is your trust – trust that she'll find her unique gift and fulfil her own dreams.

Most schools base teaching methods on the developmental norms that are appropriate for most children at their relevant ages. Realise that your child's school isn't purposely setting out to keep your gifted child from learning. The school may not have had to deal with a highly gifted child before, so it doesn't always know how to handle the situation.

In the private sector, a gifted child is sometimes put up a year to work alongside older children covering different work. In a state school, a gifted child may be given a special educational learning plan to cater to her needs. Those with a sporting, musical, or athletic talent may join a specialist after-school club to develop unique talents in the right environment.

Friends, family, and other parents can all react differently when they learn that your child is gifted or talented. Some react with delight, some with jealousy. As a teacher in my son's school, I was rather uncomfortable when he was able to read fluently at 3 years old and was videoed by the psychologist at 4½ as a rather amazing case. I wanted to keep the pressure off him and not have him 'perform' or be under pressure to get ridiculously high marks in exams.

---

## Moving on up

One major consideration if your gifted child is put up a class or two is how she copes with being emotionally separated from her peer group – and how she will go through adolescence if she's hormonally a couple of years behind classmates. Each child is unique and develops at her own rate, so take advice from your child's school if you're not sure.

From personal experience, my son's school handled his ability professionally and with ease. He moved up from the Reception year to Year 1 and because he was very well-balanced emotionally, he sailed onto his secondary school and has been always a year ahead of his peers academically. The only thing he found frustrating, as a keen footballer, was that he was always a bit smaller physically than the other players and he found getting into the top team sometimes difficult and the opposition a bit too robust at times!

Your goal should be to make your child feel as comfortable and relaxed as possible – and to accept her accomplishments as normal. Later on, when the other children catch up, her gifts aren't quite so noticeable and your child is likely to feel that something valuable has been lost.

Remember the following social and emotional tips for parenting a gifted and talented child:

- ✔ **Recognise and identify giftedness early.** Gifted children have a great thirst for knowledge. You must recognise this thirst as early as possible so that everyone can give your child plenty of opportunities to develop her talents.

- ✔ **Find a gifted child a mentor to develop her talents.** A mentor could be yourself, a grandparent, a family friend, or an interested sports or music teacher.

- ✔ **Keep things balanced at home.** Make sure that other children don't become jealous of the time and energy you give (or is demanded of you) to a gifted child.

- ✔ **Find out what your school can and will do.** A good school identifies very able pupils and meets their expectations and needs. Talk to your child's headteacher and find out exactly how the school stimulates and extends gifted children.

    All schools will have developed an agreed policy on how their most able pupils are managed – but be prepared for derision and jealousy as well as enthusiasm and encouragement.

Raising a highly talented child can be frustrating, demanding, exhausting, and brilliant fun. It can be emotionally draining as well as intellectually demanding, but the most important thing to remember is to give a gifted child a safe and secure home to discover who she is and lots of love and acceptance.

# Chapter 15

# Raising Twins, Triplets, and Multiple-Birth Children

. . . . . . . . . . . . . . . . . . . . . . . . . . . . . . . . . . . . . . . . . . . . .

## In This Chapter

▶ Preparing yourself mentally, physically, and practically

▶ Tackling the basics – with more than one child

▶ Seeking and accepting help

▶ Developing a child's individuality

. . . . . . . . . . . . . . . . . . . . . . . . . . . . . . . . . . . . . . . . . . . . .

Sixteen feeds a day, twenty nappy changes a day, and a couple of hours sleep at a stretch – welcome to the world of twins, triplets, or quads!

Raising twins, triplets, or other multiple-birth children is a monumental task. Whether you were a high-flying international jetsetter or a mum with one other child, having more than one child at the same time is exhausting, frustrating, and nerve racking. This role also requires you to be highly organised, able to delegate, and have the confidence to ask for help when you need it. (You also need to have arms like an octopus!)

The chapter offers advice for parents preparing for, giving birth to, and raising twin and multiple-birth children.

## Preparing for Multiple Births

*Nothing prepared me for this. I've never worked so hard, been so exhausted, cried so much, or felt so overwhelmed. I've forgotten how it feels to dress up, sleep longer than two hours at a stretch, and laugh with my friends or even my partner. I didn't think it was going to be like this – what's wrong with me?*

—Claire Butler, mum of twins

While nothing can truly prepare you for giving birth and then raising multiple children at the same time, you can take some proactive steps to make the endeavour more manageable.

A friend I met at a postnatal group said bringing up her twins resembled training to run a marathon – it certainly didn't feel like preparing for a sprint! Her top advice: Make sure you're prepared mentally, physically, and practically, which makes enjoying your children as babies easier.

Get yourself insured *before you have any scans* if you think you have a greater chance of conceiving more than one child – particularly if twins run in your family. Insurance is a good idea to help with the cost of everything.

Following are some additional things you can do *before* twins or triplets become part of your everyday life.

- ✔ **Complete as many of the jobs you mean to do *now*.** When the babies come, these projects (painting the dining room, clearing out the loft, or even de-cluttering your wardrobe) just won't get done. And you may wait for another five years before they do.

- ✔ **Start looking at the world as a parent with two children accompanying you all the time.** Consider, for example, car parking at your supermarket; work out the best places to park and shop with ease. Check that your washing machine is in good working order and that all your appliances are easily accessible and can be utilised with one hand.

- ✔ **Purchase all baby equipment you will need *now*.** Start to buy at least two of everything online and in bulk. Look for discounts on bottles, sterilising equipment, nappies, clothes, and furniture.

My friend with twins bought all her Christmas presents in August because her children were due in November. She knew how stressful trekking round the shops with two tiny babies would be. At the time I thought she was mad, but now I see exactly why she did it.

- ✔ **Practise using all the equipment.** Rehearse getting the car seats into the car, unlocking and pulling up the buggy and fitting a sling around your neck. If you feel confident using the equipment *before* you have the children, you can manage it more quickly when you're also dealing with two crying babies.

- ✔ **Get all your paperwork out of the way.** Pay outstanding bills, or better still put them on standing order.

- ✔ **Prepare birth announcements early.** Write a stack of stamped addressed envelopes to announce the birth to family and friends and have them ready to pop the first photos in. Preparing announcements

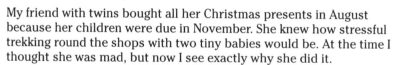

can help you feel less anxious later on. You may feel that doing so is tempting fate, but the more prepared you are the better.

✔ **Get your hair cut and coloured before your babies are born.** A fresh look helps you feel better, more groomed, and more like a human being.

# Bringing Home Your Multiple Bundles of Joy

Here are some practical parenting tips for handling your new arrivals:

✔ **Buy at least four sets of new pyjamas or light tracksuits and live in them.** They're comfortable and easy to wear – and you can have visitors and midwives calling without any worry or fuss about what you look like.

✔ **Don't pressurise yourself to get out of the house before midday.** Get a rota sorted out for any other children for the school run – and relax.

✔ **Strategically locate supplies around your home.** Keep a crib or Moses basket, baby changing equipment, and plenty of baby clothes downstairs as well as upstairs so you don't have to run up and down all the time.

✔ **Maintain your usual noise levels so your new arrivals get used to real life.** Don't make a rod for your own back by making everyone whisper in a tense and unusually quiet atmosphere.

✔ **Don't waste money on fancy nappy bins.** They fill up too quickly. Just get a large ordinary kitchen bin and line it with lovely smelling bin liners.

✔ **Get your babies on some sort of timetable for sleeping at the same time.** Doing so will be a life saver for you. See the nearby sidebar 'Lullaby baby: Getting your babies off to sleep' for tips.

✔ **Keep a feeding and changing journal.** That way everyone in your family can know where you are in the feeding and changing scenarios. In the middle of the night, you're bound to forget who had what and when!

✔ **Prepare easy entertainment options.** Stock up on magazines. Accept that you'll watch loads of 24-hour telly – and be grateful for its company.

✔ **Don't beat yourself up about stimulating your babies in the first days and weeks.** Don't obsess about black and white drawings of faces to stimulate them. Simply love them, cuddle them, and bond properly with them. Keep them clean, fed, and warm – doing so's your priority at first.

✔ **Bath your babies in the kitchen sink.** Doing so saves you an aching back and lots of time.

## Lullaby baby: Getting your babies off to sleep

Even babies under six weeks can be encouraged to help form the right sleep patterns. Follow these guidelines to help settle your babies at bedtime:

✔ The bedtime routine should be calm and quiet. Keep the lights dim, and avoid lots of talking and eye contact during the last feed.

✔ Give your small babies a full feed prior to going to bed, and make sure they're well winded.

✔ Always settle your babies in their cot before they fall asleep. If they become sleepy on the breast or bottle, rouse them slightly before putting them in their cot because this establishes the idea that the cot means sleep time.

✔ Make sure your babies are tucked in securely because this makes them feel secure.

✔ Allow your babies five to ten minutes to settle themselves to sleep. If they get upset, pick them up and offer them more to eat. Hunger is one of the main causes of young babies not settling in the evening, particularly with breastfed babies. Resettle them in their cot and leave them for a further five or ten minutes. If they're still unsettled, repeat the same procedure. Being consistent is the key to this technique working, and in the long term it's more reassuring for your baby than changing tactics at bedtime. Don't be tempted to take them downstairs because bringing them back into their daytime environment only confuses them and won't develop the routine that you're trying to establish.

✔ **Use timesaving gadgets and products.** Try a combined shampoo and conditioner. Get a cordless phone, a baby listening machine, a juicer, and anything else that you can afford.

✔ **Make food preparation as easy as possible.** Use the Internet to do your food shopping and get groceries delivered to your door. Have all the local take-away phone numbers handy.

✔ **Hire help.** You may well be house proud, into feng shui, and incredibly tidy – until you have twins or triplets. Let go and realise that your home will be untidy and messy for weeks, months (and possible even years) to come. Hire a cleaner or ask your existing cleaner to increase their hours.

## *Getting help – and enjoying it*

As the parent of multiple-birth children, you need to be comfortable asking for help. Most parents feel a bit of a failure if they ask for assistance, but if raising one baby takes two parents, then twins must require four and triplets six! So wise up and *ask for* and *accept* some practical help.

Having a couple of hours of daily support does wonders for your morale. The following strategies include ways to find and get the most out of available sources of help:

- **Let your in-laws help.** Mothers-in-law really love to feel needed. Ask for help and then take a bath, go for a ten-minute walk, or open the mail. Fathers-in-law often love to put up new shelves for the babies, change fuses, and cut the grass so they feel helpful too.

- **Organise a reciprocal babysitting circle with other mums with twins.** After you get into your stride, locate other mothers (see the nearby side-bar 'Useful organisations for parents of multiple-birth children') and give yourself a break – just some time to nip to the shops or pop to the doctor's without all the kids. Other mums with twins know the ups and downs and what to expect when they babysit for you.

- **Consider all your options for help.** Neighbours, relatives, health visitors, young teenagers, and anyone else you feel comfortable with can help. Beg favours – or pay people – to help you change a nappy, go to the loo unencumbered, or play with your little ones for a few minutes while you make lunch or a cup of tea.

- **Fully involve your partner.** Don't leave out your partner because you feel you're the best one for the job and he or she doesn't do it 'your way'. Partners want to be involved and participate in the bonding process.

## Feeding and bathing

My experience working with parents of multiples suggests that meals resemble feeding time at the zoo, with one baby balancing on a knee and the other being bounced frenetically in the baby chair by the other foot.

---

### Useful organisations for parents of multiple-birth children

Many parents of twins and triplets find joining a twins' support group helpful. Some useful organisations include:

- TAMBA (Twins and Multiple Births Association; Tel: 0870 770 3305; Twinline: 0800 138 0509; `www.tamba.org.uk`)

- National Organisation of Mothers of Twins Clubs (`www.nomotc.org`)

- Twinsclub (`www.twinsclub.co.uk`)

- For dads with twins: `multiples.about.com/od/dadsofmultiples/a/dadtwintips.htm`

Don't worry. After you get into the rhythm of having twins or more, you won't know anything else, so whatever routine you get used to is fine for your family. Trust your instinct.

Following are some tips for making meals and bath times enjoyable:

✔ **Try breastfeeding your babies, if at all possible.** Breast milk contains a natural balance of nutrients and antibodies for your babies, which protects them from infections and illnesses. Coping with two sickly babies at the same time is very stressful and energy sapping. Try expressing milk and bottlefeeding your other child with it.

✔ **Use different coloured bottle teats for each baby.** This way you know whose is whose – which can be important if they are on different formulas.

✔ **Make up batches of formula 48 hours in advance.** Formula keeps really well in the fridge. Preparing some bottles ahead saves you time and the stress of crying babies waiting for you to make up their feed. Having pre-prepared bottles is also brilliant for the night shift.

✔ **Keep a supply of ready made-up formula.** Just in case, for emergencies.

✔ **Don't be shy to feed your baby in the car.** I knew a mum who carried a sleeping bag in the car to snuggle up in or to put up against the window to create a bit of privacy. (Actually, the mother was me!)

✔ **Purchase a bottle cradle.** This device lets you feed one baby while you wind the other. *Never* leave a baby unattended with a bottle cradle, though, in case of choking.

✔ **Feed from the same bowl.** Feeding twins from different bowls can be difficult because they love to share everything. Put the food in the bowl and let them have spoons.

✔ **Make double the quantity of food.** Enjoy half now and freeze the rest for another day.

✔ **Keep a food diary.** Briefly list who loved the apple puree and who hated the carrot puree to avoid lots of spitting out and frustration.

✔ **Try starting with savoury foods first.** I wish I had done this with my own daughter as she would have got used to all the healthy vegetables first before getting all the lovely sweet fruits and yogurts. Try giving vegetables first as finger foods before fruit.

✔ **Enjoy mealtimes.** Mealtimes are a chance to engage and chat to your children. If you can create a tradition where food, conversation, and fun all come together, your children one day will see mealtimes as a place to share their day or raise their worries.

# Sleeping

When newborns first come home from the hospital, it is not unusual for their days and nights to be all mixed up. They may sleep soundly for three to four hours during the day and then may awaken every one to two hours during the night. So what can be done about this situation?

If your twins' days and nights are mixed up, reverse them by actively playing with them during the day. Exercise their limbs, play music, read books, and sing songs to them. Keep the lights on and pull open the curtains each day.

As the day winds down, calm your home. Dim the lights, pull the curtains, turn off the music, talk in a softer voice, and give your babies a warm bath. Keep to this routine and within one to two weeks, your twins' days and nights will be in synch with you and the rest of the family.

The following are some additional, practical tips for putting your twins or triplets to bed:

- ✔ **Create a *sleep rota* with your partner, even if he or she has to work.** You'll become too exhausted over time if you do all the night feeds yourself. Work out a routine where you are on duty in turns. If you're breastfeeding, try expressing for the night feeds.

- ✔ **Put a microwave oven in your children's room.** This way you can heat up feeds in the middle of the night easily without the screaming that can be really stressful. Be mindful that a microwave can heat milk unevenly and overheat it; be very vigilant that you test the bottle on the back of your hand. (Don't shake the bottle; that puts bubbles into the milk which can give your baby wind.) Also, never heat your breast milk because doing so destroys all its natural antibodies.

- ✔ **Sleep or nap when your little ones are asleep.** Don't start doing the ironing or start the washing. Sit down, read, and fall asleep – you recharge your batteries, which is far more important than a few chores around the house.

If you do lots of little things to make a difference and get as much help, rest, and support as you can, you can bond far better with your children and enjoy the whole experience more. An enjoyable parenting experience is, in turn, good for your confidence and for your children's confidence in you.

## Who? Me?

I remember working with a family who had triplets – three girls. The mum was incredibly stressed at breakfast time, trying to organise the school run, pack the lunch boxes, get the girls' teeth brushed, shoes found, and toast buttered.

As the mother and I chatted about how she would like mornings to be and what was currently

happening, we discovered that she spoke to the children as 'The Girls' – so when she asked them to go upstairs and brush their teeth, they didn't think she was speaking to them.

As soon as she began addressing them by individual names, her children did as they were asked and mornings became much more enjoyable.

# *Developing Twin-dividuality*

Your mother-in-law, sister, or grandma may become exceedingly obsessed about either dressing your children identically with matching bibs, hair accessories, and booties – or excessively worrying that you're not!

From the moment they're born, your children are unique, special, and exceptional human beings. As your children grow, develop, and begin to walk and talk, they express their different personalities, strengths, weaknesses, likes, and dislikes. Dressing the same – or not – doesn't detract from who they are or make them a cloned person.

Additionally, from the moment twins or other multiples are born, people compare and stereotype them: Which is the eldest? Which is the quietest? Which is the strongest? Which one is the most developed? It is important to realise that comparison can be a negative way to view your individual children, affecting not only how the children are seen by the outside world but also the ways they see themselves.

You're likely to find that most people consider parents with twins fascinating and ask lots of really personal questions – usually just as you're unloading the nappies, spaghetti hoops, and toilet rolls at the supermarket checkout. Keep some polite, well-practised answers up your sleeve.

Here are some ideas for developing and cultivating a sense of individuality in each of your children.

✔ **Spend one-to-one time with each of your children.** Children of all ages and stages love to have their parents' exclusive attention. However, twins and multiples are forced to share their parents' (and grandparents') time and attention for much of their lives. Orchestrate opportunities for one-to-one time.

✔ **Find a unique common interest and pursue it together.** As your children develop their own personalities and passions, identify an interest that you can share with each one. Perhaps you both enjoy a sport such as golf or ice skating, an activity such as gardening or cross stitch, or an interest in collecting china teddy bears or model building. Pursuing an interest together is a great chance for both you and your child to learn something new.

✔ **Don't refer to your multiple-birth children as a unit.** Whenever possible, avoid labelling your children as 'the twins' or 'the triplets'. If you recognise that they are individual children, they will too. Yes, calling out your children's names rather than just saying 'Come on, you two' takes more effort. But doing so shows respect for their individuality and gently encourages others to do the same.

✔ **Reward and punish individually.** When I talk to adult twins about their childhoods, I often hear a common theme of resentment when they remember being punished for a crime committed by their twin. Meting out punishment on an all-for-one-and-one-for-all basis is far too easy. You must remember that although they often act like a twin team of naughtiness, you need to recognise and address each individual's role.

✔ **Promote individual activities.** As your children get older, encourage them to seek out individual activities and interests. Each child needs to pursue an interest that is unique to them. Perhaps one can play netball and take art lessons, while the other does tap dancing and karate. While this approach may make for some complicated car-sharing runs, it offers multiples an opportunity to develop their individual talents and encourages them to explore new relationships.

Of course, don't force twins *not* to participate in activities together if they both love swimming and table tennis.

✔ **Encourage individual friendships and separate play days.** Multiples are often each other's best friends. This special relationship should, of course, be celebrated, nourished, and cherished – but it shouldn't be an exclusive relationship. Encourage your children to develop their own friendships in healthy ways. Set up different play dates for each one of them.

✔ **Adjust expectations and standards for each child.** Parents of multiples have to remember that their children are individuals. Be consistent in the way you treat each of your children, but also avoid imposing an unfair double standard on your twins or triplets. Even though they may look and act identically, they are different people with different needs, strengths, and weaknesses.

✔ **Point out and praise unique characteristics.** People seem to be infinitely curious about how twins are alike and different. Use this curiosity as an opportunity to point out and praise the unique characteristics of each of your children. Make sure you give each of them a chance to shine in the spotlight. By focusing on their great – but different – attributes, you build your children's self-esteem about themselves beyond the context of their just being a twin or triplet.

However, never compare your twins, triplets, or quads – the world will do this quickly enough. Your job is to build their self-esteem.

✔ **Celebrate individual achievements.** Celebrate each other's individual successes with equal enthusiasm, whether yours, your partner's, or each of your children individually. Individual celebrations build up your family team and recognise that each of your children is uniquely talented.

✔ **Create individual memories.** Many adult twins talk to me about a regrettable lack of individual pictures of themselves, especially as infants or small children. As a parent, I know how difficult it is to get one photo moment captured, much less separate shots of each of my children. And I know that identifying who's who after the pictures are developed can be even more of a challenge if you have triplets, twins, or quads.

Still, everyone deserves his own set of baby pictures and baby book. Take time to record each child's memories through photographs and writings. Build their childhoods with care and love.

My friend Nicky came from a large family of seven children. The attention to detail in her early photograph albums really touches her. The photos are all carefully labelled with dates and scattered with little personal remarks.

✔ **Identify possessions – his, hers, ours.** You can help strengthen your children's sense of individuality by making sure that their possessions are clearly identified or personalised. Each of your children should have something to call their own, whether it's toys, books, or clothes.

The need to have their own space and possessions increases as twins, triplets, or quads grow up, particularly when they're going through adolescence. Having their own rooms and places to keep their own things becomes very important. You can help by creating and enforcing rules that respect individual privacy and property.

---

# Useful books and Web sites

Some helpful books about raising twins and other multiple-birth kids include:

✔ *Raising Multiple Birth Children* (Chandler House Press) by William and Sheila Laut

✔ *Having Twins – And More: A Parent's Guide to Multiple Pregnancy, Birth, and Early Childhood* (Mariner Books) by Elizabeth Noble

✔ *Two at a Time: Having Twins; The Journey Through Pregnancy and Birth* (Atria) by Jane Seymour

Some helpful Web sites include:

✔ www.parentlineplus.org.uk: A national charity offering help and support through an innovative range of free, flexible, responsive services for parents.

✔ multiples.about.com/od/family issues: A wide-ranging online resource covering family and parenting issues.

✔ www.twinslist.org: Offers advice from the early days to travelling with multiples.

✔ www.twinshelpstore.com: US site offering resources for families with multiples.

---

 Don't stress yourself about whether your children are developing separate identities – develop each child's independence and his identity takes care of itself.

Sibling rivalry is very common with twins and multiple births because, from the very beginning of conception, they've had to compete for nutrition, attention, and space. I know a mum who has deliberately never told her kids which one came first to avoid petty bickering and competitiveness. See Chapter 13 for more on sibling rivalry.

# Making Me Time

As much as you love your children, you're always going to have tough days when it all gets too much. Take a step back from the wood and to try to look at the trees. If you can do something to change your negative or tired state of mind, do it.

I use a lot of neuro-linguistic programming (NLP) techniques throughout this book and with the parents I work with to teach them strategies to change their current states of mind. The easy tricks can really make a difference in your attitude and include simple things such as smiling or changing the voice inside their heads to a silly one such as Donald Duck's or Catherine Tate's. I may suggest they put on their favourite music and dance around the kitchen table – particularly if they don't feel like it. Or I ask them to consider how they would feel about the day if they only had one week to live. All these techniques are about lightening up, laughing, having a cry, and regaining the bigger picture.

I do a lot of work with stressed-out working parents in the corporate environment and in the home. One vital ingredient for a happy, confident, positive parent is 'me time' or as I like to call it 'making a date with myself'. Consider the following strategies for carving out moments for yourself:

- **Break down a tough day into smaller pieces.** If you've been up since 5.45 a.m. and have banana puree all down one side of your trousers, an upset potty, and a crying child, focus on only the next hour, the next ten minutes – or even the next minute at a time.

- **Put mess and chaos out of sight.** If the mess overwhelms you, stick it all in a cupboard and just shut the door. I used to put all the toys in a massive basket and hide it behind the settee. You can always do more – more cleaning, more tidying, more ironing. Give yourself a break; your state of mind is more important.

- **Find ways to let out your anger.** All parents need to express anger, frustration, and tiredness in healthy ways. My friend Sara told me she used to go into the garden and have a good scream sometimes. Another friend finds pillows are pretty robust for hitting in frustration. I used to hide in the stationery cupboard for a few minutes when I taught 35 four-year-olds – just to have a good silent swear.

If you feel you need some help expressing anger in healthier ways, tell your doctor, health visitor, or ring a helpline and get some professional help. Never leave it until you do something you regret.

- **Find time *every* day for you.** Sit and daydream, read the paper, have a bath (and remember to lock the door or you'll have little visitors), ring a friend, watch the soaps, have your own favourite freshly ground coffee, or whatever helps you rest, replenish, rejuvenate, and relax.

- **Take your time.** Deliberately slow down and don't rush everywhere. It's a busy world – but don't join it. Small children dawdle, walk slowly, and look under stones to find fairies, so allow them to do so. They can teach you a lot about life.

✔ **Dress up once a week.** You don't have to wear anything fancy, perhaps just your favourite jeans. Wash your hair, put on some make-up or after-shave and feel like a real person. Doing so connects you to who you really are and helps you to see your family life in perspective with the whole of your life.

## Keeping a Positive Parent Journal

I encourage all the parents I work with to fill in my Positive Parent Journal (available at www.positive-parents.com).

Filling out a page in the Positive Parent Journal each night just before bed-time helps you focus on all the things that went *well* that day. The journal helps you stay focused on all the positive things you do each day and sends you to sleep in a positive frame of mind, ready to begin the next day in a posi-tive way. The journal also helps build a store of happy memories for you as a parent and encourages you to believe in your own abilities.

The successes you list can be as big or as small as you like – they're your achievements and nobody has to see them.

When parents return to see me, we celebrate each week their best achieve-ment as a 'Pat on the Back Moment'. They're encouraged to have that glass of wine, slice of cream cake, or bowl of cherries in celebration.

## Visualising the perfect present

When being a parent becomes too exhausting and you need a boost, try this visualisation as a gift to yourself:

1. **Sit in a quiet place where you won't be disturbed and relax.**

   Close your eyes and focus on your breathing. Hear the sounds of the room around you as you deeply relax and go inside yourself.

2. **Imagine a wonderful present.**

   See the shape of the present. See the colours and the wrapping. Hear the rustle of the paper and the sound of your voice excitedly receiving the present as a surprise.

   This wonderful present is just for you. How do you feel receiving it?

**3. Open the present. It's a box to fill with positive memories and images.**

Include any and all of the following in your present:

- Your happy memories
- Your personal achievements that you're really proud of
- Your special bundles of little things that mean so much to you
- Places you've loved visiting
- People who love you
- Good times and funny things that have made you laugh

Make this the best present you could ever give to yourself – your perfect, ideal, best present ever.

**4. Enhance and accentuate the present you've created.**

Turn up the brightness of your picture. Make the colours more vivid. Bring the present so close that you can hold it in your hands. Turn up the sounds you can hear and make the wonderful feelings you feel even greater. Spin these wonderful experiences up above your head and let them go right down to the bottom of your toes.

**5. Spin the feelings, sounds, and pictures up and down your whole body.**

Let them burst into a golden shower that washes over the top of your head down to the tips of your toes.

This is your present to yourself. You can give yourself this gift any time you need it.

# Part VI

# The Part of Tens

The 5th Wave                    By Rich Tennant

"Y'know, I think some oil and a little soothing music are all we need."

## In this part . . .

This part consists of a set of little chapters full of positive parenting principles to live by, great ways to build a happy home, practical things to do when it all goes a bit wrong, and some really useful resources to support you through your amazing journey.

# Chapter 16

# Ten Things to Do Every Single Day as a Parent

. . . . . . . . . . . . . . . . . . . . . . . . . . . . . . . . . . . . . . . . . . . .

## In This Chapter

▶ Becoming a positive role model

▶ Getting involved in your child's life

▶ Creating boundaries and consistency

▶ Developing independence

▶ Being firm and fair in your discipline

▶ Respecting your child

. . . . . . . . . . . . . . . . . . . . . . . . . . . . . . . . . . . . . . . . . . . .

*P*arenting is a 24-hour a day, 7-day a week, 52-week a year job. Yes, genuine parenting dilemmas pop up every now and then, and you need to prepare yourself to deal with them. But for the most part, the daily essentials of being a good parent come down to the following simple principles that you can practise each and every day.

Think of three habits you'd like to practise on a daily basis and write them here to remind you. Each night just before you fall asleep, take a look at the things you wrote to see if you're remembering to do them and make a note to do them again tomorrow. This chapter gives you some great habits to get into!

## Be Loving

Whether you read the whole of this book from cover to cover or just dip in and out, take this one important fact away with you – you can never be too loving with your children.

Get rid of that old wives' tale that hugging them, holding them, or telling them you love them is spoiling your children. If the parents of the world paid more attention to their children, the world would be a better and happier place.

I can think of many children who suffered because their parents were too busy, too selfish, or too preoccupied to spend time with them. I have never met a child who was worse off because her parents loved her too much. That situation's just not possible.

Show affection in the words you use to praise your child's specific accomplishments when she tries hard or masters something new or challenging. Nothing makes a child stand up taller than praise from a parent – praise that's heartfelt, genuine, and specific. Check out Chapter 5 for more on effective praise.

# Act as a Role Model

Have you ever noticed that you have many of the same attitudes, habits, and opinions that your parents had when you were growing up – even though you swore you'd do it all differently?

Well, that's because your parents were your first, important role models, and you are now the same to your children.

Imitating parents is a natural part of how children develop and grow. Perhaps you're not aware of the subtle messages you send to your children all the time – but all your actions and emotions are communicated to your kids. That's why anxious parents produce anxious children and positive parents bring up confident kids!

Don't be afraid to assert authority as a parent – that's what you're there for! Rather than telling yourself you're powerless against the influence of the media or your child's friends, remind yourself that you do have a strong, guiding influence over your child. In fact, your influence is even more important *because* of these outside influences. You can set clear, fair, and consistent boundaries. So limit your child's TV viewing and video games and regulate what she's allowed to watch.

Everyone performs poorly when tired or stressed. Be aware of your own mental and physical health – and forgive yourself when you stumble. Raising a well-balanced, self-confident adult is hard work! Pat yourself on the back now and again. You deserve that glass of wine! Chapter 7 offers more advice on taking good care of yourself and your relationships.

# Involve Yourself in Your Child's Life

One of the most important things you can do to safeguard your children is to spend time with them. No one ever feels that they have enough time to do the things they have to do – much less the ones they'd like to do! But strong family ties are formed between children and their parents if a little regular daily effort is made to spend time talking, eating, and playing together.

Set aside time when you can give your full attention to your child; perhaps family dinner time, homework help, or once-a-week outings. Remember that each of your children needs some time to spend with you alone, apart from brothers and sisters. Set aside together time with your children when they're younger and the habit is likely to continue as your children grow.

The three kinds of time you can spend with your kids are:

- **One-on-one time.** Just you and your child talking, shopping, cooking, going to the playground or the park, watching television, reading aloud, or playing a game.
- **Family time.** The whole family eating a meal, washing the car, bike riding, reading aloud, cooking, going to the theatre or cinema, or playing a game in the garden.
- **Community time.** When you as a family, or you and your child, attend something in your neighbourhood such as a fete, sports event, or attending your place of worship.

Talking with and listening to your child is one of the most important quality time activities you can do and it can happen anywhere, at any time – while folding laundry, playing a game, doing the shopping, or driving home from Grandma's house.

For more tips on quality time and parental involvement, refer to Chapter 6.

# Focus on Flexibility

Your role as a parent changes as your child grows. What worked well when your child was in nursery doesn't necessarily work when she reaches junior school – and is likely to outright fail when she enters adolescence.

The drive and independence that makes your 3-year-old say 'no' all the time is actually part of the same process that makes your 13-year-old daughter argumentative at the dinner table. It is also what makes her more inquisitive in the classroom and even later on in her career.

So embrace the wider implications of your child's actions. Parental flexibility is all about getting *inside* the mind of your child at her particular age.

Flexibility requires empathy. If you can understand your daughter's new-found obsession with shutting her bedroom door because she's discovered privacy, then you can also understand why she loses the plot when you walk into her room without knocking. If you can remember how it felt to be 16 and hopelessly in love with someone who didn't even notice you, then you can more naturally say the right thing to your daughter when she comes home one night in floods of tears.

For more insights into how parenting styles can evolve over the course of a child's development, head to Chapter 9.

# Set Boundaries and Rules

The two most important things children need from parents are love and structure.

Some of the parents I work with don't want to repeat the strict upbringing that they experienced, so they go the other way and have no rules or boundaries at all. They then wonder why their children don't listen to or respect them – or why they feel so exhausted all the time.

Children thrive on routine and rules (refer to Chapter 8). Like everything in life, providing your child with structure is a balancing act. Structure makes children feel the security of love around them. If your child feels insecure, she may be reluctant to try new challenges.

The real reason for having rules and setting boundaries is that over time your child can develop the ability to set her own boundaries and manage her own behaviour. Although this premise may sound weird, you need to realise that your child's ability to be controlled by you leads to her ability to control herself.

# Be Consistent

The biggest single contributor to a kid's disciplinary problems is inconsistent parenting.

I know you're probably thinking, 'Well, being consistent is easy to say, but hard to do'. True enough. But the secret of consistency is keeping your expectations clear and always meeting the same behaviour with the same reaction.

If you're having trouble disciplining your child, the first thing to do is take a step back and ask yourself, 'Am I being consistent?'

Parents have many reasons for becoming inconsistent, but stress and tiredness seem to be the most common in today's hectic and frenetic world. When you feel like giving in or that you don't have the energy to take on the battle or argument, you can easily get distracted or lose your focus. So take control of your time with the three D's:

- **Decide** what you want to achieve each day by setting yourself just one or two goals that you really want (not need) to accomplish.
- **Discard** any tasks or jobs that aren't really important in the big scheme of life.
- **Delegate** tasks that other people or your kids can do.

This frees up your energy and helps you to stay focused and consistent with your kids.

A lot of parents I chat with ask if they need to maintain a united front with their partner when it comes to discipline. My simple answer is that it depends on your child's age. Because younger children see the world in black and white, they need a totally united front so they know where they stand. With teenagers, a united front isn't absolutely necessary because older children can reason and see two sides to an argument. (Just be sure your children aren't playing you against each other!) Whatever your child's age, however, chat with your partner over important things and make an effort to be singing from the same song book.

# Encourage Independence

From the day you play 'peek-a-boo' with your baby, you're preparing her for separation from you. From her first day at school, first sleepover, and first school trip to France – to the day your daughter leaves home. Good parenting is a step-by-step process, a gradual moving out into the big world, confident and independent from you.

You tread a fine line: Good parenting requires a balance between involvement and independence. Your child learns self-confidence from learning to manage her own self-sufficiency.

Parents who encourage independence in their children, help them to develop a sense of self-direction. To be successful in life, children need both self-control and self-direction. They also need self-discipline to balance their own individual needs with the needs of others.

Children need to feel a mixture of freedom and restrictions. Striving for autonomy and pushing boundaries is perfectly normal for your child. This push isn't always about rebelliousness and disobedience. Rather, your child needs to feel in control of her own life and not constantly controlled by someone else. Check out Chapter 6 for more on gaining independence.

## Be Firm and Fair in Your Discipline

At each stage of your child's development, you must establish your rules that you expect your child to obey. But you also need to expect that your child will, at some point, challenge you and test your limits. This behaviour's just what kids do.

Your job is to do what's *best* for your child, whether she likes it or not. You are the adult; you are the more experienced, wiser person who can see the bigger picture. Don't let your toddler blackmail you into buying that ice cream just before lunch with a screaming tantrum. Don't let your 12-year-old refuse to change her smelly shirt after a netball match because she gets all huffy and won't speak to you for a couple of hours. Don't let your teenager get away with not emptying the dishwasher because you can't bear her sulky behaviour as she does it. Remember – you're teaching life skills and helping to develop a well-rounded, helpful, self-reliant adult for the future and if it helps, remember that this phase doesn't last forever!

Your child's judgement isn't as good as yours. You are building an adult – part of tomorrow's future generation – so stand your ground.

## Listen First, Talk Later

Most people who know me find it very amusing that I'm a parent coach because I'm such a great talker. But what they don't realise, until they work with me or have a problem, is that I'm also a very keen listener.

Listening is the best gift you can give anyone – including your kids. Listening makes children feel valued, heard, and understood. It makes them feel important.

Through listening properly to your children, you help them find their own answers. They also let off steam. You may even get to ask the odd great question and your child may start to see things from a different perspective.

So turn down the TV, stop reading the paper, and stop peeling the potatoes. Look at your child and give her your full attention. Listen with genuine interest and really pay attention to what she's telling you. Keep an open mind – don't judge or interrupt her. You know how frustrating it is when your friend or partner interrupts you, half listens, or just says 'aaahh haaa' now and again. Your kids deserve better. Chapter 5 offers more insights on effective listening.

You have two ears and only one mouth for a reason!

# Respect Your Child

Your relationship with your child is the foundation of her relationships with others. If you treat your child with compassion, kindness, and respect, she'll grow up to be concerned about others, caring, considerate, and respectful towards people. If you are uncaring, rude, and dismissive, your child is very likely to have these characteristics when she's grown up. (Oh, and remember, your children choose your old people's home!)

Respect is the key to a good family – it brings everyone together. Families don't die from their setbacks, but they can wither and die from a negative, sarcastic, taunting, or guilt-ridden culture within them.

As obvious as this sounds, speak politely to your child and respect her opinion. Pay real attention when she speaks to you. Treat her kindly.

# Chapter 17

# Ten Techniques to Build a Happy Home

*P*erhaps you have an ideal vision of what your home is supposed to be like based on television shows, films, and magazines. Or maybe you define home as 'the opposite of everything *my* parents did'. However you define home, you can do little things every day to make it a better place for your kids, your partner, and yourself. This chapter offers my ten favourite strategies for making your home – however you define it – a happier, healthier, more positive place.

## Play with Your Child

You've seen them: The cute tiger cubs playing and wrestling together, the baby polar bears tumbling in the snow, the kittens chasing each other, and the puppies romping about. All young animals seem to enjoy playing exuberantly together.

Playing is an essential part of every child's development. It is your child's way of exploring the world and allows him to discover his senses. Through play, children explore and control their body movements, the ways to use language, and how to make sense of their environment and surroundings.

Being able to play freely enables your child to gain invaluable life skills, including socialising, learning about themselves and others, and discovering different ways to do things.

Play is children's 'work' – and they take it very seriously!

So what about getting down on your knees and roaring like a lion and chasing your kids round the sitting room?

# *Teach Your Child to Be Organised*

The demands on everyone's time and energy these days are numerous. You're busy, and so is your child. Unfortunately, children aren't born knowing how to manage time and organise their stuff or meet deadlines.

As a working mum, I had to teach my children to organise their sports kit on a Sunday, get them to sort out their packed lunches the night before (and put them by the front door), pack their reading books and diaries, and put their washing in the wash basket. I even taught them how to turn on the washing machine. (Now I didn't say they always remembered to use it – I'm not Super Mum!)

Teach your children to be organised because it helps cut down on everyone's stress. You can help by teaching your child strategies that make staying organised easier and (as usual) by setting a good example by working to be organised yourself:

- **Commit to change.** Deciding to get organised is like resolving to lose weight: both require discipline, and neither happens overnight! Rather than searching for a quick fix (the equivalent of a fad diet), organising your family to help themselves means committing to a lifestyle change, but it's worthwhile because it cuts down on your stress in the long term.

- **Build organisation into your daily routine.** Get your kids used to helping themselves by getting them to lay out their school uniforms the night before, and packing away their homework after they've done it. Show your kids how to sort out their laundry by putting it in a basket and bringing it down on a regular day each week, and doing their own laundry when they're old enough!

It's never too early to start training your children to be organised.

# Speak Softly and Gently

Most parents spend a lot of time talking only about a few things with their children: Wash your hands. Stop teasing your sister. Do your homework. Stop that. Go to bed.

You have more power than your child because you are bigger and stronger. But you'll have a difficult time forcing a child to do something he doesn't want to do. You may end up spending all your time yelling at your child or trying to bribe, convince, or force him (and then feeling guilty about it afterwards). That's the trouble with control: It takes over your relationship with your child. In fact, control can become the *only* thing that you and your child seem to talk about. Not a very good basis for a relationship.

Getting your child to do something by being gentle is just as easy as yelling and screaming. You can choose to yell, or you can choose to speak calmly. Your child is far more open to hearing you when you talk in a kind, gentle, and respectful way – so keep this fact in mind the next time you want to shout at him. Turn to Chapter 5 for more ideas on effective communication.

# Be Patient

If one quality was able to alter your life, it would probably be the power of patience. In this high-pressured, fast-paced, frenetic world, the norm has become to expect things to happen immediately. Most people get really irritated when things don't! Unfortunately, the consequence of approaching life like this is that you lose sight of the really important things in life – such as your relationship with your children or partner.

Patience is something you *do* – not something you don't have enough of. Think of patience as a muscle. You need to practise using it so it gets stronger.

Patience gives you self-control and the ability to stop and be in the present moment. From that position, you can make better choices – better choices in the words you use, how you feel, and the way you handle situations with your kids. Refer to Chapter 7 for advice on fostering patience within yourself.

# Respect Privacy and Personal Space

Everyone likes to have some personal time and a bit of personal space. Kids are no different. Regardless of their ages, they need time to relax, re-energise, and be alone. When my son turned 13 I noticed a distinct change in his attitude toward personal space and time; he wanted to be alone while getting changed and to spend more time on his own in his own bedroom.

The challenge lies in finding a balance between public, group time and private, personal time.

As my children have grown older, I have found establishing a policy of knocking and waiting for an invitation before entering my children's rooms to be very beneficial. They seem to really like the way I respect their space and privacy now.

If your children share a bedroom, talk about personal space and time. Teach them to respect each other's wishes to be alone occasionally. In this way, your children have a secure place where they can be alone to think, cry, create, or relax.

# Tell the Truth

I talk a lot about being a role model to your kids, and this definitely applies to telling the truth.

I hold being honest in high regard. I've always taught my own kids, as well as the kids I taught in school, to take responsibility for themselves, even if they get told off or into trouble, because being honest and telling the truth is a very important thing to do.

Children need to have a sense of what is right and wrong. If you teach the value of honesty to your children at a young age, then it won't be so difficult to expect that of them when they are older. Telling the truth will just be a habit.

The best way to teach children honesty? Be honest with them.

# Keep Your Child Safe

When your child is small, his physical safety is likely to be a major concern. Make sure your child doesn't wander off from you in a busy street or shopping centre. Hold your child's hand or use a safety harness or some reins to keep him near you.

By about 3 years old, you can start teaching your child some simple safety rules:

- ✔ Introduce some simple Stranger Danger rules such as: 'Never go off with anyone you don't know – even another child – without checking that it's okay with us first.'
- ✔ Teach your child his full name, address, and telephone number (although kids may not really remember the details in full until they're about 5 or 6).
- ✔ Teach your child safe ways to cross the road and how to ask for directions. Practise these techniques with him.

I remember my mum and dad always arranging a safe meeting place in case I got lost in a new place, so I knew where to go if we got separated (which I did in a Spanish market when I was about 6). Your meeting place can be by the checkout or central information point in a shop.

# Laugh a Lot

Life can be too serious if you're not careful. The bills and the mortgage can get you down. But, for children, life should be full of hope and fun, joy and curiosity.

What can you do to lighten up a bit? How can you create moments of silliness when you dance round the kitchen table singing to Robbie Williams or Justin Timberlake holding the pepper grinder as a microphone? Or is that only me?!

Connect with your young self. Remember how it felt to be young, enthusiastic, hopeful, playful, and free from too many responsibilities. Try to feel at ease with your child-like self – and life in general.

Perhaps you were brought up to think being an adult is a serious business. Suspend that belief for a little while and let it go. Breathe deeply and relax into a more playful attitude to life and see the changes that can occur easily and effortlessly as you lighten up your attitude to everything and decide to wear your party pants more often.

Your child will love spending time with you while you *both* grow, change, and laugh together. Laughter, humour, and seeing the funny side to things is a great way to change an atmosphere, feel less stressed, and gain more energy.

# Know Where Your Child Is

A parent's natural reaction is to be protective, but realistically you can't possibly watch over your kids all day, every day. Pre-teens and teenage children, in particular, need to see their friends and spend time away from their parents. Self-sufficient activities are healthy, normal, and essential to your child's growth and sense of identity.

Still, your most important job is to keep your child as safe as you can without arousing too much tension and fear in him.

Think and talk about a safety plan for your family. For example, remind your children that you need to know where they're going, who they're with, and when you can expect them to be back.

My husband and I ask our son for the phone numbers and addresses of his friends. We also organise practical ways for him to contact us if he's been delayed.

Chat about how you plan to try and find your children if they're not back in time. Make clear arrangements for picking up your kids if they've been out. Write down arrangements so they're easy for everyone to understand.

Being prepared isn't tempting fate – it's more like taking out insurance. After you have things covered, you rarely need it.

# Tell Your Kids the Truly Important Things

This tip is actually ten tips in one. Lucky you! Each of the following statements is worth sharing – and re-sharing – with your kids. When in doubt, try telling your child one of the following:

✔ **'I love you no matter what.'** Remember to love your child's successes and failures equally.

✔ **'You're special and you mean the world to me. I'm so pleased you're part of our family.'** Tell your child what unique qualities you admire, and encourage him to be himself no matter what.

✔ **'I'm so proud of you.'** No matter what your child achieves, the effort he puts into things is what makes your child proud of who he is.

✔ **'It's okay to make mistakes.'** Mistakes are the way to discover even more things we can do.

✔ **'You're great fun to be with.'** Let your child know that you love spending time with him – talking, laughing, playing, or just chilling out with him.

✔ **'I love listening to you – so tell me more.'** One of the greatest things you can give your child is the space to express himself, experience being heard, and feel understood. Doing so shows you are interested in what's going on in your child's world.

✔ **'Life is what you make it.'** The key to a successful life is attitude and a positive perception. Only you, as a parent, can teach your child the most resourceful ways to make his life happy.

✔ **'Get the balance right.'** Too many late nights can make your child grumpy. Too many fizzy drinks can rot his teeth and make him hyperactive. Too many hours on the PlayStation can make him restless and anti-social. Decide on a workable set of rules together, so that he can have an element of control over his activities – and acknowledge what's good and bad for him – you can still monitor them.

✔ **'Always keep laughing.'** Laughter eases stress, diffuses situations, and keeps you young. Plus, when you have a playful attitude to life, people are drawn to you.

✔ **'Be kind, compassionate, and helpful to everyone you meet. Don't judge – just try to understand them.'** Encourage your child to explore other people's points of view and to see the world from others' shoes. Encourage your child to go out of his way to undertake random acts of kindness for no reason at all. Kindness to others makes the world a better place.

# Chapter 18

# Ten Things to Do When It All Goes Pear-Shaped

*B*ringing up children isn't always easy. Many challenges, frustrations, and changes are involved in raising happy, confident, well-balanced children – tomorrow's adults.

No magic cure-all for stress exists. You just have to experiment with lots of different ways until you find something that suits you – acupuncture, aromatherapy massage, working out, having a candlelit bath, watching TV, enjoying a cup of coffee, or chatting to a friend.

Stress management is a routine part of most large businesses nowadays, because they have come to realise that positive ways to handle stress increase efficiency. Try applying the same principle to parenting – after all, if you'd asked me at 5.45 a.m. on Saturday morning how I was feeling after already taking out the paint pots, painting a rainbow, and washing up for breakfast, I'd have said 'Stressed!'

Being a parent, and particularly being a single parent, is exhausting. This role is physically, emotionally, and mentally demanding. When you're running on empty, your reserves are low. You run out of patience and energy and often react to stress in a negative way.

So what do you do if you feel overwhelmed, depressed, stressed, and unsure? This chapter offers some best first steps for finding solutions.

# Get Help When You Need It – in the Way You Need It

Parenting can be a lonely business, but remember that a problem shared is always a problem halved. Seek out support from wherever you feel most comfortable. Talk to your family, friends, neighbours, or older, more experienced people and ask their advice. Bear in mind:

✔ Some parents enjoy forums on the Internet.

✔ Some parents prefer joining a real-world group with individuals of similar interests and experiences – such as other parents with teenagers, toddlers, or kids with special needs.

✔ Some parents prefer talking to their doctor or health visitor.

The key is, whenever you feel overwhelmed, unsure, anxious, or that everything's just going pear-shaped, you must find the right support for *you*.

# Address Postnatal Depression

Nothing is quite like the joy of holding your newborn baby for the first time, or experiencing the moment when she first looks up at you, totally dependent on you.

But after the birth, sometimes emotions are so overwhelming that you can't imagine coping with the enormous responsibility of having a child. Most new mums get the 'baby blues' – on the third or fourth day after the birth they feel a bit weepy, flat, and unsure of themselves. But *postnatal depression* (or PND) is what happens when you become depressed after having a baby.

Around 1 in every 10 women has postnatal depression. If you feel you need some help, don't be ashamed to admit it. Your doctor, health visitor, and midwife want to help you get better so that you can enjoy and care for your baby – so just ask.

Just talking to a sympathetic, understanding, uncritical listener can be a great relief. You may choose to talk with a friend, relative, volunteer, or professional. If you can't easily find someone, try the National Childbirth Trust (www.nct.org.uk) or the Meet a Mum Association (www.mama.co.uk) – their local groups are very supportive, both before and after childbirth.

You can choose more specialised and alternative treatments to antidepressants, including cognitive behavioural therapy (see *Cognitive Behavioural Therapy For Dummies* by Rob Willson and Rhena Branch), that can help you to understand and resolve the depression.

In addition to talking through PND, remember the following dos and don'ts:

- ✔ **Don't** try to be 'superwoman'.

- ✔ **Don't** move house (if you can help it) until your baby is six months old.

- ✔ **Do** make friends with other couples who are expecting or have just had babies. Having friends in similar situations makes you feel supported and means you have someone in the same boat to chat with. These relationships may even lead to a baby-sitting circle.

- ✔ **Do** go to antenatal and postnatal classes – and take your partner with you.

- ✔ **Do** keep in touch with your GP and your health visitor, particularly if you've suffered postnatal depression before. You can be better able to recognise any signs of PND early, and you can start treatment at once.

- ✔ **Do** take every opportunity to get your head down. Try to cat-nap. Let your partner give the baby a bottle-feed with formula or your own expressed milk.

- ✔ **Do** eat enough and make sure you're eating healthy foods such as salads, fresh vegetables, fruit, fruit juices, milk, and cereals, which are all packed with vitamins and don't need much cooking.

- ✔ **Do** find time to have fun with your partner. Try to find a baby-sitter and get out together for a meal or to see friends.

✔ **Don't** blame yourself or your partner. Life is tough after having a baby, and tiredness and irritability on both sides can lead to quarrels. Having a go at each other may weaken your relationship when it needs to be at its strongest. Make time for each other.

✔ **Don't** be afraid to ask for help when you need it.

A useful Web site for locating support, ideas, and friendship locally is www.netmums.com/lc/postnataldepression.php.

# Manage Your Anger

Everyone gets angry. You know what anger is – whether you experience it for a brief second or in a fully fledged rage. I've even described anger as a 'parent tantrum'. The hardest thing about such strong feelings is learning what to do with them.

Being angry at times is perfectly okay. In fact, you need to get angry sometimes and let the emotion and frustration out. But you must release anger in the right way – a healthy way. Otherwise, you'll be like a pressure cooker full of boiling water with the lid tightly on; if the steam doesn't escape, the water finally boils over and the cooker blows its top. When that situation happens, it's no fun for anyone.

Never getting angry is impossible. Instead, remember that how you act when you're angry can make the situation better or worse. *Don't let anger control you* – take charge of it. Chapter 10 offers lots of great tips for better understanding and taking control of anger.

# Deal with Stress

Overwhelmed and stressed are two words many parents use to describe their situations. Although feeling stressed is normal, you must tackle your parenting challenges head on – don't let stress take control of you.

Think about how starting to take control of your stress can benefit your whole family. Stress drains your energy and has a negative impact on you and your family. If you run on empty for too long, you run out – and your family need you to be energised, upbeat, and happy.

Start to manage your stress by taking energy breaks and making dates with yourself. Write down a list of little things you can do to replenish your batteries, put a spring in your step, and make your eyes shine again. Enjoy a cup of coffee, sit down for 15 minutes, or take a long, hot bath. Just become more aware of taking time out for yourself each day, each week, and each month. And make a promise to yourself to do these little things on a regular basis. Put some dates in your diary so you get into the habit of making these treats an everyday occurrence. See Chapter 7 for more stress-managing ideas.

# Get Discipline Back On Track

Rather than noticing your child's bad behaviour, really go out of your way to notice the times when she behaves well. Encourage the behaviour you want so that you can catch your child being good. What you pay attention to happens more often: Kids love attention, you feel great, and your relationship and discipline really improve.

Rely on clear, specific, genuine praise (see Chapters 8 and 10). Everyone says things such as, 'Oh, what a great picture' rather than 'I love the turquoise blue sea and the bright yellow sun'. Children (and adults actually) like very clear and genuine statements of praise. You can apply this level of specificity to behaviour, too. Each time your child behaves well, be specific in your language and say 'Thank you for picking up that crisp packet from the sitting room floor' or 'I love the way you've tidied your bedroom'. Make sure your child knows *exactly* what you are pleased about – and watch your relationship improve in leaps and bounds.

# Keep the Glow in All Your Relationships

I find that those closest to me always put me under the greatest pressure to be patient and attentive, to play with them, talk with and listen to them, or just spend time with them. Perhaps your children, partner, friends, relatives, or colleagues all want a part of you, and you sometimes feel pulled in all directions.

As a parent, you are in the driving seat of a lot of relationships. So maintaining the glow in your relationship with yourself and with all those around you is very important.

Relationships can change, become vulnerable, and lose direction when you have children. Try writing down seven actions that you can take to improve your relationship with either yourself, partner, friends, relatives, colleagues – or all five of them. By shining a torch on your relationships, you can begin to stand back objectively and give your relationships an MOT, which allows you to make some simple, small changes with big benefits.

Start making small changes every day and notice how things feel. Write down your achievements in a journal, which can keep you motivated to continue making those small adjustments. Chapter 4 has loads more about relationships.

# Get into a Positive State

I do a lot of work during my seminars on helping parents get into *positive parent states*. This is where I help parents get into a positive frame of mind using many different practical strategies taken from tried and tested neuro-linguistic programming techniques.

The following exercise is just one way to take back control when you feel everything spiralling out of control:

1. **Relax and breathe deeply and slowly.**

   Allow your shoulders to drop. Allow your whole body to relax.

2. **Mentally give yourself a gift – the gift of being peaceful and relaxed – now.**

3. **Imagine what you really want to achieve as a parent.**

   Imagine what you can see and hear and imagine how you feel.

4. **Turn the colours of the picture up brighter and the sounds you can hear louder, and make the feelings more intense.**

   Really step inside your picture and enjoy the warm feelings of joy and success, pleasure and pride.

   See yourself smiling. Feel content and happy knowing that you have done a good job.

5. **When the experience can't get any better, bring the pictures and sounds and feelings closer to you and clench your fist tightly.**

   As you clench your fist, remind yourself of this wonderful experience.

Breathe deeply and slowly, savouring, remembering, and relishing these wonderful feelings.

6. **Breathe deeply and become aware of the sounds in the room.**

Feel your feet on the ground and your body on your chair. Start to come back to where you are now and open your eyes.

You can have this wonderful feeling anytime you want it – when your kids won't brush their teeth or tidy their bedrooms. You can have it when you're late, tired, or grumpy. You can choose to have it anytime you need it. Simply clench your fists and the feeling returns to you easily.

# Get Physical

A simple physical change you can make is to start smiling. This may sound crazy, but merely smiling actually sends a message to your brain that makes you feel better immediately. Try it!

Similarly, jumping up and down, hopping about, or pretending to be an aeroplane helps you to start feeling better. Try putting music on and singing or dancing round to it. All these actions lift your mood.

By changing your energy level, you start to change your attitude and mood, which helps you feel more in control.

# Be Flexible

A lot of families I work with come to me when they find themselves stuck. I use Neuro-Linguistic Programming (NLP) to free up the stalemate that many families find themselves in.

In my experience, flexibility is the key to making good choices and having better relationships. The person who is the most flexible holds the key to success – so, as a parent, it's a good idea to be you.

The important thing to remember is that your role as a parent changes as your child grows. Good parenting is flexible and it needs to fit into your child's stage of development. What worked well when your child was 3 and in nursery, doesn't really work when she goes to junior school or when she becomes a teenager.

Being flexible may seem obvious, but you'd be surprised at how many parents refuse to change their style as their child develops and then find themselves wondering why they're having so much difficulty communicating with their child using techniques that always worked before.

# Celebrate Your Successes

During my seminars I encourage parents to make a note of their single biggest achievement at the end of each day. Try doing so yourself for a week.

Your achievement can be as small or as big as you want – from not shouting at the kids to smiling at the mess. At the end of the week, look over your list of achievements and rank them in order, from 1 to 7, with 1 being your greatest moment.

Take time to read your chosen moments and really relish and enjoy the warm feelings of success. Picture your greatest achievement, hear the sounds associated with it, and feel the wonderful feelings. Turn the colours up brighter and the sounds louder. Feel all the great feelings swirling up from the tip of your toes to the top of your head and back down and up again. Really spin the joy of the achievements and success.

Wondering how good a parent you are is normal. Perhaps you worry about how your status as a working, single, or divorced parent may affect your child. You may fret about being firm enough – or being too firm. You may feel anxious about whether you are doing the right thing or being the right role model.

Every parent wants to get it right and do the very best for their kids. In the end, successful parenting is all about balance, loving care, and clear boundaries. Perfect parents do not exist. No parent has all the answers – just some common sense guiding principles. All children need love, affection, safety, limits, shelter, food, clothing, and to have the opportunity to learn. But after these things, you'll find many different ways to bring up happy children.

I wish you happiness on your parenting journey – learn, laugh, and grow together.

# Chapter 19

# Ten (or so) Top Resources for Parents

*E*ven with the Internet and an abundance of books, magazines, and other information sources, locating truly useful parenting resources can be a challenge. This chapter highlights ten (or so) of my top choices for finding the information you need.

Of course, you can always contact me directly at:

Sue Atkins

Positive Parents Confident Kids Coaching Ltd

Tel: +44 1342 833355

E-mail: sue@positive-parents.com

Web site: www.positive-parents.com

## Parentalk

Parentalk is an organisation committed to helping parents make parenthood fun. It produces a range of resources that are full of practical, down-to-earth information and advice on how to make the most of your parenting.

PO Box 23142

London, SE1 0ZT

Tel: 020 7450 9073

Fax: 020 7450 9060

E-mail: info@parentalk.co.uk

Web site: www.parentalk.co.uk

## Care for the Family

This organisation provides support for families through seminars, resources, and special projects.

PO Box 488

Cardiff, CF15 7YY

Tel: 029 2081 0800

Fax: 029 2081 4089

E-mail: mail@cff.org.uk

Web site: www.care-for-the-family.org.uk

## Parentline Plus

Parentline Plus provides a free phone helpline and courses for parents. Parentline Plus also includes the National Stepfamily Association.

520 Highgate Studios

53–76 Highgate Road

Kentish Town

London, NW5 1TL

Free helpline: 0808 800 2222

Text phone: 0800 783 6783

Fax: 020 7284 5501

E-mail: centraloffice@parentlineplus.org.uk

## Parents Anonymous

This is a 24-hour answering service for parents who feel they can't cope or feel they might abuse their children.

> 6–9 Manor Gardens
>
> London, N7 6LA
>
> Tel: 020 7263 8918

## Parents at Work

This organisation provides advice and information about childcare provision.

> 45 Beech Street
>
> London, EC2Y 8AD
>
> Tel: 020 7628 3565
>
> Fax: 020 7628 3591
>
> E-mail: info@parentsatwork.org.uk
>
> Web site: www.parentsatwork.org.uk

## Relate

Relate provides a confidential counselling service for relationship problems of any kind; it has many local branches.

> Herbert Gray College
>
> Little Church Street
>
> Rugby, CV21 3AP
>
> Tel: 01788 573 241
>
> E-mail: enquiries@national.relate.org.uk
>
> Web site: www.relate.org.uk

## National Council for One-Parent Families

This organisation is an information service for lone parents.

255 Kentish Town Road

London, NW5 2LX

Lone Parent Line: 0800 018 5026

E-mail: info@oneparentfamilies.org.uk

Web site: www.oneparentfamilies.org.uk

## Gingerbread

Gingerbread provides day-to-day support and practical help for lone parents.

7 Sovereign Close

London, E1W 3HW

Advice line: 0800 018 4318

Tel: 020 7488 9333

E-mail: office@gingerbread.org.uk

Web site: www.gingerbread.org.uk

## Home-Start UK

Home-Start UK provides support, friendship, and practical help for young families in their homes.

2 Salisbury Road

Leicester, LE1 7QR

Tel: 0116 233 9955

E-mail: info@home-start.org.uk

Web site: www.home-start.org.uk

# National Childminding Association

This group informs childminders, parents, and employers about the best practices in childminding.

8 Masons Hill

Bromley

Kent, BR2 9EY

Advice line: 0800 169 4486

Tel: 020 8464 6164

E-mail: `info@ncma.org.uk`

Web site: `www.ncma.org.uk`

# Fathers Direct

Fathers Direct provides information and resources for fathers.

Herald House

Lambs Passage

Bunhill Row

London, EC1 8TQ

Tel: 020 7920 9491

E-mail: `enquires@fathersdirect.com`

Web site: `www.fathersdirect.com`

# Online resources

Sources of online information are plentiful. Following are some of my favourites:

- ✔ `www.bbc.co.uk/parenting`: Includes a wealth of information, forums, and support.
- ✔ `www.raisingkids.co.uk`: Offers support, information, and friendship to everyone raising kids, whatever their circumstances or income.

✔ www.netmums.com: Netmums is a unique local network for parents, grandparents, childminders, health visitors, or nannies, offering a wealth of information and advice for anyone working with families.

✔ www.childline.org.uk: ChildLine is the free helpline for children and young people in the UK. Children and young people can call 0800 1111 to talk about any problem. Counsellors are always available.

✔ www.workingfamilies.org.uk: Working Families is the UK's leading work–life balance organisation, offering help and a voice for working parents.

✔ www.familyonwards.com: Links to articles, book reviews, and other useful Internet sites.

✔ www.growingkids.co.uk: Offers a wide range of tips and advice for healthy, happy, growing kids.

✔ www.parentscentre.gov.uk: Information and support for parents on how to help with your child's learning, including advice on choosing a school and finding childcare.

# Index

## • *P* •

● **S** ●

• *U* •

• *V* •

# Notes

# FOR DUMMIES®

## Do Anything. Just Add Dummies

## UK editions

### PROPERTY

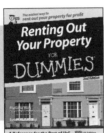

**Buying and Selling a Home For Dummies**
0-7645-7027-7

**Renting Out Your Property For Dummies**
0-470-02921-8

**Buying a Property in Eastern Europe For Dummies**
0-7645-7047-1

### PERSONAL FINANCE

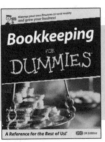

**Investing For Dummies**
0-7645-7023-4

**Bookkeeping For Dummies**
0-470-05815-3

**Sorting Out Your Finances For Dummies**
0-7645-7039-0

### BUSINESS

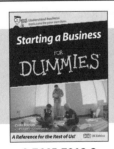

**Starting a Business For Dummies**
0-7645-7018-8

**Marketing For Dummies**
0-7645-7056-0

**Business Plans For Dummies**
0-7645-7026-9

Answering Tough Interview Questions For Dummies
(0-470-01903-4)

Arthritis For Dummies
(0-470-02582-4)

Being the Best Man For Dummies
(0-470-02657-X)

British History For Dummies
(0-470-03536-6)

Building Confidence For Dummies
(0-470-01669-8)

Buying a Home on a Budget For Dummies
(0-7645-7035-8)

Children's Health For Dummies
(0-470-02735-5)

Cognitive Behavioural Therapy For Dummies
(0-470-01838-0)

Cricket For Dummies
(0-470-03454-8)

CVs For Dummies
(0-7645-7017-X)

Detox For Dummies
(0-470-01908-5)

Diabetes For Dummies
(0-7645-7019-6)

Divorce For Dummies
(0-7645-7030-7)

DJing For Dummies
(0-470-03275-8)

eBay.co.uk For Dummies
(0-7645-7059-5)

European History For Dummies
(0-7645-7060-9)

Gardening For Dummies
(0-470-01843-7)

Genealogy Online For Dummies
(0-7645-7061-7)

Golf For Dummies
(0-470-01811-9)

Hypnotherapy For Dummies
(0-470-01930-1)

Irish History For Dummies
(0-7645-7040-4)

Neuro-linguistic Programming For Dummies
(0-7645-7028-5)

Nutrition For Dummies
(0-7645-7058-7)

Parenting For Dummies
(0-470-02714-2)

Pregnancy For Dummies
(0-7645-7042-0)

Retiring Wealthy For Dummies
(0-470-02632-4)

Rugby Union For Dummies
(0-470-03537-4)

Small Business Employment Law For Dummies
(0-7645-7052-8)

Starting a Business on eBay.co.uk For Dummies
(0-470-02666-9)

Su Doku For Dummies
(0-470-01892-5)

The GL Diet For Dummies
(0-470-02753-3)

The Romans For Dummies
(0-470-03077-1)

Thyroid For Dummies
(0-470-03172-7)

UK Law and Your Rights For Dummies
(0-470-02796-7)

Winning on Betfair For Dummies
(0-470-02856-4)

**Available wherever books are sold. For more information or to order direct go to www.wiley.com or call 0800 243407 (Non UK call +44 1243 843296)**